The Addiction Counsellor's Toolbox

The Addiction Counsellor's Toolbox

WILLIAM A. HOWATT

Howatt HR Consulting Inc.

ISBN 978-1-894338-82-0

Published 2007

Howatt HR Consulting Inc.
6585 Hwy. 221
Kentville NS B4N 3V7

Preface

ADDICTION counselling is not a perfect science. In fact, I cannot give you an agreed upon definition of what an addiction counsellor really is. What I can tell you is this is an exciting field that is evolving each and every day.

The future of addiction counselling points toward one important action: increase the overall competency of the front line addiction counsellor so when a person comes to counseling, the counsellor has sufficient tools to match the client's needs, vs. the client having to match the counsellor's orientation.

Three things determine a counsellor's effectiveness in this field:

- *Education* – Have a solid foundation in all the competencies needed to be an effective addiction counsellor.
- *Experience* – Have a mentor to help you meet the challenge of taking theory and putting it into action. This process will not happen over night. Experience in this field is a critical element for professional development. After about 6000 hours of field placement, you should be in a position to start to understand what this field is. It took about 10 years for me to finally say, "OK, I think I have some idea what I need to do." I am not trying to scare a newcomer; just pointing out the need to be realistic in one's expectations to make the point there are no shortcuts. We all need to be willing to do our book learning as well as practical learning; they are core elements for building competencies.

- *Intuition* – This may not be something that can be taught; it is something we learn to trust – what many refer to as our *gut*. I teach all my students to learn to trust their gut. Since this science is not perfect, addiction counsellors need to be aware that they always need to be critically thinking and evaluating. Assessment tools and measures cannot think for you; they are tools, not law.

Finally, I encourage all of my students to build their own addiction counsellor toolbox. As you start to develop your orientation and select what you think works well and fits your needs as a professional addiction counsellor, take time to organize your thinking and challenge it on a regular basis.

Take out the old and put in the new. I say that because if you stay tuned in this field there is always something new. By reading journals, going to professional development sessions, listening to peers, and reading books on this topic, each year you will realize you will never know everything there is to learn in this field.

After nearly 20 years of studying and writing I have figured out that I do not have to know everything. I just need to keep the commitment to continue my learning so I am able to stay as current as I can for my professional development and for my clients. This helps me develop new tools and strategies that may make the difference in helping clients make new and better choices.

Addiction counselling is a dynamic process that requires counsellors to have their own life in order, balance, and health before they are ready to become professional helpers. In addition, they need to focus on developing strategies that will provide energy and focus to work with the addiction disorder population. This calling can be draining and frustrating, but at the same time rewarding and exciting by helping people make new choices.

The demands of the profession require new and experienced counsellors to have a comprehensive set of addiction counselling competencies, such as provided in this book.

Chapter 1, *Conversation Skills,* deals with the importance for addiction counsellors to develop a solid communication strategy. Without a strategy for effective communications, counsellors cannot counsel.

Chapter 2, *Communication Micro Skills,* introduces communication micro skills that facilitate conversation and decrease miscommunications. Micro skills bridge conversations and counselling.

Chapter 3, *Addiction Counselling Theories,* presents popular addiction counselling theories, therapies, and techniques.

Chapter 4, *The Rubik's Cube of Addiction Counselling,* offers some of the core skills needed, as well as a six-step problem solving model that can be used to incorporate the counsellor's communication model, theories, and best practices to assist a client.

Chapter 5, *Addiction Recovery Tools*, gives an overview of popular and proven addiction recovery tools.

Several appendices support the materials found in the five chapters and offer additional addiction counselling tools.

Addiction counsellors who have a foundation and experience in the field may choose to jump to appendix D, where they can do the counsellor tune-up. This is a self-evaluation of perceived competencies and points the counsellor to sections in this book that deal with competencies they need to develop.

BILL HOWATT

Contents

CHAPTER 1

Conversation Skills

"I listen! I heard every word you said – how else could I have told you what was wrong with it?"
– Connolly and Rianoshek, 2002

A S an addictions counsellor, it may sound obvious that before one can counsel a client one must first have effective communication skills. Since addiction counsellors are actually engaged in conversations with their clients a vast majority of the time, they require good communications skills, such as listening.

Typically, counsellors spend probably close to 90% of their day in conversation, including all elements of communication, such as e-mails, memos, voicemail, phone, and meetings. So it behooves them to have strong communication skills as the foundation for conversation skills before jumping into what is traditionally thought of as counselling skills, such as theory, techniques, and problem solving models.

Self Assessment on Communication Training:
- How much training have you had on developing conversational communication skills?
- What is the difference between counselling skills and communication skills?
- What is your communications style? (See Appendix A to complete a self-assessment.)
- What is the value of developing a communication model?

The general paradigm of this chapter is to help counsellors enhance their verbal communication skills, regardless of the medium (e.g., in person, phone, video conference). However, there are obvious applications that are useful in all areas of life.

Communication skill development is similar to all learning; it takes time. It is a process, not an event. Being able to talk does not equal the skill of communication. One important component in any counselling conversation is the ability of the counsellor to safely communicate, as well an understanding of the client's model of the world.

Miscommunication can lead to assumptions, conflict, and ineffective counselling. Effective communication can lead to more effective client interaction. This chapter provides counsellors with a set of tools and strategies for improving the effectiveness of their *conversational* communication skills.

Communication is any verbal or nonverbal exchange of information between two or more people. The way an individual receives communication determines its meaning. Without conscious recognition, people receive information and automatically sort the message and determine its meaning. No two people, however, hear the exact same thing. This is where most communication conflict begins.

The conflict debate is usually tied to a misunderstanding of fact and opinion, or, rather, what one person processes as meaning compared to another person's interpretation. One general observation is that many people have two conversations going on at a time: one in the external world and one that goes on internally. We will explore how a person's internal stories can be automatic, and how listening involves both a science and an art.

We can only truly understand and learn the meaning of content when we make the conscious choice to stop, focus, and examine the meaning and implications of the information we have just received. The crucial learning is that one must adhere to this conscious choice or they will continue to be at risk of misunderstanding the true meaning. Why? Because we all have internal processing programs that determine how we filter the world.

We all see the world a little differently, based on our life experiences, values, and beliefs. The goal is to provide a set of tools to be more effective in conversation. Our aim is to break down communication into a process that makes sense and enhances its effectiveness.

The Process of Communication: How People Communicate

Communication for most people is not difficult when the stakes are not high or there are no perceived risks. People naturally enjoy open communication when they perceive it as being mutually rewarding and safe. Whether they are introverted or extroverted, each has their own perception of safety.

Communication can also be spontaneous and simple. For example, imagine you are at a conference and while getting a cup of coffee you meet a complete stranger and start talking with a few polite hellos and gestures. Fifteen minutes later, you find yourself saying goodbye, and as you reflect on the conversation, you have a positive feeling that you have known this person for much longer than 15 minutes.

This example shows how two people can meet and within minutes have an effortless and wonderful conversation. The other side of the fence is when we have a one-sided conversation with people we know, and perceive that the person we are talking to is acting as if their point of view is the only one of value. This is a simple example of a complex challenge for many counsellors, day in and day out.

I place both of these examples under one umbrella I call communication; and many people break it down as being good or bad, depending on how they feel in the conversation regarding their level of internal comfort.

Labeling Communication as Good or Bad

People typically do not like being in conversations where they perceive risk. When an individual thinks there is a risk, the dynamics of the conversation can change within seconds. Unfortunately, too many often judge communication as being a matter of absolutes, either all good or all bad.

It is of critical importance to learn to listen and obtain all data and content accurately, as well as to develop the skills to keep a conversation safe so all parties involved have an opportunity to learn and agree. When I say safe, I mean when parties in a conversation, regardless of the stakes, understand that they have a point of view, are allowed to share it, and do not fear attacks or reprisals.

This section explores how communication works, and how people respond. This is an important topic, as clients often do not feel safe to communicate and express their points of view.

Circle of Communication

For communication to be effective with a client, the first step is to find some common interest (e.g., sport or hobby). This allows the counsellor to better build rapport. There is seldom a time when we are not communicating, so the first learning point is the need to be aware of our impact on others. Intention and actions are not the same thing! Figure 1-1 illustrates the Circle of Communication.

Whenever there is a difference between what we want and what we have, we perceive pain. Pain is the way the mind tells us that we are not

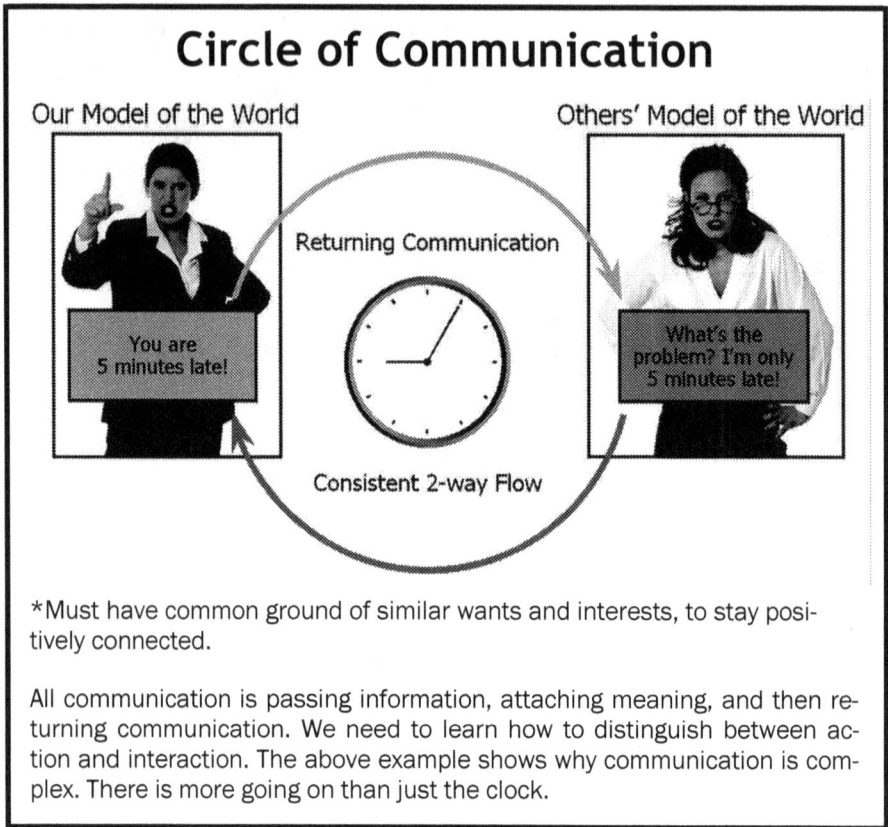

Figure 1-1 — Circle of Communication

getting what we want. When we do not get what we want, it is common to create behaviours to close the gap.

The underlying law in all communication is that the amount of perceived pleasure and pain determines the value of the communication, or if it was a good or bad conversation. When both parties perceive the conversation as being one of pleasure, the communication moves forward effectively, and the relationship can be proactive and positive.

On the other side of the continuum is, of course, pain. Confrontation is something most people will do anything to avoid or postpone, in order to avoid pain. This is why counsellors, to be effective, are coached to avoid confrontation.

To be a great communicator, it is helpful to realize that great communication starts with flexibility, and one of the most relevant books you can read to learn flexibility is *Green Eggs and Ham*, in which Dr. Seuss teaches the importance and benefits of behavioural flexibility. In that classic children's story, Sam-I-am is trying to get his friend to eat green eggs and ham. When the friend says no, Sam-I-am continues to make the same request, all the time remaining non-judgmental, and using his own creativity. The key is to not judge one's self or others.

The ability to be creative, non-judgmental, professional, and not take things personally is challenging to learn. Although, as you practice and learn, you will find having a "full-intervention-toolbox" – learned knowledge and skills for communications – an invaluable resource for success and happiness on the job and in your personal life.

A counsellor with behavioural flexibility has the capability to create or use alternative behaviours to solve a problem that is leading to internal frustration. The more skills and behavioural flexibility you have, the lower the chances of communication breakdowns and the better the chances of being heard.

Many Hear, Though Do Not Listen

Many people hear, but do not listen. This simple statement is an important one to capture and retain as we explore the rest of this section. As a counsellor, one of the most important skills to have is the art of listening. We will explore some reasons as to why this is true.

A person hears sound because sound waves impact the eardrum, which creates a chain reaction that ends in activity in the brain. Hearing is just the first action in listening. It is where one's first perceptions come from in reference to conversations. For example, the unexamined view of perception is similar to a mirror of sensation. This perception system operates much like a camcorder by making an objective recording of external data. This leaves the assumption that this recording has only captured the physical world.

Researchers and authors like William Powers, who have studied perception and filtering of information, teach that this kind of assumption is dead wrong. For example, Powers developed an 11-step perception hierarchy based on intensity, sensation, configuration, transition, event, relationship, category, sequence, program, principle, and system concept.

Each person's perception 'camcorder' has a set of filters, which process all information one takes in from the external world. Each individual's filter system is personalized, and is influenced directly by past learned experiences. This system functions outside a person's conscious level of awareness, before conscious analysis can occur. Knowing it is in place is important in assisting a person to understand the need to keep these filters from negatively disrupting a conversation.

Powers' point is that filters play an important part in how a person processes the world. People are not built solely on a set of reflexes, reacting in predictable ways. We all process the world differently, and this is how information can get lost as it is passed from person to person.

The key to improved communication is for people to learn how to take control of this automatic process and be consciously in control of how they communicate. When one is able to understand the difference between hearing (automatic processing of the external word) and listening (actively processing true meaning and facts) one is more effective in their conversations, and has more sense of control. Once we do this, we learn that hearing is not listening, and that we have choices. We are able to turn off our automatic filters and take time to fully understand what the sender is sending. The first part of effective conversation is to ensure that perception does not shade reality.

Why People Misunderstand Communications

Neuro Linguistic Programming (NLP) teaches an important insight about how people normally process the external world and incoming information. Without realizing it, people distort incoming information. Below we explore three ways that information can be distorted as a client attempts to process information from a counselling session or simple conversation. These points show how people can filter out information that can impact their understanding of the content and derived meaning.

Three ways that meaning can be distorted by a listener:
- *Deletion* – People can delete chunks of content from the message, which impacts the final meaning.
- *Generalization* – People can generalize information, and make connections that are not accurate. Much like semantics, content gets connected to incongruent meaning.
- *Distortion* – People consciously or unconsciously shade and change the meaning of the original intent of the message.

The process of communication is not only a science; it is also an art. Understanding the science of communication provides important insights, which can assist in motivating them to listen. It also helps them stay in control of their emotions. Powerful emotional drivers such as looking to set an impression, work pressure, defending a position, and attempting to win a point of view are but a few of the challenges that lead many to misunderstand and have misgivings about life. All these are rooted in how they have been communicating and processing the external world.

Perception, Meaning, Communication, and Actions

The four components below indicate how people typically process information. These elements provide the underpinning support and rationale for the communication macro process that will be covered later in this chapter.

Perceptions – If counsellors are not tuned in to their perception filter system, it operates automatically and outside their level of awareness. To be more effective as a counsellor it is important to not let perceptions be formed without all of the facts. Thus, accuracy is important for factual perceptions.

This means the facts are observable, measurable, have evidence, and are demonstrated to the observer. Counsellors gather facts in a conversation by asking questions, not forming assumptions. If the content of the conversation cannot pass this test, then the perception may not be accurate, as critical facts may be missing. Many people cannot tell the difference between facts and referential constructs.

For example see how a referential construct can influence perception in a statement I make to another person, "My daughter Emily is a wonderful child." This referential construct does not relate to fact. When I study this statement, it is obvious that my daughter is Emily, and "wonderful child" is an opinion.

The point is that few people treat these two as separate. For example, in the counselling world, consider the implications of the statement, "that father is a bully." The implication is that bully becomes treated as fact, and the automatic perception is created. It is important to be mindful of how *words* impact and influence one's perceptions.

Another common example in addiction counselling occurs when a client says, "I only have one drink per day." But under questioning the counsellor learns the drink is really a 40-ouncer. This is why counsellors are asked in any and all questioning around addictive disorders to always get the facts on frequency, duration, and intensity, to avoid referential constructs.

Meaning – There are two modes of how a person obtains meaning: the automatic meaning that can negatively impact how we process what the client is saying, and proactive meaning, where the first step is to make a conscious choice to turn off the automatic meaning.

Later in this chapter is a macro conversation process whose outcome is to effectively learn to find the meaning of what a client is saying. However, counsellors must accept that they will need to be proactive and interested in learning what clients are really thinking.

There is a need for curiosity and interest. Questions like "what else could it mean?" are important for moving away from the automatic mode. This type of internal questioning helps to keep the counsellor in more right-brain thinking vs. left-brain thinking. It is too common that when we rely only on left-brain thinking we run previously learned programs. The point is not to allow oneself to be automatically convinced of the meaning of a conversation. This mindset helps keep emotions in control, and the process more cognitive than emotionally reactive.

Active communication occurs when a counsellor seeks to get the true meaning of a message and its intention. To be proactive and use active communication, the primary outcome is to avoid miscommunication by not assuming the meaning of a message and by looking for the facts and intention.

Those who do not do this can end up in *parked communication* that often can form misperceptions. This is when one or both sides of a conversation hold on to their frame of reference and take no action to reduce miscommunication or to clear potential misunderstandings when they occur. This can lead to communication breakdown and negative feelings about the communication.

The good news is that it takes two to have a miscommunication, thus if you actively partake in this process, you do not need to get frustrated because your focus will be on having meaningful and factual conversations. Clients often come to counselling under stressful situations and can be expected to get upset and jump to conclusions. It is the counsellor's job to stay calm and focused on ensuring conversations are safe, informative, and meaningful.

One objective in the early stages of conversations is to assess clients' perceptions and meaning in regard to their behaviour in relationship to characteristics of addiction, such as compulsive use, loss of control, and continued use despite adverse consequences. The *hows* of assessment will be discussed in coming chapters.

When a counsellor looks for a client's meaning around tough questions such as behaviour, sometimes a question can lead to a client becoming upset. Counsellors need to have empathy for this and be clear that, to keep the client in counselling, it is necessary to keep open communications. Without safe and healthy communication, the benefits of addiction counselling will never be realized.

When dealing with an upset client, the below statements may create an opportunity for active communication:

"It seems you are upset. I suggest we continue our conversation when you are not so upset."

"I really want to have a conversation with you, and I am not interested in fighting or avoiding you. However, I can't engage you when you are this upset. How much time do you need to calm down, so we can have a safe conversation?"

"I think we both see this issue differently. I need to let you know I am OK that we disagree, and I am willing to take as much time as needed so we both can be heard and work for an agreement."

"How is getting this upset going to help us come to an agreement that is beneficial and positive for you?"

Actions – As with meaning, there are two kinds of actions. There can be the *automatic actions* that often lead to miscommunications, or there can be *learning actions*. Learning actions occur when one person makes a commitment to learn what the other is really saying, and how two or more parties can meet their needs and purposes.

A person who seeks to learn the other's point of view with passion and curiosity is in an effective position to truly listen to another point of view. Thus, any action taken is based on learning and has a much greater chance of keeping civility in the conversation. Conversation with civility is not about right or wrong; it is about honesty, dignity, and integrity.

The outcome is to improve relationships. The goal is not to judge or hurt others. This kind of action will only increase trust and goodwill, with less fear and more tolerance. People make mistakes, and when there are reserves of trust and goodwill, there is more opportunity for understanding, learning, and active communications.

Often, miscommunication, as we have suggested, can lead a person to perceive the conversation as being bad. This can engage powerful emotions. These emotions can overwhelm some people and lead them to act out to the point where they lose their composure. I call this outrageous conversations.

Evolution of Outrageous Conversations

Typically, all communication that moves from safe conversation to perceived risk can result in pain and miscommunication. Because many people are not aware of their automatic hearing filters system and the *fight or flight* response system (for more information, see Appendix A), they respond with the chain reaction of miscommunication and interpersonal struggles.

In the realm of communication, the person may fight (externally judge, attack, and be overtly upset) or flee (avoid, withdraw, lie, deny). One may question the effectiveness of this internal wiring today. As you review the model below, consider how, in a loving partnership/relationship, a conversation can move from peace to war in seconds. Very often in post interviews of a typical miscommunication, neither of the two, when asked, understood how they went from calm to anger so fast. Most were clear on why they were upset, though not on the process that occurred internally.

One apparent reason for this escalation is that the way human beings are hardwired puts them at risk of becoming overloaded quickly if they do not know what is happening with their bodies. Some say that the human mind is not effectively wired for dealing with conversations, and that the original purpose of the *fight or flight* response may have served us well a million years ago, though today it is creating problems.

Why? The brain does not have the ability to determine the level of risk. In other words, the same amount of chemicals will be released regardless of the threat. Thus, many people get more apprehensive than the risk warrants, and end up in outrageous conversations when there really is no need or value to be that worked up.

Social theorist Alfred Adler teaches that all human beings want to get along and to be liked. The challenge for many is that for this to happen, individuals need to learn how to overcome the obstacle called outrageous conversation. Figure 1-2 illustrates how a conversation can go from safe to outrageous.

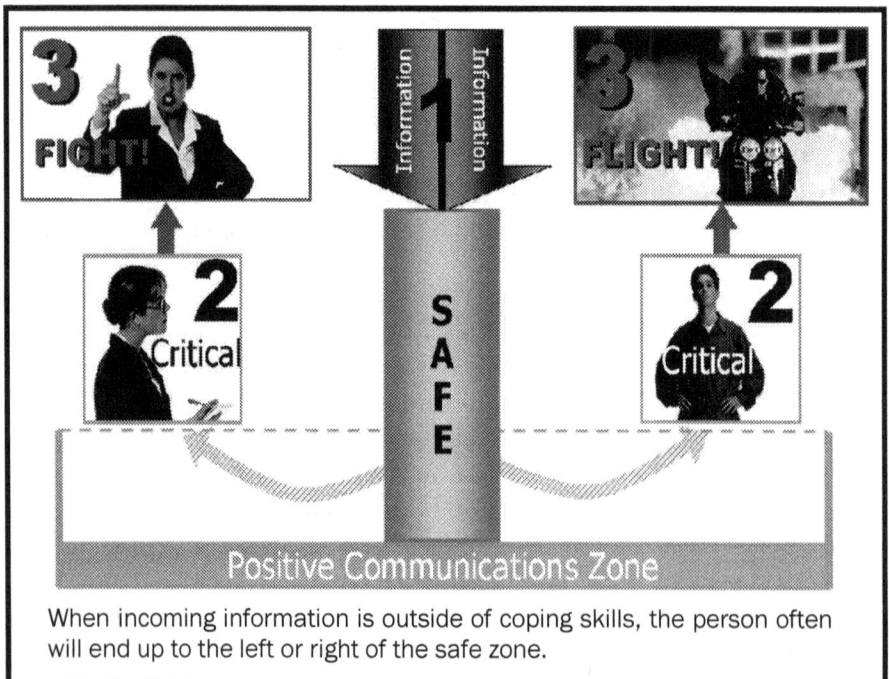

When incoming information is outside of coping skills, the person often will end up to the left or right of the safe zone.

Figure 1-2 — Three Steps to Outrageous Conversations

- *Common Conversation* is when the risk is low and all parties are feeling safe and in control.
- *Critical Conversation* is when one or more people perceive a potential risk issue in a conversation (e.g., they sense a challenge of sorts, pressure, judgment). If people in this phase are not aware of how they filter the world, they are at risk of becoming emotionally overwhelmed.
- *Outrageous Conversation* is when a conversation has gone bad, is highly charged emotionally, and the risk for relationship damage is great. It can occur in two forms: 1) covert (flight response), e.g., avoid and lie; and 2) overt (fight response), e.g., anger and frustration. The concern is the damage that can be created after the original exchange. For example, two individuals may have miscommunication over a deadline, which turns into a huge yelling match. Now there is a secondary issue to resolve if they are to move on. Pride, ego, and personality all can impact the intensity, duration, and frequency of outrageous conversations.

Cause and Effect of Outrageous Conversation

Outrageous conversation puts a conversation into a communication vacuum. This is where facts are lost due to high emotions and misperceptions, and the conversation goes to a destructive level where the truth no longer seems to be important. The communication vacuum keeps individuals within their own logic and emotion; they continue to loop within what they believe is right, and communication stops. Being caught in a communication vacuum can shut out the truth and result in damaged interpersonal relationships. Overall, the need to be right rules.

The rationale for calling this the communication vacuum is that this kind of fallout too often takes away the will and energy needed to fix the miscommunication. When this vacuum remains, and outrageous conversations are allowed to continue, it will take longer to fix the problem because of all the secondary issues created and relationships damaged.

Risk of Miscommunication

Communication is either effective or not effective — we are *always communicating*.

Below are examples of ways people miscommunicate that can lead to outrageous conversations that impact the quality of the communication and relationship. Counsellors want to do all they can by actively listening to a client to avoid any of the below examples:

- Only look at their own side of the story and are not willing to learn the other.
- Communicate only from their position, and not listen.
- Express their need for more attention and feel no one is listening to them.
- Ask for help because of the pain they are in, and are frustrated.
- Find a new option for their life.

Figure 1-3 illustrates a four-step model of how communication often breaks down. Communication breaks down when there is not enough active listening, focus, interest, and common ground to establish rapport. To have healthy communication, people need to have an overlap of interest. If this is not present, one person may start to resist and resent the other one, and if rapport is not established, then the process is at risk of becoming outrageous.

Many are not aware that they have an internal threshold for how long they will tolerate another person and the breakdown of communication. Once they go beyond their threshold, they are at risk of being negative. This is a concern, because once negativity occurs, it forms a lasting impression, as well as the potential for the development of secondary issues (e.g., gos-

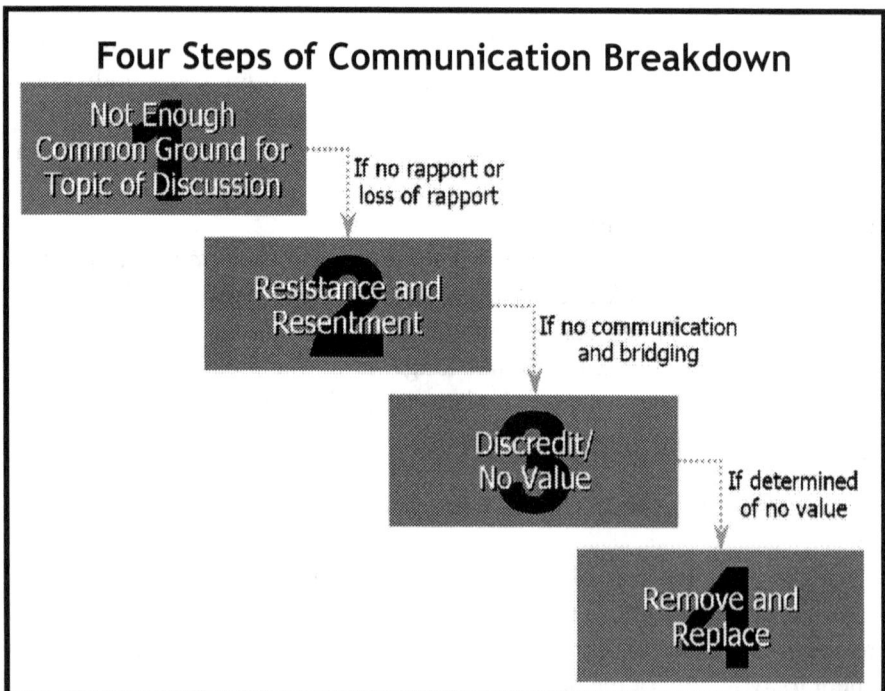

Figure 1-3 — Four Steps of Communication Breakdown

sip). Each person has their own tolerance thresh-old, but with education and practice, it can be increased.

When we feel overwhelmed with a particular communication, we spend time focusing on it. What we focus on can expand and grow. If a person defines something as negative, it will negatively impact and influence the quality of communication. Often people in this state perceive they are not being understood. The frustration of being misunderstood can lead some people down a path of less effective behaviour, such as depression, drugs, and alcohol.

One of the biggest causes of miscommunication is perceiving the other party's intention and meaning. If we are negative all the time, everything can seem negative. Counsellors need to be mindful that clients who come to counselling often have had many conversations that resulted in miscommunications and as a result are not as trusting of others' meaning and intentions.

A counsellor who maintains a positive attitude and supports the active listening concept of truly being interested and understanding what others are communicating will reduce miscommunications and outrageous conversations. The challenge of effective communication is that a large crosssection of the general population is programmed by automatic listening.

Macro Process for Effective Conversation

When people feel fear or threatened, it is common for them to perceive they are lost, out of control, and that the environment is controlling them (external locus of control).

For many, the thought of mapping a conversation is foreign. It is true all conversations will be different as the number of variables involved will change the context, dynamic, etc. However, the macro process below provides an effective model regardless of the conversation. When you have mastered this process, you will be able to adapt micro skills to assist in keeping critical conversations important and in control.

One metaphor that may be of value is to think of this macro process as a desktop program that must be kept running in the background. Anytime a conversation is starting to move from common to critical, a dialogue box pops up on your screen, reminding you of self-awareness and control.

In any conversation, it is OK for the parties to agree that they disagree, and they will need to look at their options for finding an agreement or new action. What is not acceptable is the cost of not agreeing to disagree, and becoming angry and hurtful. Outrageous conversations infect and debilitate environments.

MACRO COMMUNICATION PROCESS

A. Self

1. Self refers to the importance of one looking inward and accepting the choices one has. Each person in the conversation is responsible for their own actions and behaviours. An excellent resource for learning more about the power of choice is William Glasser's Choice Theory. (For more information see Chapter 3.) Many clients, unfortunately, are not aware of internal locus of control (the idea that all behaviour is created internally, and people have a choice as to how they respond), and that once individuals learn insight they are able to better manage their behavioural systems. When people operate from an internal locus of control, they are ready to master the art of conversation mapping. To begin, the person will tune in consciously to the important *conversation drivers*, the variables that are unique to each person and that impact how they perform in communications. Some examples of communication drivers are communication style, personality style, active listening, action vs. parked communication, perception filters, emotional intelligence, understanding of *fight or flight* response, Meta programs, micro skills available, stress level, mental health, locus of control, awareness of communication process, personal congruency and integrity, self-esteem, position of authority, and cultural differences.

2. Discover and learn about your internal automatic programs. These are the stories that we run in our head when we hear information. These programs are automatically filtered and influence our perceptions. The goal is to avoid becoming parked in communication and allowing automatic conclusions to determine the destiny of the conversation. The two points below will assist you in re-engineering and designing new, effective internal programs:

    a. *Clearly Defined Personal Boundaries* – Personal values, ethics statements, and life goals are helpful in establishing personal boundaries. They also help you to be clear on who you are and what you stand for. The aim is to design and determine what is and is not acceptable, and to be prepared to communicate violations.

    b. *Installing New Personal Internal Programming* – Once a individuals have a clearly determined set of boundaries, they are able to install their new personal internal programs of what they really want and can accept. These will help measure where they are in any conversation. For example, if a person wants to be in emotional control but is acting outrageously (e.g., complaining to others about the boss, instead of expressing concerns directly with the boss), the core skills of this program can help them develop an internal awareness of choosing behaviours that are not as effective as they could be. In other words, this program can help people learn how to stop and get out of automatic hearing and move from outrageous conversation back to critical, so that safety can be restored and the conversation can move forward. Self-evaluation of what one really wants is a powerful and true guide to getting focused. The sad reality is that many people are not aware of what they really want; however, they are clear of what they do not want, which can leave them in a victim mentality. Too many professionals are aware only of the present moment in time, and do not look beyond immediate needs. To move beyond this, a person needs to have positive internal programs running.

How well one knows oneself and their choices will influence the first two parts of this section. The not-so-obvious benefit is that individuals promote the importance of separating *facts from opinions*. It helps people to stop the automatic stories, created from past history and experience, from being the filter they use for all conversation. It helps create a new beginning as to how they perceive the world, and how to ensure they are not only hearing others, but that they have a strong interest in listening as well. It also prevents *fight or flight* from ruling conversations.

Many people who take communication training fool themselves into thinking that all they need is a new neat set of tricks so they can be more effective and win. This is seldom effective over the long term because most novelties wear off or are replaced by the new flavour of the month.

Questions for this phase:

- What are some of my communication drivers that are presently helping me in conversations?
- What are some of my communication drivers that are presently limiting me in conversations?
- What can I do to improve how I take control of myself?
- How does knowing myself help in any communication process?
- Why do many people find it hard to look critically at themselves?

B. Awareness of Stakes and Discovering Common Hooks

This is really part one of the process in action. The previous component is the prep work for this process to be effective. Following is the application.

1. *Awareness of stakes* is the first macro step in action. In any conversation where you perceive that either person senses a risk, the conversation has the potential to move very quickly from common to critical, then to outrageous.

   Indicators:

   Physiological – Face color changes, tone and/or pitch changes, breathing changes.

   Psychological – Starts to stutter, talks faster, repeats themselves.

   Behavioural – Sudden shifts in body, body part starts moving, tapping, pointing fingers.

   Once we perceive and become aware of any of these factors in the other person or ourselves, it tells us that safety and risk issues are present. We know that unless the situation becomes less threatening that the *fight or flight* response may take over, and the situation may become outrageous.

   Whether or not the above has occurred, the first step is to be consciously in control, and avoid escalation to outrageous conversation. For this to happen, both sides must have a sense of safety so that there is an opportunity to build trust and respect. The conversation cannot more forward unless both parties are safe.

2. *To build safety and defuse potential fight or flight response,* it is important to listen for *common hooks,* the similar interests, purposes, intentions, values, goals, outcomes, and rationales exhibited in safe communication. To do this with another person, you need to be willing and motivated to actively listen to the person's point of view and purpose. When you are able to do this, you have taken control of your automatic hearing and are capable of listening. This step is really your awareness of the science of conversation.

3. *General guidelines for conversations.* Spend the first few minutes of any conversation connecting or reconnecting to discover common links. This builds reserves you can go back to if the conversation becomes critical. This helps to determine similarities, common needs and purposes, and safety. It also shows the other person that you are willing to learn their needs and positions. This opens the gate for reciprocal listening. The bottom line is that until it is safe, there will be no active conversation. For example, a person may want to avoid you, and just

tell you what you want to hear to get rid of you. For conversation to work, fear must be removed.

In all conversations it is important to be aware of safety and communication hooks. A conversation will not be congruent unless both parties are able to present their views.

Questions for this phase

Monitor yourself by asking the following questions:

- Am I acting as if I am interested in the other person's points of view?
- Am I in control of my emotions?
- Am I acting in a threatening manner?
- Do I feel safe right now?
- Is there ever an excuse to get angry with another person? If so, where is the evidence that learning and relationships are built?
- Is anger is an emotion whose sole outcome is to control?
- Do I want to control people or work with people?

C.   Presentation of Point of View

Once safety is in place and emotions are in check, it is time to engage in the *art of* communication. This is where your communication micro skills will be very important, and mastery of these skills will help this stage move forward.

1. *Fact Finding* – The intent is to engage and clarify each side's point of view with the goal of seeking out the facts. Openly define the meaning and purpose of the conversation so both parties know what it is about (scope and potential outcomes). It is important that you be clear of your point of view's facts. This will assist you in staying in a cognitive vs. emotional mode. When people are not sure of their facts, they are at much greater risk of feeling threatened and losing their composure. A guiding principle is to speak the truth of what you know, based on facts, and present an opinion as just that – a point of view. Often, the differences between a person who influences people and one who does not are homework, research, knowing the facts, and being able to present facts in a timely manner. It is critical to accept others non-judgmentally.

2. *Presentation of facts* – Support others in presenting their facts clearly; sharing their personal internal programs (discover how they are processing the issue); and clearly stating their purpose, intentions,

means/methods, as well as their desired outcome/results. As you do this, if you are unclear of the facts, it is important not to make any statements that could be perceived as judgmental. Ask open-ended questions (see micro skills section) in seeking to understand. This stage is a presentation of their point of view. It is not the time for you to cross-examine and to blow holes in their presentation, as this may put the conversation at risk. This is a common mistake. Resist the temptation and be committed to active communication.

3. *Seek permission to be listened to, if necessary* – Once the individual has presented their point of view, it is important to understand that if you are not asked for your position, it is appropriate to seek permission to present it. Once you have presented your facts, it is helpful to seek feedback on what you have presented, as well as the other's views. This provides you an opportunity to question the other person about your facts, to help clarify your point of view.

Questions for this phase:

- May I present my perceptions?
- What is it that I want to happen and why? (Asking self)
- What are my facts? (Asking self)
- Does this really matter? (Asking self)
- I don't feel that you're listening to my point of view. What can we do about this?
- If we can't listen to each other and work this out on our own, I suggest we get a third party to help us. Do you agree?
- I am prepared to stay here as long as it takes so I can fully understand your facts.

Note: It is normal to move back and forth among the above points 1, 2, and 3 until both parties perceive they are clear and have all the facts, intentions, and meaning of the conversation.

D.   Research and Agreement

When A, B and C are done correctly, this phase moves forward. Unfortunately, people often rush to this part of the process, and end up in outrageous conversation and parked communication. Make a commitment to prevent this from happening. It was once said, "he who speaks first will lose." There is a great deal of wisdom in this statement. Again, in this stage micro skills are paramount.

- Determine outcome and goals; find common ground; and research new common ground as needed. These will help all parties clearly perceive that purpose and needs have been taken into consideration.

  Example: I'm hearing that we are agreeing to … Is that correct?

- Agree on common interests and needs, and align conversation for agreements. The outcome is to establish a clear and precise set of agreements and actions to which both parties agree. It is important to ensure that the agreements are clearly laid out with timelines and measurable criteria to avoid misunderstanding. In some cases, putting them in writing is of value. Most of the time there is no need to be this formal.

  Example: It appears to me we have an understanding of each other's purpose in this case, and I think it is time to put our final agreements together. Do you agree? Can we agree that I will do … and you will … within the next two business days?

Questions for this phase:
- What is the common ground for both of us on this matter?
- How can we make this a win/win for both of us?
- Is there any more fact collecting we need for this matter?
- Can we put our agreements together?
- What are the timelines and measurement criteria you would like to use?
- Are there any other parties that you believe need to have input in this matter?

E.   Follow-up and Adjustments

Too often left out, this is an important part of the process as it establishes credibility, accountability, and congruency. It is a common mistake for professionals to not attend to follow-up as much as to making the agreements. Not following up when you say you will may promote the attitude that you are not reliable, which decreases the possibility of success. It is a best practice to follow up on all agreements, small or big, to promote consistency and your commitment to your agreements.

In the event of a relapse, there may need to be necessary adjustments. If there are any communication barriers and the stakes are becoming high again, it is recommended the parties go back and start this process again from the beginning.

Questions for this phase:

Follow-up:

- Hello, we agreed to follow up in 10 days; when can we talk to review our agreements?
- When can we make our follow-up agreements?

Relapse:

- It appears we have hit a potential roadblock. I suggest we slow the process and start over again so we can both be listened to. Is that OK with you?
- What are the consequences if we don't correct this matter now?

Summary of the Macro Process in Action

A great deal of miscommunication and/or struggling conversations are directly due to a lack of self-awareness, such as not having an integrated macro conversation process, and micro communication tools and strategies. Three parts are important for all effective communication:

- Self (A)
- The Science (B)
- The Art (C, D, E)

In the end, it will be your job to learn and practice the above macro process to be an effective communicator, which is a critical element for effective counselling. It will keep you from making the ineffective choice of responding to the world via your automatic hearing system. This process will help you balance and master the self, the science, and the art of communication.

Macro Communications Process	Study Review Template
Self	**Questions**
1. **Self – The starting place where all people first need to look inward and accept the choices they have.** a) Discover your communication drivers. b) Discover and learn about your internal automatic programs. c) Clearly define personal boundaries. d) Install new personal internal programming.	• What are some of my communication drivers that are presently helping me in conversations? • What are some of my communication drivers that are presently limiting me in conversations? • What can I do to improve how I take control of myself? • How does knowing myself help in any communication process? • Why do many people find it hard to look critically at themselves?
Macro Process in Action	
Science of Communication 2. **Awareness of Stakes and Discovering Common Hooks** a) Awareness of stakes is the first step of the process. It is important to be aware of fight or flight and Emotional Intelligence. Indicators: • Physiological • Psychological • Behavioural b) Discovering common hooks is establishing common purpose, needs, intentions, and wants.	**Questions:** • Am I acting as if I am interested in the other person's points of view? • Am I in control of my emotions? • Am I acting in a threatening manner? • Do I feel safe right now? • Is there ever an excuse to get angry at another person? If so where is the evidence that learning and relationships are built? • Anger is an emotion whose sole outcome is to control. Do you agree with that? • Do you want to control people or to work with people?

Macro Process in Action (Cont'd)	
Art of Communication	**Questions:**
3. Presentation of Point of View a) Fact finding is where the conversation's intent is to engage and clarify each side's facts, purpose, and meaning. b) Presentation of facts supports people in presenting their facts clearly. c) If needed, seek permission to be listened to.	• May I present my perceptions? • What is it that I want to happen and why? (Asking self) • What are my facts? (Asking self) • Does this really matter? (Asking self) • I don't feel that you're listening to my point of view. What can we do about this? • What are the facts and where is my evidence? • What do you mean when you say more … ?
4. Research and Agreement a) Determine outcome and goals; find common ground; research new common ground as needed. These will help all parties clearly perceive that purpose and needs have been taken into consideration. b) Agree on common interests and needs, and align conversation for agreements. The outcome is to establish a clear and precise set of agreements and actions to which both parties agree.	**Questions:** • What is the common ground for both of us on this matter? • How can we make this a win/win for both of us? • Is there any more fact collecting we need for this matter? • Can we put our agreements together? • What are the timelines and measurement criteria you would like to use? • Are there any other parties that you believe need to have input in this matter?
5. Follow-up and Adjustments To be congruent, commit to follow up on all agreements, regardless of the stakes involved.	**Questions:** • When can we make our follow up agreements? • It appears we have hit a potential roadblock, I suggest we slow the process and start over again, so we ensure that we can both be listened to. Is that OK with you? • What are the consequences if we don't correct this matter now?

CHAPTER 2

Communication Micro Skills

"The art of life lies in a constant readjustment to our surroundings."
— Ka Kuzo Okakiwa

ONE of the most frustrating experiences for many professionals is human conflict, and one of the biggest culprits is poor communication. This is often a result of misunderstandings due to a lack of micro skills to assist the macro process. Internal conflict and a lack of understanding of the communication process can cause individuals to talk themselves into situations not based in reality.

The following micro skills are provided to support you in the communication process. They are intended to help you maintain control of self, science, and art. Create your own toolbox of resources for your personal development over the next few years. Mastery will take time; take on the following skills one at a time.

Read through the entire list and pick 10 points that jump out as a place to begin, and practice one at a time. These are to be used to support the Macro Communication Process. There is no expectation that you have to know all of these to be an effective communicator. However, a great communicator is much like a person who fishes; the one who baits the most hooks will get the most fish.

The person with the most skills will be the most effective in both the science and art of communication (macro process). As you can see, communication is an art that can take years to master; there is a difference between talking and strategic communications. This is not a complete list, so feel free to add to it.

Self-Talk – The father of self-talk is Albert Ellis. The following examples are based on Ellis' notion of how much control thinking has over our bodies. You can, by thinking negatively, cause yourself undue mental stress. The opposite can happen if you have positive self-talk. Ellis describes how using positive self-talk will put you in a position to keep your feelings of fear from becoming unmanageable, leading to irrational thinking. When in a crisis situation, positive self-talk will help you maintain a lower anxiety level, which will help with problem solving creativity.

Examples of positive self-talk that you can use:

- I can handle this.
- I won't take it personally or get emotionally involved.
- This person has a problem; help them get through it.
- If I were they, what would I want to see, hear, do?
- Just stay calm — take a deep breath.

Deep Breathing – Deep breathing helps to settle the autonomic nervous system. By being able to use relaxation breathing, you can quickly change your physiology from nervous anxiety to calm. When you are calm, you are able to think more clearly. When you think more clearly, you are able to perform more effectively and healthily, provided you have the knowledge and skills to know what to do.

Be Aware of Personal Space (proxemics) and Cultural Differences – Each of us has own own criteria for the imaginary circle around us – our personal space, or comfort zone. When one violates another's space without permission, it often raises that person's anxiety. Figure 2-1 shows average imaginary boundaries to which people adhere.

In regard to personal space, two important points to remember are: a) no two people have the same personal space limitations because of interpersonal variables; and b) cultural differences influence individual comfort zones (e.g., Asian people have closer personal space zones than people in the Western world). Be mindful of personal space. Always work from the 4-12-foot area, so you are not perceived as a threat.

As in any of the micro skills, it is imperative that you become more aware of cultural differences. Many of us have good intentions when working with people from another culture; however, this good intention is not enough. We need to look at them through the eyes of their own culture. When families choose to come and live in North America, it is important to remember that they still live by the values of their own culture. We are not expected to be experts on all cultures, but simply asking questions will show them that we are interested in and respect their culture. When in doubt, ask

Your Comfort Zones for Proxemics and Communication

Your Public Zone

Your Social Zone

Your Personal Zone

Your Intimate

*   *

*   **YOU**   *

*   *

1 - 12/18 inches

18 - 36 inches

Important:
always be aware
of cultural
differences in
relation to
proxemics

4 - 12 feet

* = the area that is recommended to work within to stay professional

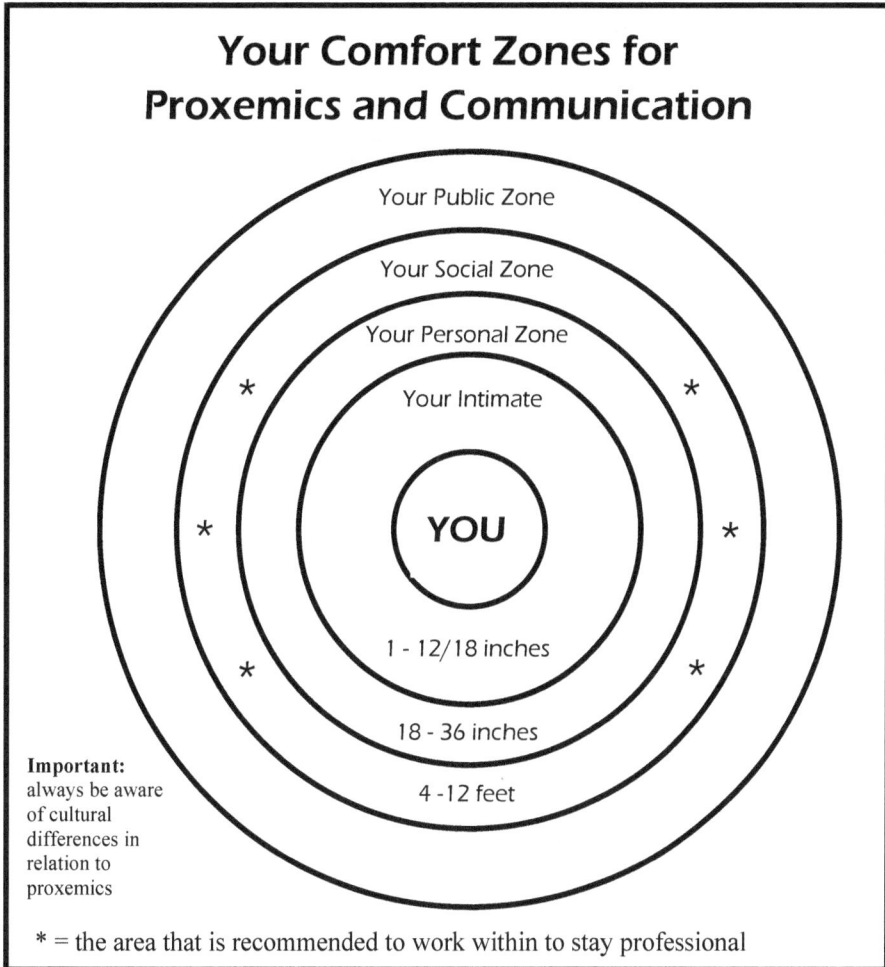

Figure 2-1— Your Comfort Zones for Proxemics and Communication

questions. Once you learn about others' culture, you can teach them about the North American culture and our cultural expectations. This way, barriers can be brought down.

Kinesics — The term kinesics represents the science and study of non-verbal body language. Non-verbal language includes facial expression, gestures, and body language. There are arguments and research that suggest that over 60% of all communication is non-verbal, because what people see often projects a stronger meaning than the words they hear. As a counsellor, it is critical to pay attention not only to what your client's body language is saying, but also to what your body language is projecting.

Be Aware of Your Paraverbals – Paraverbals are the art of self-monitoring and controlling one's tone of voice, volume, and rate of speech (figure 2.2). They represent the power of the word. When speaking, it's not always what you are trying to say, it might be how you are saying it that is important (e.g., volume, pitch, rate of speech, tone). You need to be aware of how the meaning of words changes as the variables change.

For any of the four body messages, you will be able to recognize that the person is outside the normal range. Non-verbals are the first sign that they are upset, and recognizing this provides an opportunity to lower anxiety by intervening in a non-threatening manner. Staying in the social zone and standing in a position that is approximately at a 20-degree angle to them, will provide you with a safe and non-threatening approach. As you interact, and work to interpret the other person's non-verbals, you must also be aware of your own non-verbals.

Diane Gossen provides two important rules to ensure words do not change the context of the message:

Figure 2-2 — Effectiveness of Variants in Communication

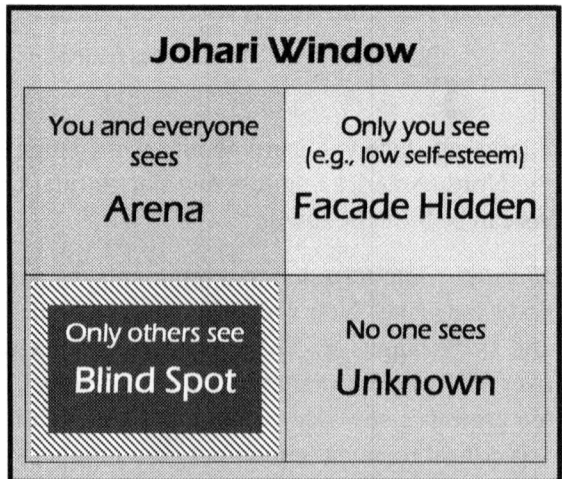

- Avoid rhetorical questions (e.g., "You know the rules, don't you?").
- Stick to the communication facts, avoid personal opinions (e.g., You did it before, so you'll probably do it again).

Be Aware of Blind Spots – The Johari Window explains that all humans have an area of their behaviour that is not in their awareness (figure 2.3). This area is called the blind spot, the area that we do not see in ourselves. It usually is the little nuances that we have which, if we do not become of aware of them, may be the reason communications breakdown.

Many are not aware of how their blind spots may be a part of the reason for poor communication, thus we need to

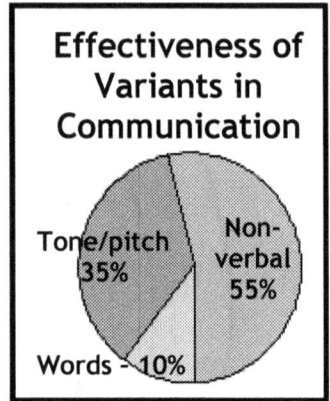

Figure 2-3 — Johari Window

have a system of learning about our blind spots, so we can overcome them. The use of a client survey regarding your service, and feedback from peers, are good tools for helping to reveal your blind spots.

The Johari Window explains how a person interacts with the world. It is useful for understanding how two people may not always see, hear, or feel the same thing. Following is a brief breakdown of the four panes:

Arena — The window which you and everyone sees as the same (e.g., the color of their shirt).

Façade — The window only you see, hear, and feel (e.g., "I am not good looking, so no one will see me as good looking").

Unknown — The window no one sees (e.g., your future).

Blind Spot — The window you are not aware of (e.g., your voice tone in some conversations is aggressive, and you turn people away).

Active Listening Skills – When trying to find out what is going on in any communication, you will be more effective if you use Active Listening skills. This is when the client knows you are fully engaged. To achieve Active Listening, you must be totally focused and have empathy because each person has their own emotions and view of the world. The following three points are an adaptation of Egan's work on how to use Active Listening skills:

- You must want to hear what the other person has to say.
- You must genuinely want to be helpful to them at that time.
- You must see the person as someone separate from yourself — a unique person who has their own feelings.

Dugger teaches that using Active Listening during an argument is the first step for improving the safety of the conversation. The following five-step technique has been modified for you:

- Focus on the issue or behaviour, not the person.
- You do not have to agree with others, but it is crucial that you respect their right to a difference of opinion and acknowledge their sense of value.
- Avoid absolute statements such as "you always" or "you never."
- You should own your position by sending "I" messages (see point 8 for an example of "I" messages).
- You will be more productive when you focus on the content, use your skills, and suspend your emotions.

In order to really get the client's perspective on the problem, counselors must attend to all aspects of communication. They must take into account the fact that clients come with their own opinions and ideas. Active listening uses many micro skills.

COUNSELLOR: "I understand your frustration." (Counsellor is carefully observing client.)

CLIENT: (Voice is high-pitched, nervous.) "My job is just so busy. We don't have time for any fun." (Client is fidgeting and seems restless.)

COUNSELLOR: "Fun?" (Client relaxes and counsellor maintains eye contact. Voice lowers, speak more slowly.)

CLIENT: "Yeah. What I wouldn't give to have enough time to just take a walk a few days a week."

By using Active Listening, you may not always be able to avoid miscommunication; however, you will be able to minimize it and continue to work on building rapport. The power of listening is invaluable; however, as Scott Peck teaches, just because something sounds simple does not always mean that it will be easy.

"I" Messages (Assertion Statements That Promote Self-Responsibility) – An "I" message is a dignified, clear way of expressing pleasant and unpleasant feelings or thoughts. An "I" message contains three components:

- A statement of behaviour directed to the peer that is found to be objectionable (e.g., *"When I saw* you . . .")
- How you felt (e.g., *"I was* concerned that . . .")
- Reason(s) for your feelings and/or expectations of better future behaviour (e.g., *"Because it* is disturbing what we agreed on . . .")

Assertion Statement Formula: "When I saw/heard/felt you . . . I feel . . . because . . ."

The power of "I" messages is that you are role modeling the importance of taking responsibility for your own perceptions.

Reality Therapy Questioning – Reality Therapy is a powerful method for positively moving a conversation forward. Reality Therapy is action language — it gets a client to self-evaluate the action quickly, in order to make new choices.

- What is it you want to do?
- Is what you are doing helping or hurting the situation?
- What is my job?
- What are the alternatives?

The key is to ask questions, and avoid making statements.

Press your Internal Pause Button – Sometimes in a conversation it is helpful to press your metaphorical pause button as an automatic protocol to take charge of racing emotions. If you allow your body to dump chemicals, your ability to communicate is greatly reduced.

Responding to a Critical Client – The following is an adaptation of McKay and Fanning, and is intended to help you deal with a critical peer.

a. *Acknowledgment:* This is where the counsellor clearly states being aware of the situation, acknowledges the value of the client's views, and shows support. This type of response allows you to simply agree with your critic. Quick and effective acknowledgement deflates a critic. When the other party hears you agree, both parties are able to protect their self-esteem.

    CLIENT: "I wish you'd pay more attention. I'm having trouble follow-ing your directions."

    COUNSELLOR: "You're right. I should not assume you understand what I am saying all of the time."

b. *Clouding:* This type of response is not necessarily accurate; it is a token response. You are appearing to agree, and the critic can be satisfied with that. But the unspoken, self-esteem-preserving message is, "although you may be right, I don't really think that you are."

    CLIENT: "My life is harder than most people could ever imagine."

    COUNSELLOR: "You're right, and if you believe this, then making de-cisions as to what to do next will take planning and action."

c. *Probing:* This is a response to vague criticism. You must use probing to see the person's intent and meaning. Probing questions are open ques-tions intended to encourage the client to go into more depth.

    CLIENT: "You never listen."

    COUNSELLOR: "Never?"

    CLIENT: "You don't even care."

    COUNSELLOR: "Don't care?"

Does It Really Matter? – Gossen promotes something we truly believe — does it really matter? If it does, then you should intervene. She believes that by asking oneself, "does a particular behaviour really matter?" or "is it a be-haviour worth intervening in?" and answering "no" lets them selectively ignore the behaviour. The basic premise is, your overall attitude and beliefs may create problems.

Finding Reality – There may be times you become frustrated by a client's behaviour and, if this continues, you will lose your objectivity. To move beyond powerful emotion and find the reality in situations where you are becoming upset, ask yourself this question, "What else could this client's behaviour mean?" Keep asking this question over and over and answer it honestly. You will become aware that this client's behaviour is not directed at you as much as it is the result of the client's current circumstances. The client's behaviour is not your problem; your role is to help clients help themselves. If you cannot help them, refer them to someone who can.

When it Gets Too Emotionally Hot – Barbara Coloroso explains that in a crisis situation, when you perceive that conflict is turning into a dangerous personal attack, it is always acceptable to:

- Call time out. (e.g., "We are both too angry to talk right now, let's take a break, and then talk.")
- Refuse to take abuse (e.g., If a client is becoming abusive, do not stand for it).
- Insist on fair treatment (e.g., You do not treat the client with disrespect, and in return you should receive fair treatment).

Meta Model Question Strategies – The Meta Model is a process to break down language to learn how to be more effective in responding to Meta Model statements. The chart on the previous page shows how to break down a statement and how to respond (see figure 2.5).

Be Aware of Denotative vs. Connotative Meaning in all Communications – Denotative is the literal definition of a word from a dictionary, while connotative is the application of the word, which depends on the context and association. People too often focus on the denotative meaning, which may lead to assumptions of the connotative application to the situation. Miscommunication occurs when we do not seek a clear frame of reference for the meaning of words in terms of their application. We cannot assume we understand where a person is coming from, thus a core skill is to avoid assumptions and become clear on the meaning behind words, phrases, and statements. If you do not know, then it is important to ask until you are clear.

CLIENT: "I was out all night!"

COUNSELLOR: "My understanding of 'out all night' is till about 4:00 a.m. What's yours?"

Gain a clear understanding of the connotative meaning and don't assume that you and the client share the same frame of reference.

Semantics – Ensure you understand people, not just the words they speak.

COUNSELLOR: "When you say time off, do you mean you are going to take sick time or vacation time?"

People communicate with words, and sometimes they connect syntax together using a different route, which can leave two parties sharing similar meaning though the content is different. Do not assume, but spend time ensuring that you understand each other's internal frame of reference.

The Meta Model – Figure 2-5	
What the Client Says	**How to Respond to the Client**
Distortion	
1. **Mind Reading:** Claiming to know someone's internal state. Ex: "You don't like me."	"How do you know I don't like you?"
2. **Lost Performative:** Value judgments where the person doing the judging is left out. Ex: "It's bad to be from that part of town."	"Who says it's bad?" "According to whom?" "How do you know it's bad?"
3. **Cause-Effect:** Where cause is wrongly put outside the self. Ex: "You make me angry."	"How does what I'm doing cause you to choose to feel angry?" (Also, Counter. Ex: "How, specifically?"
4. **Complex Equivalence:** Where two experiences are interpreted as being synonymous. Ex: "She's always questioning me, she doesn't like me."	"How does her questioning mean that she . . .?" "Have you ever questioned someone you liked?"
5. **Presuppositions:** Ex: "If my boss knew how much I am hurting, she wouldn't do that." Three presuppositions in this sentence:1) I hurt; 2) My boss acts in some way; 3) My boss doesn't know I suffer.	"How do you choose to suffer?" "How are they reacting?" "How do you know they don't know?"
Generalizations	
6. **Universal Quantifiers:** Universal Generalizations, such as all, every, never, everyone, no one, etc. Ex: "He never listens to me."	Find Counter Examples. "Never?" "What would happen if he did?"

7. **Modal Operators:**
  a. **Necessity:** As in should, shouldn't, must, must not, have to, need to, it is necessary. Ex: "I have to take care of her."
 	
  b. **Possibility:** (Or Impossibility.) As in can/can't, will/won't, may/may not, possible/ impossible. Ex: "I can't tell him the real picture."
	a. "What would happen if you did?" ("What would happen if you didn't?" Also, "Or?"
	
	b. "What prevents you?" ("What would happen if you did?")

The Meta Model – Figure 2-5 (Cont'd)	
What the Client Says	How to Respond to the Client
Deletions	
8. Nominalizations: Process words which have been frozen in time, making them nouns. Ex: "There is no communication here."	"Who's not communicating what to whom?" "How would you like to communicate?"
9. Unspecified Verbs: Ex: "They rejected me."	"How, specifically?"
10. a. Simple Deletions: Ex: "I am uncomfortable." **b. Lack of Referential Index:** Fails to specify a person or thing. Ex: "They don't listen to me." **c. Comparative Deletions:** As in good, better, best, worst, more, less, most, least. Ex: "She's a better person."	a. "About what/whom?" b. "Who, specifically, doesn't listen to you?" c. c. "Better than whom?" "Better at what?" "Compared to whom/what?"

Inferences – Language can lead us and give impressions that influence our thinking. We may reach conclusions that are not correct. It is important not to judge clients by their words, only their actions. People are much more than the words they speak.

CLIENT: "I had a hard time getting to this appointment today."
COUNSELLOR: "When you say 'hard,' what do you mean?"

Chronemics – This is the study of how people use time. As a counsellor, it is important to gain factual information regarding time intervals, and not be led by language to form assumptions. It is important to be clear on time, location, and accuracy of recall. This is true when working with persons who have potential substance abuse issues.

CLIENT: "I was out for a bit last night"
COUNSELLOR: "How long is a bit? Can you tell me how many hours you were out?"

Physical Environment – This may be out of your control; however, it is highly recommended that you do all you can to create spaces without barriers and boundaries. NOTE: This must never be at the expense of personal safety to the client or yourself.

Eye Contact – Match the natural style of the person you are talking to, rather than force your style on them. Maintain eye contact only when it is comfortable and safe.

Voice Tone – As in eye contact, it is important to work to match the client when appropriate. Be aware of your speed, volume, tone, timbre, and pitch.

Vocabulary – Use vocabulary appropriate to your client. Also be aware of your regionalisms and colloquialisms – eh!

> COUNSELLOR: "Has a precipitous episode with your betrothed hastened your pronouncement that the nuptials are terminated?"
> CLIENT: "What does that mean?"

Accentuation – Be mindful how you are using your non-verbals to communicate your message so that you are not overpowering the person you are working with. Example: As a counsellor, sit back in your chair at the same level as the client. Do not point at the client when you are talking or trying to make a point. Be aware of how your body language is being used in the conversation.

Favorite Phrases – Become aware of the person's favorite words and phrases and when appropriate use them respectfully in your language.

Reflecting – Reflecting is where you repeat key words used by clients, with the goal of showing you are in tune with them. It is also an effective tool for encouraging clients to tell you more without directly asking for it. The goal is to allow safe and comfortable lead-ins for further conversation.

> COUNSELLOR: "What I am hearing you say is that you have been challenged in understanding what we are expecting from you. Is that correct?"

Shadowing – Repeat what the client has said, using your own words. It is an effective way to show that you are focused on the client and truly engaged.

> COUNSELLOR: "Am I correct in saying that you do not feel appreciated by your peers, and that you would like them to be more aware of your challenges?"

Contextual Listening – Listen for content and details, as well as how the events are impacting the person, cognitively and emotionally.

> COUNSELLOR: "I recognize that you are concerned about your current situation. Help me understand how it is preventing you from coming to treatment."

Use of Silence – Present yourself as calm and patient. Sometimes it is of value to slow the pace and take a few seconds for silence. Allow five to six seconds to go by before making your comments. Be mindful that this can be uncomfortable for some.

> Example: Client seems upset. One strategy is for the counsellor to wait 5 or 6 seconds for the client to calm down before addressing the situation.

Innocent Probes – These are sounds such as "Hmmm, I understand, yes, etc.," to keep the conversation going. It shows the client you are engaged and listening.

> CLIENT: "Today is just a bad day. Nothing is going right."
> COUNSELLOR: "Hmmm tell me more, Gertrude."
> CLIENT: "I woke up late, spilled my coffee in my car, got a speeding ticket, and was late for a business appointment."
> COUNSELLOR: "Oh my! I understand what you are saying. Continue, please" (counsellor leans forward to show interest, nods head. This shows how the client that you are listening and want to hear more).

Clarification Statements – Clarification is when you explore clients' thinking with them to ensure you are processing and understanding the intent of their message. This is a helpful strategy for avoiding misunderstandings.

> COUNSELLOR: "A few minutes ago, you said you drink nine beers a day; now you are saying you drink 12 in an average day. To help me understand your current risk, how many beers do you really have a day?"

Reframing – With reframing, you provide the person with another meaning for a situation, to help them attach a different meaning.

> COUNSELLOR: "This situation has affected your relationship both at home and at work. Am I close?"

Open Ended Questions – These are questions that cannot be answered with a simple yes or no. They encourage the client to provide more information. They also are an excellent way for clients to explore their internal frame of reference for meaning and evidence.

> COUNSELLOR: "When do you think will be a good time for us to chat?"

Justifying Questions – Ask the person to explain what you perceive as various incongruencies, which you have picked up in the conversation. This must be done in a non-threatening manner. It provides clear evidence that you are listening, as well as tracking the conversation accurately.

COUNSELLOR: "You said you get into trouble every time you think about going to a treatment program. Can you please explain to me what you mean by every time?"

Consequence Questions – This means asking clients what the consequences of their actions are, with the goal of ensuring that clients are aware of the cost and impact of these choices on their future.

COUNSELLOR: "What are the repercussions for drinking and driving?"

Encouraging Statements – Provide clients with encouragement to give more information, as well as to show your support and commitment to their success.

CLIENT: "I feel frustrated."

COUNSELLOR: Nods head as the client is speaking, and utters a verbal sound of "Ummm" to keep the client talking about feelings of frustration.

Positive Assets Statement – Be sure to point out the client's capabilities. Unfortunately, too many people who have life management issues forget their special talents. This is independent of validating; it is a frank and honest observation.

CLIENT: "I have been a homemaker so long I don't feel confident to start over by myself."

COUNSELLOR: "It takes a great deal of organizational skills to successfully maintain a home and family, and you did this well for 15 years. Let's start with a list of the skills you have. Then we can start to explore what the options are for you. OK?"

Selective Attention – Ask a question to get the person back on task with the primary focus of the discussion. This is a way to help keep you both focused on the present situation and needs.

CLIENT: "My car broke down again, the power company is threatening to shut off my power and I'm afraid my job will end at the end of this month."

COUNSELLOR: "Have you received formal notice that your job will end this month?"

CLIENT: "Well no, I've just heard a rumor so far."

COUNSELLOR: "Is it possible that it may remain just a rumor?"

Filter all Communication with a Non-judgmental Ear – Judging your client may limit opportunity.

Reflective Listening – This is when you listen to the person's whole message. The purpose is to show that you are listening and to close any gaps of misunderstanding – a powerful tool for addressing conflict. You suggest that you hear a theme and check in to see if that is what the client is saying. It is a way to ensure you both are on the same wavelength.

Emotional Filter – Be mindful of your emotions when another person is talking and ensure you are monitoring the person's emotions at the same time. As a counsellor, you must be in charge of your own emotions.

> CLIENT: "My mother recently passed away; I really miss her."
> COUNSELLOR: "I know how hard it must be. My mother recently passed away as well. We will support you the best we can as you work through this family issue."

Avoid Overpowering Communication – Be aware of your position and the power it can have on a person. Understand the counsellor's role is to assist people, not to control them. It is often not the words that make a message; it is the delivery of the message.

> Example: A client is being abused by a spouse and tells the counsellor. It would be wrong for the counsellor to tell the client to leave the spouse. The counsellor's role is to help the client sort out what action would be best. If the counsellor tells the client to leave the spouse, the client may do this unprepared, only to try to please the counsellor, thus possibly end up in another crisis situation.

Discover the Person's Internal Mental Filters – We all have personal frames of reference that impact how we perceive and deal with the world. It would be impossible to truly understand clients without some understanding of their frame of reference. You do not need to know all of their baggage, though you do need to know how they make decisions and the criteria they use for forming them, e.g., motivated by the stick or the carrot.

> Example: If people see the world from an external locus of control, they could base their decision making on fear of consequences they think may arise. If they view the world through internal locus of control, they would use a different frame of reference for their decisions. This will help counsellors to more fully understand their client's frame of reference.

Avoid Assumptions and Conflict – The counsellor's role is not to assume or to create conflict with clients. Monitor the client's and your own communication, to ensure you do not fall into conflict. We talk with people, not at them. A debate is different. Counsellors do not need to agree with clients; they need to ensure they do not fight with them.

Be Aware of Visible and Invisible Cultural Differences – Seek to understand what you need to know to be effective with all new clients. If you do not know, ask, or you may never know, and you may do more harm than good in your efforts to communicate.

CLIENT: Stares at his hands and shifts in his chair when he looks up and sees the counsellor attempting to make eye contact with him.

COUNSELLOR: Noticing the client's discomfort, says, "I've noticed that you have not made eye contact with me during this session. I am wondering if eye contact is discouraged in your Japanese culture. Or is there another reason you're not making eye contact?"

Be Clear, Focused, and Internally Congruent – Stay in tune with your true intentions and motivations each and every time you talk with a client. This is an underpinning principle that cannot be forgotten. Believe that people have potential, and stay committed to this belief as a client helper.

Example: A counsellor is trying to project active listening to what the client is saying. To do so congruently, the counsellor uses open-handed gestures, eye contact, leans forward, and uses concise language.

Movement Synchrony or "Mirroring" – This is a form of communication through the use of body language. When communicating, a person may unconsciously mimic another's hand gestures, body position, and movement. A counsellor may also use this form of communication to help make a client feel more relaxed or comfortable in a counselling session.

CLIENT: "I don't feel right talking to you about this." (Sitting back in the chair and pushing it back slightly.)

COUNSELLOR: "I understand this must be difficult for you. Understand that I am here to listen." (Also sits back to allow the client to have personal space.)

Non-Attention – It is sometimes necessary to NOT attend to statements made during communication, as when clients revert to talking about the same thing over and over, or when they continually dwell on negative thoughts. By not making eye contact and not paying attention to changes in body posture, vocal tone, etc., the counsellor can move the conversation forward rather than stagnating. This helps the counsellor to not buy into the other person's automatic actions and is helpful in keeping the conversation in the safe zone.

Positive Regard – This is non-judgmental caring, when one's positive regard does not change for another regardless of what choices or actions the other takes. The counsellor lets clients know by non-judgmental response that their choices are seen as valid ones.

> COUNSELLOR: "You have shown a strong commitment to attending your program. I think you are starting to discover you are capable of doing more than you believe."

Chunking – This is the ability of the mind to categorize the information it receives into groups instead of bits and pieces. This helps the brain organize and store information into similar segments. This is something that is done unconsciously. We do not decide to do this; our brain does it automatically.

Summarization – This is a technique used by a counsellor to ensure that a client's story has been heard properly. Summarization may be used at the beginning, middle, or end of the session to sum up what has been discussed thus far. Summarize their message, using your words, to ensure that what you perceive is what they said, and to show that you are listening.

> COUNSELLOR: "So what you are saying is that you're stressed about what issue you need to address first, and this is stopping you from doing anything. Does that sound close?"

Re-story – This is effective in helping clients construct a new story by listening to their past story and assisting them in identifying strengths. A new story is developed related to how they talk about themselves on the basis of identified strengths and is the beginning of taking their story in a new direction. This is an important tool in empowering clients to take action and make change possible.

> CLIENT: "I haven't done anything of great educational value."
> COUNSELLOR: "You told me that you have finished your MBA; that's very important."

Monitoring Paralinguistics – This is the self-monitoring of one's vocal expression: rate, pitch, tone, etc. This helps to ensure that you do not overpower the person you are communicating with and that your paralinguistics are appropriate for the situation.

Generalizing – Generalizing is when a person, problem, idea, etc., is referred to in common terms, rather than a singular, unique subject.

> CLIENT: "Everybody's the same; no one understands me."
> COUNSELLOR: "What do you mean everybody is the same?"

Influencing – This is the art of providing your point of view in a manner that is non-threatening. It is important to be interested in the other's views first, so you have an opportunity to influence them on your point of view. To influence a person, the key is to first listen, then pause and wait for your turn. Speak with people, not at them, and avoid repeating yourself. Be passionate; don't sound like a salesperson.

Paraphrasing – This is rewording and simplifying a client's comment to clarify the meaning, and to ensure that the counsellor is pacing the client correctly.

> CLIENT: "It's not fair that he does not want to stop drinking and take care of his responsibilities."
> COUNSELLOR: "You're concerned he doesn't show an interest in meeting your expectations of what a husband needs to do for his family?"

Reflection of Feeling – This is to give feedback to key feelings, sometimes hidden ones, with the use of key feeling words and paraphrasing.

> COUNSELLOR: "You did make a really tough decision for you and your future."

Monitoring Discrepancies (also known as incongruity and mixed messages) – Discrepancies can be found in internal or external behaviour and thoughts. Body language may not be in sync with verbal language. Clients say one thing, yet their tone of voice, body posture, etc., show that they may mean something else. Other instances of discrepancies appear in a backhanded compliment, the non-apology and "lint-picking" behaviour. A client's ideal world is often not in sync with the real world.

Decatastrophizing – Questioning clients using "what if . . ." questions so they can see the real extent of the problem and potential risks. Very often people will make something bigger than it really is. The *what if* question helps them to stop catastrophizing.

> COUNSELLOR: "John, what if your wife does not agree with your point of view on this matter?"

Observing – Gather information on an ongoing basis so that you are able to stay congruent. Pay attention to what is happening around you and provide feedback accordingly. Observing involves collecting information from your perception of the environment, as well as the person (e.g., if the background noise is disrupting the conversation, move to a quieter location).

Transactional Analysis – This is a popular psychology term which provides a clear explanation of how people communicate and get into communication difficulties. Transactional Analysis explains that humans have three main ego states, (parent, adult and child) which they draw from for all communication. Once you become aware of what you are doing (which ego state you are in), you will have an opportunity to create a new behaviour from a more appropriate ego state.

The three ego states provide a clearer understanding of how a counsellor's behaviour and that of a client influence the way the client responds. For example, if the counsellor speaks from a Critical Parent ego state (speak in a raised voice) and the other person responds from their Rebellious Child ego state (in a protective manner) it is obvious that there is a problem in the communication patterns.

Where Transactional Analysis is helpful is not only understanding that the best ego state to work from is the Adult ego state (neutral) and the Free Child (creative and fun) ego state, but also to be aware of the not-so-obvious ulterior transactions that are damaging and lead to false relationships (see figure 2-4).

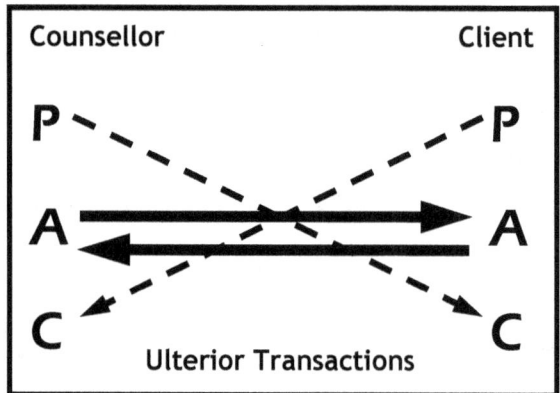

Figure 2-4— Transactional Analysis Ego States

Since these blind spots of transaction occur, and often are not heeded, they can be extremely damaging to a relationship. To keep the communication open in crisis and conflict, be congruent, aware, and true to your beliefs.

Contrast – Contrast is the art of showing what else something could be. Many times we can get caught up in our own model of the world and become blind to what others deal with every day. Sometimes by providing other people with contrast, they can become aware of more than their own reality. This can be done by questions like, "Do you know what it is like to make a mistake that changes your world? How do you believe John feels now since he made this mistake? Is it possible John knows he made a mistake and he is hoping there are people who love him and will help him find a new path? And is it possible that he can't really do this without the support of his family?"

Refocus Agreements – There may be times that your creative system will frustrate other people. You may have had agreements, but they call you on a point because they do not think it is fair. It is not necessary to always change or say you're sorry. You should only say you're sorry when you have done something wrong, not to appease someone. If you have not done anything wrong, you may consider asking a question like: "Did we agree I could not ... ? How have I done something wrong if my intentions are not malicious? Can we refocus the agreement and clarify the issue?"

Enforce Agreements – Be fair, consistent, and predictable. If someone breaches an agreement, call them on it immediately. You could do this in the following manner: "We agreed if there were any danger you would use the support line ... now it seems you were in danger over the weekend and you did not. What happened?"

Use Metaphors – Use stories to explain a point. Stories help to move the focus to a neutral topic so that individuals may not feel they are being confronted. This can lower defenses and help them make the needed associations. Metaphors help to dissociate the focus of the conversation and can covertly make your point without resistance.

Meta-cognitions – These help tune your awareness of how people are forming their present cognitions. For example, when people are tuned in to, and hearing their own thinking, they are Meta-cognitating. To promote the skill of becoming aware of one's own thinking, consider the following ideas: ask clients what internal dialogue they are having. Instead of asking for the right answer, which is an absolute, have them focus on the process and the strategies they are using to come up with an answer. One good question is to ask clients to come up with four reasons why something would be the wrong choice. The art of comparison and critical thinking comes from focusing not on what we think about, but how we come up with what we think about.

Practice the Three Rs – <u>Rapport</u> – People must perceive that they are safe. This takes into account the environment, comfort, confidentiality of the conversation, ability to find common interest and common ground, safe non-verbals, and that you are aware of your tone, volume, and pitch.

<u>Respect</u> – You must come across as non-threatening, non-judgmental, open; your language is appropriate and you are aware of individual differences.

<u>Relationship</u> – Be aware of cultural sensitivity issues and multicultural differences and needs.

Use Creative Ploys – The power of creativity may help open a person's perception to process information in a different manner. For example, one effective question is, "What if we ...?'" This may open up an active mastermind dialogue. The key is to suspend right and wrong, and encourage brainstorming and creativity.

Playback – Sometimes it may be necessary to do a complete play-by-play review of all the facts that have been shared in the conversation. The key is to highlight only the facts, and to avoid adding your opinion.

COUNSELLOR: "Can I play back all the key facts I have heard so far?"

Separate Behaviour from the Person – If clients do something you do not appreciate, separate them from their behaviour so they know what your issue is. This can be done by using the following kind of strategy: "I am prepared to help you, however, you are missing appointments without notice. How can I help you if you do not show up, and how can I keep booking time others could use if you are not committed to attending treatment?"

Speak from Your Heart – Speak from your heart when you communicate; speak truthfully and with passion. Obviously, the intensity will depend on the situation, but it is important to be real and congruent with what you believe.

Establish Common Purpose – Often when the stakes are rising in a conversation, the focus is lost. When this happens, go back to defining the common purpose. When you perceive an individual's agenda is being promoted, ask, "What is our common purpose in this matter?" Then help flesh out what is needed to develop common ground and increase safety.

State Your Intentions – When you perceive a person is becoming defensive and the conversation is becoming less safe, it is important to qualify your intentions. This helps open the door to perception, and aligns the conversation to what needs to be enhanced and established so it can move forward effectively.

COUNSELLOR: "My intentions are . . .; they are not to upset you."

Take a Time Out and Challenge Your Decision – If you are not sure why you are debating a point, it is helpful to request a break so you can determine what you are talking about and the rationale behind it. This takes courage, though it is important to help you keep oriented to facts rather than emotions, where too often ego rules. For example, "Do you mind if we take a break so I can research my position to ensure I am expressing my point of view from a position of facts and logic, and not ego?"

Stop Repeating Yourself – If you find you are repeating content over and over, you may want to ask yourself, "Do I know where I want to go with this client?" Often the response is "no," and you are lost or stumped as to what you need to do. Whenever you feel you are lost or repeating yourself, one way to refocus is to ask questions such as: "So what have we agreed to so far? What have you learned so far in counselling?" Their responses will help get you focused and directed as to where to take the conversation.

Transactional Communication – Often people have communication difficulties when one person is focused on the content dimension (e.g., counsellor says, "You appear to have a challenge with drugs") and the other is focused on the relational dimension (e.g., the client responds with a comment such as, "You think I am a druggy"). From a Meta communication point of view, in any conversation, when one party focuses on content, and the other on relational dimensions, there will likely be difficulties. You need to match the other person's communication position to build rapport and move on. For a breakdown:

COUNSELLOR: "You appear to have a challenge with drugs." (Content)

CLIENT: "You think I am a druggy." (Relational)

COUNSELLOR: "I want to confirm if you think you have a problem with drugs. How I can do this without you thinking I am judging you?" (Matches and responds in relational context)

A New Way to Listen, Using Meta Programs – To become an outstanding communicator, you need to understand that we all have different ways to interact and process the world. One way to learn how to communicate and understand other people's models of the world is to learn their Meta programs. These are the programs that we have in our heads that we use to filter and process information. They help to keep us from being overwhelmed by all the sensory information.

If we can learn others' Meta programs, we can tune into them and be effective in how we interact with people. First, I will explain how to recognize the different Meta programs and then provide one or more questions to use in finding which program the other person is using. Once we learn to listen for the person's Meta programs, we are in a position to use them to enhance communication. These programs are the source of understanding how to motivate others.

Assessing Meta Programs (internal filters)

Direction sort — This determines how a person is motivated. People are basically motivated towards (by reward and pleasure) or away (moving away from pain and discomfort).

Q: What do you want from your favorite counsellor when you are learning?

A: *Towards* — A counsellor who provides an opportunity to learn and a path for growth as a person.

Away — A counsellor who is not mean or fearful.

Frame of Reference — This determines if people are motivated from an internal locus of control or external locus of control. This is important to see if they get their direction from what they think, or by others as they interact with the world.

    Q: How do you know when you have done a great job?

    A: *Internal Locus of Control* — I just know inside, no one has to tell me.
       External Locus of Control — Someone has to tell me.

Note: Listen for the answer. Some people need a little of both. Find the desired preference, so you know how to work with them.

Convincer Strategy — This is the program that decides when a person is competent. We all have a formula we use to measure competency in another person. This is important to know when we are working to convince someone; it tells us how much we need to work to convince them.

    Q: How many times does someone have to demonstrate competency for you to be convinced?

    A: One time.
       More than once, thus many times (_____ fill in the number from each person).
       Over a period of time (_____ length).
       Need to prove every time — they have a constant need of convincing, they are hard people to be convinced.

Convincer Representational System — This is the program that helps you learn what the person's primary method of communicating is with the outside world. Some people are visual (see), audible (tell) or kinetic (feel). When asked a question, what they answer determines how they like to communicate.

    Q: How do you know someone is doing a good job?

    A: I need to see them — a visual person, they like visual language and pictures.
       I need someone to tell me about how they clicked, or have a talk with them.
       I need to read about them or do it with them so I know how it feels.

Action Filter — This tells how people work if they go into great detail before they proceed and if they react quickly.

    Q: When you come across a new opportunity, do you usually react quickly after you size it up, or do you need a detailed study before you proceed?

A: *Reactive* person acts quickly.

Reflective person needs time to prepare and study it before they proceed.

<u>Reason Filter</u> — This filter tells if people look for the possibilities in a situation for motivation, or they get motivation from xxx and have to see xxx in a situation.

Q: Why are you choosing to do what you do each day at work?

A: *Possibilities Response* — They see all the practical options and possibilities they will get for their present actions.

Have-to Response — They report that they have no choice. They must do what they are doing at work. They do not see the options, only limitations.

<u>Chunk Size</u> — This determines how people like to receive information. Do they like the big picture first or do they want all the details?

Q: If we were going into a business opportunity, would you want to know all the details first or the big picture?

A: *Details* — If they respond with details, find out how much of the big picture they need.

Big Picture — If they respond with the big picture, find out how much detail they need.

<u>Relationship Filter</u> — People can either notice primarily the *sameness* or matching properties of something, or the *differences* or mismatching of something when compared to another. For instance, do you first notice that three coins on your table are all tails, or that one is upside down?

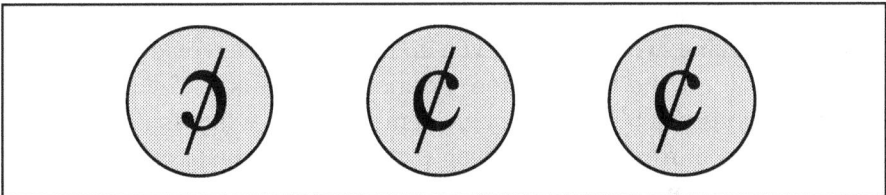

<u>Attention Direction</u> — This filter helps you determine if they filter the world through "I" or other. People who focus on self first appear to be in their heads a great deal and not paying attention. If they sort by others, they are in tune and active. There is no question per se, just observe the person. The most successful people are those who sort by others.

<u>Affiliation Filter</u> — This determines if a person likes to work with people or by themselves.

Q: Think about a situation in your life where you were the happiest. Was it when you were alone or was it with a group of people?

A: It was when I was (story of being alone) — independent player.

It was when I was (story of being with a group or team) — team player.

With practice, in five minutes you can find out all of the Meta programs of the people you are working with by using the above questions. The value is you will have a method to directly link and hook up with the way they process the world. It is an excellent tool to enhance communication.

Neuro-Linguistic Programming Communication Strategies – A science called Neuro-Linguistic Programming (NLP) provides a powerful method to take advantage of non-verbal communication, as well as other strategies. Since the majority of communication is done through body language, most people pick up cues at an unconscious level and then rely on words to communicate their desires. This section provides an example of how you can use non-verbal communication to develop rapport and effectively allow yourself to maintain communication in a congruent manner, to reduce conflicts.

<u>Pacing and Leading</u> – Pacing (mirroring and matching others' behaviour) can be used to duplicate someone's behaviour. When you mirror or match, you are modeling their behaviour at a conscious level; however, they will receive information only at an unconscious level. You do not need to be concerned that they will notice you modeling their behaviour, because you are communicating to their unconscious only.

If you follow these guidelines, you will do just fine and start to build instant rapport.

An example of matching: when the other person moves their right arm first while talking; when you talk, you do the same. You would match body posture, head tilt and foot position. Position yourself at a 45-degree angle, so your actions will be less obvious. All mirroring is acting as if the person is looking in a mirror, while matching is moving the same parts (e.g., if they move their right arm, you move your right arm).

You should flip back and forth between mirroring and matching to be less noticeable. Practice this skill at home and with friends until you feel comfortable. The purpose of mirroring and matching is to build rapport, to help lower tension and build a safe environment to open lines of communication. When you can start to match a person's behaviour in a non-threatening manner by using non-confrontational language, you are on the road to building rapport.

Once you have built rapport by mirroring and matching, you can start to lead, and clients will model your behaviour, outside of their level of awareness. You will find that pacing and leading techniques (mirroring and matching in action) will become a powerful tool in building rapport, which will quickly lower tension.

An Example of Pacing and Leading Using Matching and Mirroring

CLIENT: Telling you about a run-in with their spouse. Client's hands are moving slowly, and sitting with legs crossed.

COUNSELLOR: When you respond, you start to match and mirror the client's behaviour. Note: Things to watch are the client's breathing pattern, eye blinking, head tilt, posture, lower body position, hand movements, and speed when speaking.

CLIENT: Starts to increase behaviours during the discussion. Client is raising the voice, beginning to talk faster, breathe faster, and move their faster.

COUNSELLOR: You start your response by pacing (matching or mirroring) behaviours, to build instant rapport. If client behaviour starts to escalate, you stop matching and mirroring, and move to have client pace you.

You now lead client by shifting away to a calmer voice, use slower hand movements, and move slowly to another location. NOTE: In the rare situation that the client does not follow, go back to pacing again. The key is rapport.

CLIENT: As client starts to pace your movements (at an unconscious level) and begin to relax (e.g., breathing slows down) client will appear calmer and ready to problem solve. **Remember, this is done outside the client's level of awareness.**

Bandler and Grindler developed a system for building rapport with language, based on how people move their eyes. They discovered that the eyes told a story of how a person accessed information. Figure 2-5 shows the visual accessing cues of a normally right-handed person (note: If you are left-handed, just flip the graphics. The Vr, Ar and Ai would be on the left side of the page and the Vr, A, and Vi would be on the right).

What Bandler and Grindler found is that where a person's eyes moved when answering a question told what internal representation system the person was using. They determined that people choose from three primary systems and usually have a primary one which they use most.

For Right-Handed Person (it's usually opposite for a left-hander)

<u>Visual</u> – In this representative area, the person looks up to the right to remember, or to the left to create. When speaking in a visual modality, people use words like see, look, and picture. These people usually also talk fast.

<u>Auditory</u> – When a person's eyes look in this area, they are accessing sounds. They use words like talk, sound, listen, and they talk more slowly than visual people; they like to hear the words.

<u>Kinetic</u> – When accessing feelings they look down to the right. They use words like feel, grasp, and understand. They talk more slowly, and experience the world through emotion.

Using NLP

Visual Accessing Cues (for a normally organized right-hander)

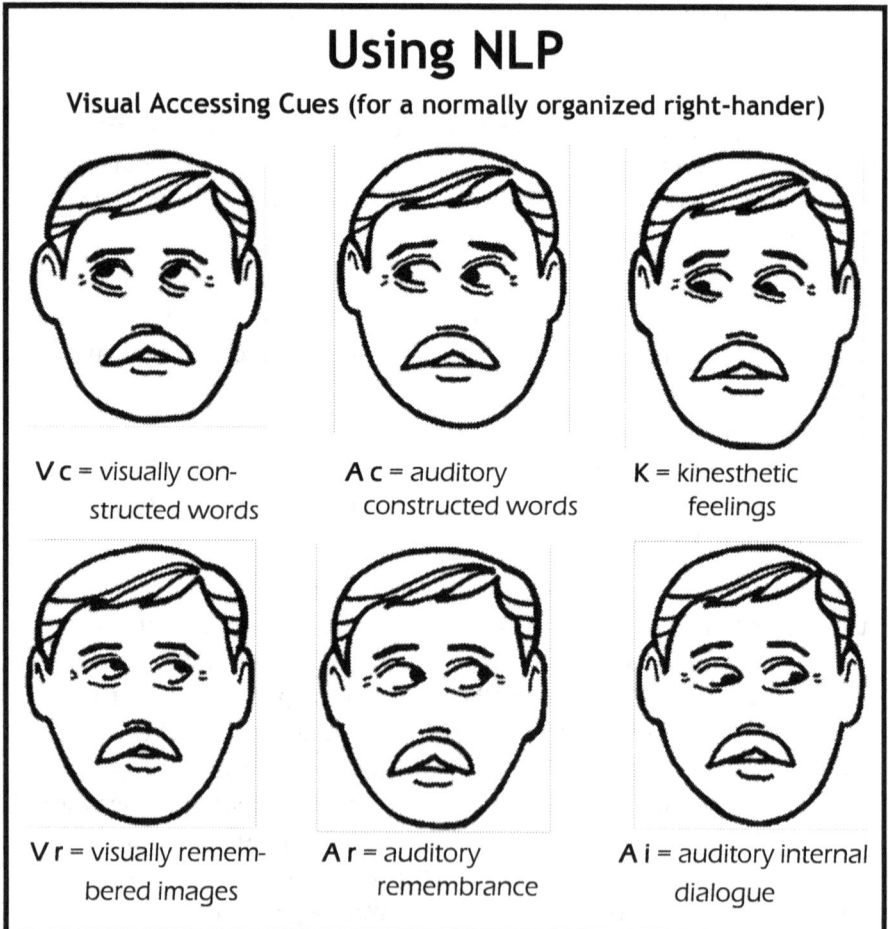

V c = visually con-
structed words

A c = auditory
constructed words

K = kinesthetic
feelings

V r = visually remem-
bered images

A r = auditory
remembrance

A i = auditory internal
dialogue

Figure 2-5 — Using Neuro-Linguistic Programming

Communicating Using Eye Movements – One useful technique is to learn what representation system people use with their eyes when they are in a conversation. For example, if you ask, "What do you want?" and the person moves their eyes up to the Vc position (figure 2-5) while thinking about what to say, you know they are using a visual modality and are visually remembering what they want. So if they said, "I don't know," you could respond using the visual modality with, "I know you don't know, but what do you see?" This matches their modality and your words.

Matching Verbal Predicts – The key is to match the client's language in the conversation. See the examples below to explain the technique.

Kinesthetic Matching:

CLIENT: "I feel I have no idea of who I am."

COUNSELLOR: "When was the last time you *felt* you knew who you were?"

Visual Matching:

CLIENT: "I *see* no hope of getting her back."

COUNSELLOR: "How long have you *seen* this picture?"

Auditory Matching:

CLIENT: "I really do not know what you are *talking* about."

COUNSELLOR: "When you *hear me speak*, what do you find *hard to understand?*"

With practice you will find that Neuro-Linguistic Programming techniques are powerful communication methods that allow you to use body language and verbal language effectively to establish rapport.

Non-verbal Communication – Earlier in this text we referred to non-verbal communication being a large part of how people "read" others. The need for congruency is critical to ensure that your verbal content matches your body language, or you will negate the positive points/information you are trying to communicate. Without this congruency you will never make the emotional connection that allows the listener to trust you. Without trust, active listening is limited and impedes the positive transfer of knowledge or ideas.

When you initiate communication, keep in mind that you succeed or fail in the first 30 seconds. A client has probably consciously or unconsciously sized you up before you speak. Knowing this is half the battle to ensure that your body mirrors your words. Strive to suit your words to your actions, and your actions to your words.

Posture is another key element in body language. Behavioural psychologists tell us that humans read the authority of an individual from the trunk and chest of their body. It conveys authority or the lack of it. Always stand or sit up straight, with your chest up and your shoulders down to maintain good posture. Congruency is key here, as you never want to contradict the spoken word with negative body language.

Cultural Micro-rhythms – Each culture has its own micro interactions that show up in the form of non-verbal and verbal conversation rhythms. These interactions occur outside the person's level of awareness. In conversation it is normal for people to use what is called super reflex. This is how the body adjusts its physiology to stay fluent and seamless within the conversation, so the conversation has a good beat and rhythm. For example, when a person makes a point they may make a certain gesture and you may automatically respond with a gesture of your own. When you notice a pattern, it is a good sign that the conversation is in a natural flow and that the person's super reflex is tuned in.

Motor Mimicry – This is the power of controlling a conversation by facial expressions, which are directly correlated to emotion. By simply smiling at appropriate times, you can pace a conversation and increase its safety and effectiveness.

Ostensible Head Movements – Head movements also can impact the response of another person's emotions. A simple nod can promote a positive response, just as a side-to-side head movement can promote a 'no.' As again non-verbals are more powerful than verbal cues for determining how a person will respond.

Environmental Imprinting – Fundamental attribution errors point out how many people make the mistake of overestimating the importance of fundamental characteristics (core skills and competencies) and under estimating the importance of the situation and the context of the environment. Avoid judging and be aware that it may not be a person who is the challenge when we are communicating; it may be the impact of the context of the culture.

Drivers of Change – Be mindful in a conversation of drivers that have impacted and influenced a person before. Some are influenced by reward, others by fear. The analogy often used is the carrot and the stick. To determine how a person is motivated, simply ask them a general question, such as, "How did you know it was time to buy a new car?" If they bought it to avoid repairs to their old one, they are motivated by avoiding pain (stick). If it was for some kind of personal satisfaction, they are motivated by reward. This kind of information can be helpful in positioning a conversation.

Conclusion

The key to success in counselling is effective communication. There will always be communication challenges when working with a client, but counsellors who use the tools presented in this chapter will have fewer communication concerns and will build rapport and trust with their clients.

CHAPTER 3

Addiction Counselling Theories

The only person who is educated is the one who has learned how to learn ... and change. – Carl R. Rogers

EVERY addictions counsellor needs to develop their own personal integrative addiction counselling orientation, which includes a wide spectrum of knowledge and skills, such as addiction theory, models, and ethics.

Regardless of the theories one ultimately chooses, it is important to have a general awareness of the core theories presented in these chapters, in order to better understand the language and frame of reference of some peers when discussing what they are doing with their clients and the rationale for their counselling.

An addictions counsellor's role is not to judge clients or peers – ever. One important function of being an effective and non-judgmental counsellor is solid preparation and understanding of human behaviour. This is why addictions counsellors are tested in core competencies from all the theories, because of the importance of having general knowledge and understanding of mainstream theories and their explanations for human behaviour.

Personalizing Counselling Theory

What is counselling theory? Why do we need to know it? How is counselling theory connected to addiction theory? One of the main goals is to provide answers to these and many other questions.

Once you are aware of the core components of some of the most popular current counselling theories, you will be better able to respond to the three above questions. It is important to note that there are literally hundreds of counselling models and theories.

This chapter provides traditional counselling theories, which have been tested and proven over an extended period of time. The ideas from these are still impacting theories, and are still relative. The main criterion in picking theories to include is that they had to be mainstream leading theories. The goal is to put them in a format which teaches the core ideas and themes that will be of real use and value as you counsel clients with addictions.

Basically, these chapters offer tools and ideas that can be used at any level of training. Those with post secondary degrees will find the information is geared for effective addiction counselling, regardless of your degree. However, if you have mastered other tools that you are qualified to practice, please continue. The intention is to meet the wondering why questions, such as: "Why is theory X not here?"

As you work through this chapter, keep in mind the importance and benefits of working with the central ideas of each theory that you believe you can personalize in a manner that supports your integrative personalized counselling orientation. This occurs when you are able to take core ideas from a number of theories, and develop your own counselling model that is based on proven theory. There is no need to be a purest anymore, though there is a need to have a model based on proven theories.

Obviously, there is more than one theory that works or we would not have literally hundreds of theories in modern day counselling. However, for your own risk management, at the very least you should make sure in your development as an addictions counsellor that you have a solid grasp of at least one counselling theory, and build on it.

Jacobs, Harvel, and Masson (1994) maintained that a counsellor who did not have a working knowledge of at least one counselling theory was likely going to be ineffective. An integrative approach still needs to have core theoretical underpinnings and is derived from proven works. Young counsellors cannot make it up as they go. This will not serve them or their client, and can put both at great risk.

Developing Your Integrative Counselling Orientation

Consider this short case study: You are working with an alcoholic who took their first drink when they were 12 years old, and now after 18 years of drinking every day, finds themselves in your office looking for help.

If you were asked what happened for this person to become an alcoholic, what would you say? When you become aware of addictions theory, you will be able to provide a theoretical explanation as to why the person became addicted, based on an addiction model.

Counselling theory provides important theoretical explanations as to 'why people do what they do,' not only addictions. It comes from clinical observation and clinical research, and from observing human behaviour enough that the theorist is able to predict how and why people behave (Kottler, 2002). "All action taken by a counsellor or therapist depends on their particular theory that is adopted as an organization framework."

The theorist model provides a theory and breakdown of the fundamental antecedents and origin of human behaviours. From there, the theorist works to develop a map of strategies and protocols, which form the basis of what is known as the counselling therapy. Therapy is the process the theorist uses to help the client get back on their desired life path.

In counselling therapy, the tools of the trade are called counselling techniques. These are what allow the therapy to come alive. A counsellor who does not have at least one tested and proven counselling theory and therapy in their toolbox will not be effective working with persons with addictions.

Counselling theory is not an option; it is a must in the field of addictions counselling, as it is in all other fields in which counsellors work. The good news is that a counsellor can often take a theory they like and combine it with another to develop their orientation.

Forming A Personal Integrative Counselling Orientation

One needs to ask themselves a few important questions when starting to study any counselling theory or therapy, to develop their own personal integrative counselling orientation.

- "At my level of training, what are my counselling limitations?" If you are not trained as a medical doctor, psychologist, or psychoanalyst, spending time reading and studying Freud may not be in your best interest. As an addictions counsellor, there are clearly defined limitations to the level and kind of counselling you are able to do, and you will need to determine this before you start your employment. Addictions counsellors cannot practice psychoanalysis without proper training and supervision. The bottom line is that you are spending time ensuring that the theory you want to learn is a fit for your level of training and your role as an addictions counsellor.

- How does the counsellor explain the theory to the client? For a client to buy into your personal integrative counselling orientation, you need to be able to explain in simple layman terms that make sense to the client's model of the world, how you counsel, and why you have chosen your methodology. It is important to be able to defend what you do. To do this, you need to understand what you are doing, and why you are doing it, at any moment in time when you are in the counselling process. That is why it is paramount to personalize, and have a well-defined personal integrative counselling orientation.

- How does treatment planning include addictions theory and counselling theory? When you work in addictions, you will have one model of addictions that your agency may advocate more than another (e.g., biopsychosocial model of addictions). However, very often before you have this model you will have the underpinnings of a counselling orientation in place, or one you are developing. Addictions theory explains the cycle of addiction, and provides a recommended outcome and path for what needs to occur for a person to be able to move into recovery. Counselling theory provides the 'hows' in terms of understanding human behaviour. When you are thinking of adding any knowledge or skills to your personal integrative counselling orientation, as an addictions counsellor you must also be thinking about how your chosen counselling theories will support and work in treatment planning and your practising addictions model. To better understand these points, consider how the theories you are using in your counselling orientation can be taught to the client as they follow their treatment plan. For example, if your client is looking to feel more a part of society, you may have aspects of Adlerian psychology in your orientation, because Adler believed that was a core outcome of all humans. In the treatment plan, you may promote the use of support groups like AA, not only because it works with the medical model, but because it is also backed by a well-accepted counselling theory.

- What is counselling therapy? The therapy is the actions and the doing part of counselling. It is the process that allows the theory to become alive for the client, and helps them learn, grow, and make new insights as to how to improve the quality of their life. The therapy is the process the counsellor uses to help the client find what they are looking for. It is important for any new counsellor to have a clear understanding of the difference between theory and therapy. For example, William Glasser's theory is called Choice Theory, and his counselling is called Reality Therapy.

- How can I develop a counselling model based on theory and therapy? As you learn theory and therapies, you will need to put them into action, and you may want to develop your own model. The main point is that regardless of the theories and therapies you choose, you will need to put thought into how you are going to pack-age them to make an effective helping model. The intention of this chapter is not to teach helping models; it is to point out that all help-ing models are based on proven theory and therapies.

- What are the micro processes in the counselling therapy called? Most theories that have an effective counselling therapy have strategies called counselling techniques, which the counsellor uses. When forming a counselling orientation, it is important to define and mas-ter various counselling techniques that can be used with your coun-selling model. This is why you should be diligent as you format your orientation. A clinical supervisor or your counselling professor will be a good resource. All the techniques and aspects of the theories listed here are appropriate for addictions counselling and this level of training competency.

- The 3 Ts are a mnemonic that stands for Theory, Therapy, and Tech-niques. When learning a counselling theory, be clear of how these three parts come together and work within your addiction counsel-ling model.

Before you can truly develop and put together your personal integrative counselling orientation, you need a clear idea of the following:

- Target Population – Age, sex, multicultural considerations, diversity issues, population primary concerns (e.g., gay/lesbian/bi).
- Agency Policies and Procedures – Policies that govern your range and scope of counselling and other functions of responsibility.
- Agency Standing Orders – Daily roles and functions as an addictions counsellor.
- State/Provincial legislation – Legal considerations in terms of prac-tice.
- Addictions Certification – Professional criteria in terms of bounda-ries of practice.
- Personality – The theory needs to be congruent with your personal-ity. All counsellors bring value, beliefs, and personality traits to wher-ever and whatever they do as a profession.

The development of your personal integrative counselling orientation is a process, not an event. However, as you become ingrained in the profession, it is important to study and be purposeful in your learning and mastery of the skills that you will be able to use as an addictions counsellor.

As previously mentioned, the key to developing your counselling orien-tation is to first survey counselling theory, then select core ideas that meet the above criteria. To do this effectively, you should start to develop your own counselling resource toolbox by simply taking theories, therapies, and techniques that you like from various reading ideas and strategies. Once you start processing these tools and integrating them, you will be on your way to developing your own original tools, such as client worksheets and educational handouts. As Stephen Covey (1989) promotes, one of the best ways to learn is to teach. A great counsellor is also a great teacher. Your job as a counsellor is to work yourself out of a job, by supporting and educating your clients to live life on their own. An important goal is to avoid dependency issues.

Directive vs. Non-Directive Counselling Theory

When working in the field of addictions, there may be times when the counsellor needs to be more non-directive than directive. For example, when the client is coming up with a clear plan of what they need to do, the counsellor is often more effective by staying out of the way and providing support. The other side of the coin is that when a client is in crisis and does not know what to do, it may be important to be directive for your own safety. Sometimes the client does not even need to be in crisis; the fact they are in counselling may be enough to create stress and anxiety. To put the client at ease, the counsellor might suggest to the client where to sit, how long the session will be, or describe the counselling process.

The debate wages onover whether non-directive or directive counsellors are more effective. All counselling theories have an innate directive or non-directive component to them; however, both the style and the personality of the counsellor impact the final outcome as to how the message is sent to the client.

You will be able to tell the tendency of each counselling theory discussed in these chapters, but whether the final delivery is directive or non-directive will be determined by how you send the message and how the client receives it. As you look through your window of the world, be mindful of what you are doing, and be clear as to your rationale for being directive or non-directive. For most, a personal integrative counselling orientation will lean one way or another most of the time, but it is important always to be aware of where you are in the counselling process and why.

Stages for Learning a Counselling Theory

For some, going to the dentist may be more fun than learning counselling theory. Why? Fear of theory in general, since for many it has been categorized as something for scholars or university professors who have nothing else to do than read theory. Just talking to a client without theory can be called Ma and Pa counselling. You are just having a conversation and are flying by the seat of your pants. Counselling is much more than a conversation. It is a strategic dialogue that knows the end of the story once the client starts engaging in its logic, and, as with any learning, it takes time and patience. Learning theory first very often means learning a new vocabulary so that you can process the words to understand the theory.

In addictions counselling, always remember you are working with lives. What is each life worth? Would you want a person experimenting with your life or doing what has been proven? The correct answer, of course, is someone who is using models that are proven and that work. Before you see a client, be clear on what you can and cannot do, based on your training and theoretical orientation.

When you are learning a counselling theory or anything else new, consider the following:

Understanding The Four Stages of Learning – All learning starts out in one of four stages:

1. Unconscious incompetence – In this stage, an individual is not aware of what they do not know. For many, this is the stage of awakening to find out something is possible.

2. Conscious incompetence – One is aware of what learning is, and even knows what the outcome is; however, they do not have the skills to get there. This is a frustrating stage of learning where many feel overwhelmed.

3. Conscious competence – This is the stage where the person has the skills they need, though they must really work at it. They are on a quest to obtain more information, and get more practice. Each person will identify a couple of core skills they think they must work on to overcome the limitation or standard they are working at, so that they can raise their own bar of excellence and success.

4. Unconscious competence – This is the automatic stage. The new skills and knowledge have been assimilated into the person's life, and they no longer have to think about it. They handle challenges naturally, and do it very well.

All learning is a process; failure is only a part of the learning process. Edison did not invent the light bulb the first time he tried; in fact it took him well over 1,000 attempts to get the experiment right. It takes the average person 12 to 18 months to master any new skill. To move from conscious competence to unconscious competence is normally where many people give up, due to frustration. In the stage of conscious competence, lapses are normal. If you do not continue to practice, you will not retain knowledge and skill level. The same goes for any addict. They are at risk of a full-blown relapse if they do not keep working and stay focused. Theory takes time. Spend time and effort mastering skills so your orientation is sound, effective, and effortless.

Important Legal Consideration

You have just heard that a 16-year-old male with a cocaine addiction that you worked with for six months has killed himself; and the family wants to sue the agency where you are working.

The best defence is a proactive offense. In addition to your understanding of professional ethics, laws, policy, operational and clinical procedures, you may be faced with the task of defending your *personal integrative counselling orientation*. A well-defined and practiced personal integrative counselling orientation is a best practice, as it provides clear evidence of your competency. This kind of preparation provides the groundwork to be able to demonstrate that your ethics and personal integrative counselling orientation are sound. This is important when you are before a court and are attempting to prove you were not negligent.

If you are asked what counselling theories you used with the client, and you reply that you did not use one, or have one, how will that look to the courts or onlookers as to your competency for being a counsellor in the first place? Ignorance is not a defense. You need to be able to defend everything you do with a client at any time. Counselling theory helps to provide and support your rationale for your counselling orientation.

The above situation may never happen to you, but you need to know it could, and best practice is the best defense. There are no shortcuts to mastery; it takes work.

Importance of Diversity and Multicultural Awareness

When working with any of these theories, be mindful and seek out information in terms of diversity issues and multicultural considerations. Whatever personal integrative counselling orientation you design, ensure you screen it with diversity issues and multicultural considerations. "As professional counsellors, we must learn about the clients' values, interpretations, and beliefs before we can be of any use in helping change to occur" Howatt (2000).

The first step is to build your orientation. Once you have your orientation, make sure what you do is always sensitive and that you are aware that diversity and cultural differences impact and influence how your message is received. If you want to be a master and work within these differences, you need to do the following:

- Ask questions about the culture (e.g., what is it about your culture that I need to know so that I may be able to work more effectively with you?).
- Study the cultures and diversity of populations you are working with, via readings and programs (e.g., heroin addicts' lifestyle).
- Act professionally, take these issues seriously, and do not blow off their importance.
- Understand what works with one culture and population may not work with another, so there is no need to personalize it. Be flexible; listen and avoid language like, "I know what you mean," unless you really do. Be open, interested, and willing to learn and adapt to the client's needs.

For the most part, white Anglo-Saxon males have written all the theories offered. Their models are sound, though they may not take into account gender issues, age, sex, race, etc. Design your counselling model with diversity and multicultural awareness.

PERSON-CENTERED COUNSELLING: CARL ROGERS

"The person-centered approach focuses on the client's responsibility and capacity to discover ways to more fully encounter reality" (Corey, 2001, p. 173).

Reader Notes: Rogers' Model is grounded in a humanistic psychology, and is congruent with existential psychology. It is known for being more non-directive than directive.

Impact on Counselling Profession

Carl Rogers became one of the most influential figures in the promotion of the Humanistic Psychology Movement, not so much because of his theory as a stand-alone model, rather by the fact that almost every modern day counselling theory promotes and advocates core components of his humanistic ideology.

It is fairly universally accepted that people need to feel the counsellor is a trustworthy person and is genuinely interested in their well being, for counselling to be effective or to work at all. Rogers promoted his counselling himself as more a philosophy for living life and coexisting as human beings than a counselling theory. Rogers was committed to the education of the whole person (Rogers, 1980).

Micro skills are the study of how to communicate most effectively so that the counsellor can help the client discover their potential and new solutions. Skills like active listening, contextual listening, paraphrasing, and strategies for building rapport and the counselling environment often can be attributed to the original work of Rogers.

Theory Overview

Rogers believed that all human beings had the potential from within to overcome any life challenges, even an addiction. For this to happen, the counsellor needed to help the client bring out their own personal internal resources. Rogers taught that the main purpose of counselling was to work with the client to create a supportive and caring environment to aid them in the process of realizing their internal potential and then to support them to take new actions.

Rogers referred to this as the actualizing tendency of the person (Rogers 1986). He believed that practicing the three core conditions of counselling – Warm Regard, Congruence, and Empathy – provided the client with the support needed to enhance their self-concept with the end result being self-actualization.

Abraham Maslow

Abraham Maslow was another important author active in the humanistic movement. He developed a model that provided a visual for the process of becoming self-actualized. Maslow's hierarchy of needs is in ascending order, where biological needs are placed at the bottom and social needs at the top. This model indicates that we satisfy our biological needs before our social needs (Plotnik, 2002, p. 332).

Knowing these five levels will be helpful in counselling clients on the path to finding their internal peace of mind. This model also clearly lays out the steps needed for life balance and personal fulfillment. Maslow's five-step model is straightforward. For a person to advance to the next level, they must have the level below in place. For example, in Maslow's model an addict cannot jump from Level 1 to Level 4. This is an important consideration when doing treatment planning with any addicted person. The treatment plan must have a logical progression and be paced for the client's success.

The five steps below will be built into a pyramid diagram with Level 1 at the bottom.

Maslow's Hierarchy

Level 5 Self-Actualization – When a person has reached their full potential. It is defined as being able to define and obtain the fulfillment of their individual and unique potential.

Level 4 Self-Esteem – When a person is able to get the sense that they are acceptable to others and themselves. They believe that they are receiving appropriate recognition for their work, and they feel a sense of value and importance as a human being. They like who they are.

Level 3 Love and Belonging – When a person knows that other human beings not only accept them but also have important caring relationships, and feel a sense of belonging. They know that others care about them, and they care about others. They are able to clearly express where their present sources of love are.

Level 2 Safety Needs – When a person is able to feel they are protected from harm. They do not fear for their life, and can sleep with a sense of peace. They know they have a safe and secure living environment.

Level 1 Physiological Needs – When a person is able to have food, water, sex, and sleep. These are what Maslow called basic survival and primate needs. We must be able to satisfy these needs before we are able to move to Level 2.

Therapy Overview

Rogers' model of counselling is not a linear one; it is more a global model that expands beyond the counselling relationship. Many counselling therapies have a rigor or a model of recommended action steps. The therapy process of Rogers did not. Rogers' model was to be present with the client, and that by living the three core conditions authentically, the process of therapy would occur as a natural byproduct of these actions. The focus was not on a set of techniques more than the qualities, attitudes, beliefs, and behaviours of the counsellor.

Thorn (1992) pointed out that the role of the counsellor was to be real, and to demystify the counselling process so that it was an encounter between two people who were equals, committed to the counselling relationship as the major vessel for driving the therapeutic process, and for its success.

When the client comes to counselling, Rogers (1977) recommended that the entire focus of the counsellor needs to be a willingness to work with the client to understand their challenges and perceived struggles by being fully present. By doing this, the counsellor is able to listen to who, what, where, with, how, why, and when. As they listen to the client in a non-threatening or non-judgmental manner, they are able to be genuine and help the client act on the internal resources and ideas they develop in the process.

Rogers' therapy in action was built on the practice of the following three core functions:

- *Empathy* occurs when the counsellor is able not only to listen to the client, but also respond with evidence that they are interested in the client's model of the world. When empathy occurs, Rogers purports that this human interaction provides the client with the support needed to unlock and free them from the limiting beliefs that have been holding them back. Rogers believed the power of believing in another person's potential was not only helpful but absolutely needed.

- *Congruence* is when the client is fully aware of their internal thoughts, as well as their external behaviours. The counsellor is fully authentic, real, genuine, honest, fully focused on the client's growth, and clear not to judge them. The counsellor also has to be congruent with their own values and beliefs. Rogers was clear that the counsellor does not need to agree to or accept dangerous behaviour.

- *Warm regard* (unconditional positive regard) is when a counsellor accepts and supports the client's choices and behaviour and does not overpower them with their own views or values. The focus is on understanding and responding in a positive manner to the client's choices, and in a manner that is congruent with empathy. Rogers believed it was important to allow the client to come up with their own choice and behaviours so that they were in control of their own destiny and empowerment. Rogers (1965) taught that every action or non-action is seen as a valued choice, as long as it is not one that puts the client in danger.

Some have viewed Rogers' model as being passive and non-directive. For the most part, it may well fit into this category. However, Rogers (1942) himself was convinced that one had to be congruent and genuine to themselves as well as to the client, meaning that Rogers would ask questions and not agree with everything a client would say if it was not safe. Rogers was interested in the process of self-discovery and allowing the client to find their own solutions.

Techniques Overview

Rogers' theory emphasized the tone and nature of the counselling process more than it focused on specific techniques (Rogers, 1961). While the process of building the counselling environment and rapport may not be a specific technique, it is of value to take a look at some processes.

Checklist for Building Counselling Environment and Rapport

- Develop core micro skills, such as attending, non-verbal, active listening, reflection, paraphrasing, open-ended questioning, and closed questions. Micro skills are the specific skills that you can learn and master to help a client believe that you are role modeling Rogers' three core functions.

- Live Rogers' core functions daily, both at work and at home, so that they become ingrained in your person, and they are no longer turned on and off.

- Be aware of multicultural and diversity issues.

- Be aware of risk and active usage. To develop rapport, be fair, firm, and consistent, especially with high-risk addicts. This message needs to be sent early, with dignity and respect.

- In the first few minutes of counselling, ensure a few housekeeping issues are taken care of, such as a client service match. If there is not, help the client find the right resource; ensure they are comfortable, and know where the restrooms are. Explain who you are, what you have done, what your agency does, and the kind of success you have had. Tell the client that if they have questions at any time to feel safe to ask, and explain confidentiality, permission, and consent statement. All of these are to be done in a helpful and caring manner.

INTRODUCTION TO EXISTENTIAL COUNSELLING

" ... Everything can be taken from a man but one thing; the last human freedom is to choose one's attitude in any given set of circumstances, to choose one's own way -- (Frankl, 1962, p.109).

Reader's Note: This section is an introduction to the core ideas of existential psychology in regard to defining the meaning of life as a core theme in addictions. Overall, this is a non-directive model.

Impact on Counselling Profession

The entire field of psychology has a great deal of its origin in philosophy (e.g., Plato). Existential psychology's roots are still aligned with many famous and profound philosophical thinkers, such as Kierkegaard, Nietzche, and Satre. These may not be household names, though in the world of existential psychology they are the fathers.

The simplistic explanation of existential psychology is that it is the study of the meaning of being a human being. Van Deurzen-Smith (1997) explained that existential therapy is not a method or model for fixing the sick, like the traditional medical model; it is a model to help people find their own solutions.

Consider, for a moment, the modern-day Monty Python cult film *The Holy Grail,* which provided one stair on the meaning of life. Why are we here? What is the meaning of life? We all have asked ourselves this question one time or another. Many of us spend our entire lives looking for the Holy Grail that may not exist in the form we are seeking.

Existential philosophy helps people examine core life questions and methods of examining them, so that they can have a much more authentic existence (May, 1981).

Theory Overview

There is so much writing on existential philosophy and psychology that to do any justice to this work is outside the scope of this chapter. Not only is there a tremendous amount of writing on this topic, unless you have a degree or background in philosophy or other in-depth training in existentialism, to understand the original works is a heavy undertaking. It is, though, of great value to share some of the major core life themes of existential philosophy that help when working with addicts.

May and Yalom (1995) teach:

- *Responsibility* – All human beings are responsible for their own choices, and this awareness, when fully understood, is the key to unlock the prison of the person who feels they are a victim of life.

- *Isolation* – All human beings know that they will die, and in the end, they do this alone. We all try to build relationships, though in the end we need to be at peace with the fact we all will be alone.

- *Self-Awareness* – All human beings, to fully be alive, must live in the present. The past and the future are not real, and living there, you are missing what it is to be a human being. All we truly have is the moment, and everything else is dead.

- *Personal meaning* – All human beings spend a great part of their lifetime struggling to find their purpose and meaning in this world. It is up to each person to define their own meaning, and come to peace with this choice to feel fully alive and free.

- *Angst* – All human beings have anxiety. We all spend a lifetime coping with anxiety, and we cannot hide from it. If we accept it as a part of life, we can understand that it is normal as we address and face all the existential themes.

- *Death* – All human beings will die, and this will be the end of our existence in this form. We all need to address this reality, and not hide from it. When we accept death, we can live life in the now, and not fear our natural and logical end.

- *Freedom* – All human beings have choices each and every day. We all live with the fear of making wrong choices. To be free, we need to understand that we need to learn to make our own choices, and not look to others all the time to make choices for us. We need to be brave and believe in our life choices, and then live with them as they come.

In a counselling session with an addict, it would be common for any of the above themes to be brought up, one way or another. These themes, from an existential point of view, are for many the core roadblocks that keep them from living a fulfilling and authentic life.

Counselling Overview

For the most part, there are no real templates of what to do in an existential counselling process. Basically, the counselling process is flexible, and can take a great deal of reflection and processing by both the counsellor and client to make any gains as the client learns to address their core life issues. The goal of counselling is to help the person move from what is known as the existential vacuum, which can be defined as a condition of meaninglessness (a mental state), due to not being able to find meaning for their life.

Mahrer (1996) developed a four-step process to work through one of the above themes. The model is what one would expect for existential counselling, because its mandate is to help the client find meaning for their life.

Mahrer's 4-Step Existential Helping Process

1. Being in the Moment – The first step for a counsellor to learn is to be in the moment, and to be in touch with their feelings and thoughts. Once they have done this, they are in a position to teach their clients. The model is for both the counsellor and the client to identify the emotions that come up in the counselling process, and for both to put names to emotions and thoughts as they come up. The goal is to reach the deepest emotions, because the deeper the emotion, the

more the person is on the road to being authentic as they process this present reality and make sense of it.

2. Integrating the Felt Experience into Primary Relationships – In Step two, the counsellor helps the client to take the present emotions and relate them to their primary relationships. This helps the client to take the trust of the present experience and explore how the emotions play out in other relationships.

3. Making Connections to the Past – Step three is about taking the present resources, thinking about the past situations that caused difficulty, and discussing with the counsellor how things would be different if they were able to use their present skills. The point is to promote that the future is pure, and that the client can improve it by being more in touch and aware each and every day.

4. Integrating What is Learned – This means taking all the lessons of how being authentic and facing their old fears will help the client in the next chapter of their life.

This template leaves a great deal up to the counsellor's understanding of the core life themes in terms of their own life. The goal of therapy is for the counsellor to learn the client's model of the world, with the objective of being present with the client, and supporting them in their discovery of contentment. Howatt (2000) explains phenomenology as the exploration of one's subjective reality and experience as a human being. In this process, the person has the opportunity to discover what they need to know, so that they can move forward in life without the pain they once had.

Techniques Overview

There may be many techniques in existential counselling. Below are five:

Existential Elucidatio – This is an extension of the core listening skills, through supporting and challenging the client to explore existential themes, such as death awareness, freedom, choice, and the quest for meaning. The strategy is to search for existential issues that may be causing the addict troubles, and may be their primary obstacles (Frankl, 1961).

Identification of Core Life Theme – This is where the client is asked to write out 10 of the most important aspects of being a human being. To do this, the counsellor asks the client the following question: "What is the hardest thing about living for you?" The outcome is to help the client to become aware of some of the internal fears and anxiety that they have had, so they can put a name to them, and start to work to overcome them.

Present State Description – This is where the client works to define their present thinking about where they are at this moment in time, then to form some conclusions as to what is happening to them in the moment that is fueling this state of being. It is helpful when a person verbalizes this with a person they trust, so that they can start to create the state they want daily in life (May, 1983).

Deflection of Problems – This is where the client is asked not to focus on the theme of death that may be causing them a great deal of internal conflict. They are asked to look beyond the issue to the choices that they have been making (e.g., will not fly in an airplane). This is to help the client tune in to the fact that they are capable of making healthy choices, and to become aware of how these choices are impacting their quality of life. The point is that we all live in fear and are concerned about death. The challenge is to deflect to the present the resources a person has, and to help them become alive in the now, and not fear what is real and unavoidable. In this case, self-preservation may be the problem, thus learning to make different choices and conclusions may be the key to feeling alive and not worried about death every moment (Frankl, 1961).

Presence – This is not a technique as much as it is an awareness by the counsellor to allow themselves to be in the moment with the client, and to be authentic. The key to many people with addictions is to have a counsellor who is congruent, is really with them, and does not look at them as a number or paycheque. Addictions are a challenge to work with day in and day out, and to learn to work with each client one at a time in the moment is a great gift for the helping process (Yalom, 1980).

Many of the above themes and interventions are done in many AA meetings and one-on-one sponsor meetings. The goal of these techniques is to get the client thinking about who they are, and how to define meaning, then to determine what they need to do to achieve this meaning.

JUNGIAN PHILOSOPHY: CARL JUNG

"Every form of addiction is bad, no matter whether the narcotic be alcohol or morphine or idealism." – Carl Gustav Jung

Reader's Note: This is a model that helps the client to explore and develop their spiritual self in addition to their physical and psychological wellness. Overall, this is a non-directive model.

Impact on Counselling Profession

Carl Jung was the originator of the study of extrovert and introvert personalities. He has had a major impact and influence on professional exploration and questioning of the different kinds of personality, and how these personality traits can impact the person's interaction with the world. Jung believed we all have common life issues, though our personality types influence how we communicate and process the world, and that this was the main difference between human beings. One of the most popular personality assessments is the Myers-Briggs Type Indicator, which is based on the writings of Jung.

Jung not only looked at the mind and body; he took into account the spirit of a person. Today we are seeing a movement back to people wanting to find their soul and passion for life. Jung was a significant figure in promoting the need for balanced body, mind, and spirit.

Theory Overview

As an addictions counsellor, understanding the basics of Jung's theory will help you to assist a client to explore the dark parts of their behaviour, and where to begin. These dark behaviours (e.g., I am stupid and cannot learn) can often be the antecedent of the addiction. Addictions, in the mind of Jung, would be only the symptom of some underlying issue. While it is common knowledge and well accepted that addictions and high-risk behaviours are dangerous, why do people continue to develop addictions when they know this kind of behaviour seldom gets them long-term peace? Perhaps Jung's theory may shed some light on this question as we move through his fundamental ideas.

Jung's theory promoted the need for a person to become aware of the need to develop a healthy balance between their conscious mind (external world) and their unconscious mind (internal world). He believed that the unconscious mind was also broken into two parts: the collective unconscious mind and the individual unconscious mind. Jung was convinced that the collective unconscious mind was shared and universal, meaning that all human beings shared this same mental pool of energy, thoughts, and awareness. He established what he called core archetypes, which were sets of symbols that represented the bridge of commonality among all people. These symbols explained and defined the different potential behaviours, motivations, and actions of a person (Jung, 1964).

Jung defined what he called the shadow archetype as the part of the self the person did not like or want to acknowledge in the conscious external world. This was his way of saying that we are all in the same game of life, together, not one at a time. Jung used archetypes to demonstrate the universal experiences and thoughts that are shared by all human beings, which originate from one collective pool. For an addict to learn that they are not the only one who is thinking a certain way is important and helpful for their recovery. Jung's psychoanalysis and archetypes are outside the scope of this training; however, what is not is the fundamental idea that we all have common experiences. Jung's model can help people to normalize and process these views of the world for what they are, so that they can move beyond the shadows that are holding them back from their potential dreams and quality of life.

Examples of two other archetypes that are common themes in addictions counselling:

- Persona is the archetype of adaptation that mediates how the person's mind works with the information they get from the outside world and their internal psyche.
- Self is the archetype that represents what a person believes of themselves, and defines for them the meaning of life.

Most of us have some personality traits and behaviours that we may see in others but that we do not like; however, Jung pointed out that we all share the same universal pictures and metaphors of life. We cannot exist alone, and we, as a common species, share all we know in one common, conscious, collective pool. Very often, the solutions for life are in front of us, and all we need to do is tune in to this universal body of intelligence, and listen and learn how we can be more effective as human beings. Perhaps this is why the number one way people stop addictions is spontaneously and on their own. They simply form a thought that says, "No more," and from that point on are no longer addicted. How does that happen? Where did this intelligence and the knowledge of how to be able to just stop come from? Perhaps there is more to Jung's theory than some may like to think.

Jung (1956) identified five core themes that we all must face. These themes are universal to all human beings, and need to be dealt with for one to find life balance:

Relationships – Jung was known to promote that there is not a big difference between the sexes; that we are more alike, and in fact are closer to bisexual than the two common ends of heterosexual. He believed that the male unconscious was female (anima), and the female unconscious was male (animus). The challenge of defining our gender role and sexuality is a common theme.

Spirituality – Jung promoted that our understanding of God is an individualist experience. However, it was one that we all need to have fulfilled as human beings. He believed that spirituality was the missing component for many people and the potential missing link for their internal peace. He felt that without spirituality a person was incomplete and would not be able to truly find the full meaning of life.

Mid-life Crisis – Jung worked with many people who were in their 40s and were experiencing mid-life crisis in the fact that they were still looking for the meaning of life so that they could settle in with who they are, and enjoy the life that they had left. It is a common challenge for many people to find themselves at the ages of 35 to 50 wondering what life is all about, and why they are where they are. Examples of issues one may present in a mid-life crisis are marriage, career, money, spirituality, and health.

Death – Jung spent a great deal of time exploring death. He believed that we all are immortal, that we die only in the physical form, and that our soul continues. He believed it was important for people to come to terms with their own death, and to understand that life is a journey and only a first step. There is much more, and we need to learn not to fear death.

Individualism – In addition to the two basic instincts, sex and aggression, he learned from his famous teacher, Freud, there is also hunger and thirst, and one he coined as the individualism instinct, which is a person's effort to find their individual place in the world. Each person is driven by an internal force to find who they are, and this drive influences what a person will do, and how they will behave.

Therapy Overview

Jung's actual therapy, for the most part, involved dream analysis and interpretation of archetypes to help the client to discover and grow, with the goal of addressing one or more universal themes that were creating issues for the person.

In addictions counselling, you will not be doing this kind of work unless you have special advanced training in Jungian psychoanalysis. Kufmann (1995) explained that to work with the unconscious mind, which is the driving force of analytical psychotherapy, takes a great deal of training and expertise. However, what you can do is counsel your clients to explore the core life themes that Jung pointed out, as a way to help the client put commonality to their life issues. One of the most effective learnings from Jung to pass on to the addictions counsellor is the importance and power of learning and understanding our world we live in each day.

Techniques Overview

When working with an addict, the following strategies may prove to be of value when you are looking to help the client define meaning of life, spirituality, and individuation.

   Exploring the Meaning of Life – The following three-stage model was developed by Lance Secretan (1998), the famous Canadian who wrote *Reclaiming Higher Ground*.

   You can use these three stages to facilitate discussion on the meaning of life.

Phase 1 – Immature phase – This is when a person is motivated by penalty and power. All their behaviours come from these two driving forces.

Phase 2 – Traditional phase – This is when a person is motivated and driven by their ego, so that they can fit in with society and meet the standards of the status quo. The person is controlled by their internal self-doubts and is ruled by fear and failure. They are scared that they will make a mistake or not fit in to society. Many people spend a lifetime in this phase.

Phase 3 – Evolving phase – This is when the person is ready and determined to tune in to their conscious mind and is looking for a clear meaning of life. They are motivated to find the connection between their soul and their physical realities. When they are able to do this, they are in a position to define their meaning of life.

   The point of this intervention is that it is difficult to have a client explore their soul and spirituality before they are able to move through phases One and Two. As an addictions counsellor, be aware that talking about the soul and developing it are two different things. Help the client to look at these three phases as a way to prompt a discussion around the kind of experiences a person needs to find meaning in their life.

Development of Spirituality – For clients who want to discuss this in counselling, it is important that the addictions counsellor be comfortable with allowing them to expand on their needs and purpose for spirituality. To do this, the counsellor would be wise to develop a frame of reference for themselves, to be clear on AA and what the underpinnings of this model are, and how they tie in to what Jung was talking about.

Jung believed that the development of spirituality was one important key to opening the door to life balance in terms of mind, body, and soul. As a counsellor, be aware of your community resources and different religions in the area where you are working. You do not need to be an expert; you just need to be aware. To help a client who wants to enhance this dimension of their life, encourage them to attend their religious community's meetings, to read on the topic, and to go to study groups. A religious activity does not always mean or equal spirituality or development of the soul; however, it can be a real path and option for many people looking for new solutions. Religious practices have helped many people find their spirituality, thus this is an option and one that may be worthy of exploring in some addictions cases. It's free, and in more cases than not supportive for a person's development, which is the outcome Jung was suggesting to help a person become fulfilled.

INDIVIDUAL PSYCHOLOGY: ALFRED ADLER

"It is easier to fight for one's principles than to live up to them." – Alfred Adler

Reader's Note: This model is based on helping a client's personal insights into why they are having a life challenge, then finding the right individually-designed action plan to help them fit into society and be fulfilled.

Impact on Counselling Profession

Adler is perhaps one of the most influential theorists of modern times, arguably the true father of modern day counselling theory. He was a sick child, and had to fight through his own sense of not feeling of value or importance.

Adler started in medicine as an eye doctor, and then became a psychiatrist. He broke away from Freud, and started to develop his own thinking. He did not buy into Freud's sexual instincts theory as the driving force of the unconscious mind, and ultimately human behaviour. Leaving Freud and prompting his own thinking may in fact be the most important impact he had on the field. Adler was interested only in the conscious mind; he wanted to work with what both he and the client could experience and see in the now.

Theory Overview

Adler's theoretical model is detailed. Corey (2001) reports that one of Adler's key themes was, "It is not what you are born with; it is what you do with what you are born with" (p.109). Adlerian psychology views personality as being holistic and systematic. Adler's focus in counselling was on the here and now. He also is well known for his belief that clients were more discouraged than sick; that the role of the counsellor was to do whatever they could that was legal and moral to help the client find their own potential, and see that they could have their desired quality of life.

Adler was known for what he called the five family positions: oldest, second of only two, middle, youngest, and only. He was interested in the dynamics of the family unit, and believed that all family members took on one of these basic roles, which were not necessarily determined by chronological age. Adler believed the family of origin had a major impact on a person's development and thinking. He found that each position had a common set of challenges, and that it was important to understand from the client how their family unit may have impacted their development – good or bad – with the goal of teaching them where some of their beliefs and rules may have ignited.

Adler had what he called the five life tasks that all human beings have to achieve to feel they can fit into the community, or what he called the social interest.

- *Friendship* – Each person needs to have a system of friends who are interested in their well being, as well as people for the person to care about. The relationships must be supportive and non-judgmental. Adler believed that a person's happiness can never be at the expense of another human being.
- *Work* – Each person needs to find a meaningful career and work to feel they are a contributing part of society.
- *Love* – Each person needs to know that they are loved by another and/or others, and that they are able to not only receive the love, but are able to return the loving.
- *Self-acceptance* – Each person needs to feel they are accepted as a valuable and important person.
- *Spiritual dimension* – Each person needs to find a connection with their spiritual being, so that they feel a sense of fullness, and are grounded as a person.

Adler believed all people want to be a part of and accepted by the social interest. In doing so, each person is driven by an internal force to feel superior so that they have the strength to drive their behaviour, and obtain acceptance from others so that they feel they are a part of the social interest (community).

Six Adlerian Considerations:

Person – Each of us is unique, and has our own personality, views, beliefs, and goals; however, we all want to end up at the same place.

Life Purpose – Each of us defines our own life purpose. We do this by creating an internal set of rules called fictional finalism. These rules are the driving forces behind our life goals, which are what we think we can achieve and become. They impact our daily lifestyles.

Fear of Inferiority – We all have a fear of not being good enough. When this becomes dominant, it increases our anxiety. If our internal rules are too rigid and limiting, we are at risk of making mistaken goals, and forming faulty assumptions about who we are and our potential to succeed.

Discouragement – When a person feels that they are inferior and not good enough, and any of the above five life tasks seems impossible, they risk forming behaviours such as addictions to help them feel a sense of superiority. Paradoxically, the more the person does these at-risk behaviours, they are in fact moving away from the social interest.

Private Logic – The role of the addictions counsellor, from an Adlerian perspective, is to help the client explore their private logic; to help them discover and create the internal "AH," that what they are doing is not helping them take control of their life; in fact, it is harming them. The process of addictions counselling is to help the person to reduce their life anxiety, through what Adler called encouragement.

Social Interest – The goal of counselling in Adlerian therapy is to help the person lower their anxieties so they can start to feel accepted by the social interest. To do this, the person often needs to change their internal rules; make a new set of life goals; change their life purpose; have a healthy lifestyle; and be committed to the five life tasks on a daily basis.

Therapy Overview

Adler had three clear stages of his counselling:

Rapport – The first role of the counsellor is to build a trusting relationship with the client. Corey (2001) explains, "Adlerian counsellors seek to make person-to-person contact with clients, rather than starting with the problem" (p. 117).

Assessment – Adler used a prescribed assessment format, and most addictions agencies have an assessment package. The counsellor needs to find out from the client in a structured interview where the client is, and use the appropriate measures to help both themselves and the client form a clear hypothesis of the core issues that need to be addressed in counselling.

Awareness of Commitment – This is the insight and comment stage, where the client and counsellor determine the core issues and find the AHs. The counsellor does what Adler called playing the hunches as to what the issues may be. The counsellor may say, "Could it be . . .?" and fill in the blanks. Once the discovery is done, the counsellor determines the client's level of motivation and ownership.

Techniques Overview

A favorite insight from Alder (1958) is when he explained that one of the main goals of counselling was to help the client gain personal insight, so they could move from discouragement to encouragement. Adler wanted to help his clients build the courage to succeed, and to achieve the universal want of all human beings: to be accepted. He was not one who focused on techniques; he was more focused on the client's need, and how the counsellor could help them.

Below are 10 techniques Adler used in counselling to help the client develop insight and encouragement. Adler believed that it was ultimately the counsellor's responsibility to discover the appropriate intervention with the client, which was the combination for unlocking the client's ineffective private logic.

Acting As If – The goal of this technique is to help the client set a mindset of success. The expression "fake it until you make it" holds true for this technique. The client is encouraged to act (e.g., happy at work) in a manner that would represent that they have the resources and internal beliefs that acting in a particular manner is natural. The underlying premise is that with practice the behaviour will feel more natural.

Catching Oneself – This is a technique in the counselling conversation through which the counsellor helps the client become aware of some self-destructive behaviour or irrational thoughts that are perhaps a part of their fatal assumptions. For example, the client may express how dumb they are. The counsellor points this out, and then encourages the client to monitor their daily activities, catch themselves, and move away from this inferiority thinking. The client learns to anticipate events and change their patterns. This may be useful with people who catastrophize, are perfectionists, have eating disorders, or exhibit obsessive-compulsive behaviour.

Encouragement – One of the counsellor's responsibilities is to help the client recognize and accept their positive qualities. The counsellor does this by helping the client identify and label their positive qualities as a way of increasing their courage to address and take on their personal life's tasks. Use encouragement throughout counselling as a way to counter discouragement, and to help people set realistic goals.

Family Constellation – Adler had the client fill out a family constellation questionnaire that looked at parents, siblings, and others living at home. The questionnaire was then summarized and interpreted to give a picture of the client's individualized social world. It looked at the conditions that prevail in the family, specifically the psychological position in the family (birth order), and interactions between siblings and parents. The point was to discover the family of origin impact on the client's life, and to help them see its relevancy.

Immediacy – This is when the counsellor helps the client become aware of the importance of present time. This involves addressing some kind of faulty thinking, and dealing within the present moment. It may help the client to see what is occurring in the session, which is a sample of what goes on in everyday life, and how it may be limiting them from reducing their life anxiety.

Magic Wand – This is a straightforward metaphor in which the client is asked to pretend that they have a magic wand. The client is asked to wish for anything that they do not presently have in their life. The counsellor encourages the client to wish for what they do not have in order to promote growth, and to move outside their mental box that may be limiting their creativity and dreams.

Offering Advice – This is a directive approach where the counsellor sees an opportunity and need to make a suggestion to the client, with permission. This is a way of showing alternatives and options. This gives clients options to explore many avenues that are available to enable them to grow, and take responsibility for their own lives.

Paradoxical Intention – This involves having the client consciously pay attention to and exaggerate debilitating thoughts and behaviours. Also called prescribing the symptoms and anti-suggestion, this brings into the client's awareness how out of proportion the symptoms are to the situation. However, from a risk management perspective, be careful not to have the client exaggerate high-risk behaviours, such as anger and depression. The purpose is to show the client that they are in control of their actions. For example, if a client says they worry about getting their GEDs, the counsellor may ask them to consider worrying from 6:00 to 7:00 p.m. daily, so they can get their worrying in, and do other things in the day, too. It helps put clients through a threshold, and teaches them they are more in control than they want to believe if they can turn a behaviour, thought, and emotion on and off.

Push-Button Technique – The counsellor requests the client to close their eyes and alternately picture a pleasant and unpleasant experience while paying attention to the feelings accompanying each experience. This teaches clients that they can create whatever feelings they wish by deciding on their thoughts.

Spitting in the Client's Soup – This is a method used by the counsellor when they determine that a client is using a maladaptive behaviour, but is getting some reward from it. The intent is to spoil the reward for the client by bringing awareness to them about their actions in the actual counselling session. This helps to expose the natural consequences of the true lack of usefulness of this behaviour. The goal is to help the client learn to decrease this behaviour so that they can move forward to obtaining the goals and lifestyle they really want.

CHOICE THEORY AND REALITY THERAPY:
WILLIAM GLASSER

Choice Theory explains that, for all practical purposes, we choose everything we do, including the misery we feel. — (William Glasser, 1998, p. 3)

William Glasser was training to be a psychiatrist in the late 1950s when he first observed that positive mental health occurred more frequently in clients who took responsibility for their actions and decisions than in those clients treated principally with psychotropic drugs (Glasser, 1965). And he rejected the general therapeutic trend of reliance on medication as a treatment strategy except in extreme cases such as schizophrenia. Glasser expands upon this logic in his groundbreaking book *Warning: Psychiatry Can Be Hazardous to Your Mental Health* (Glasser, 2003).

During his psychiatric training, Glasser also rejected Freud's work (Glasser, 1965), because he could not accept Freud's thinking that human behaviour was controlled by the unconscious mind and early childhood experiences. For the past 40 years, Glasser has been committed to developing alternative mental health treatments. The result of this commitment was the development of Choice Theory and Reality Therapy. Both Choice Theory (theory of human behaviour) and Reality Therapy (model of counselling) are phenomenological and cognitive-behavioural in design. Over the course of his career, Glasser founded the William Glasser Institute (http://www.wglasser.com/), developed the *Journal for Reality Therapy,* and published 20 books on Choice Theory and Reality Therapy.

Theory Overview

Choice Theory hinges on the idea of an internal locus of control, which purports that a client can manage their choices internally (Rotter, 1982). Glasser (1984) argues that the majority of the population operates on the premise that an external locus of control, or their external environment, controls them (Howatt, 2000). Because of this perception, many clients think they are trapped and have few choices. Glasser (2000) explains that this manifestation of stimulus response thinking is at the root of most mental health challenges.

For a client to take control of their life, they need to understand that they manage their own success by internalizing the perception of choice. Glasser (1998) explains that when a client achieves this insight they become empowered to make choices. These new choices then motivate the client to change their present behaviour. Glasser (1965) taught that a client becomes motivated to change when they determine present behaviour is not achieving desired wants, or they learn that they have the ability to make new choices. When the client obtains either frame of reference, they have the opportunity to learn how to live a more fulfilling life.

Choice Theory begins by teaching that all human beings are motivated by genetically driven basic needs (four conscious and one unconscious):

- *Fun* – enjoyment and pleasure.
- *Freedom* – ability to move freely and choose activities.
- *Recognition and self-accomplishment* – acknowledgement and self-worth.
- *Love and belonging* – supportive relationships.
- *Survival* (unconscious need) – food, shelter, and reproduction.

Choice Theory postulates that every client creates their own internal photo album for fulfilling these basic needs and has the choice of what to put in it – meaning that all humans have the same five basic needs, but each chooses different pictures (wants).

Glasser (1998) explains that clients filter the external world through their basic needs. When a client receives external stimuli different from what they want, they experience a brief and involuntary sensation of frustration. The purpose of this frustration is to alert the client that their needs are not being met (e.g., child not listening). Choice Theory teaches that this signal occurs in the comparing of places, when the client compares what they want to what they have. This sensation of frustration occurs only when the client perceives that their needs are not being met, and last only a few microseconds; after that, they make a choice.

Choice Theory postulates that the client's menu of behavioural choices is stored in a cognitive database called organized behaviour. Glasser (1998) argues that all a client can choose is what they know or what they create. Because of potential limitations in these stored learned behaviours, the client can get trapped in ineffective behaviour. For example, if a client learns that alcohol reduces stress, they may rely on drinking to deal with stress to the point that alcohol use becomes problematic. Glasser believes that each client has the ability to create new behaviours. In the above instance, for example, if alcohol no longer appears to meet the client's needs, they may choose to use exercise to replace alcohol.

Glasser (1984) explains that all behaviour can be described as total behaviour. Hence, when a client changes their behaviour and thinking, their feelings and physiology change as well. Glasser employs a car metaphor to underscore the interconnected nature of behaviour. The car in question is front wheel drive.

The front wheels symbolize behaviour and thinking, while the rear wheels stand for feelings and physiology. The engine corresponds to the five basic client needs (universal to all, but each client determines what meets their needs) and the steering wheel represents the choice each client has to direct their car.

This metaphor promotes the concept that a client can take control of their life by controlling their actions and thinking. Because all behaviour is total, any actions a client takes using the front wheels (action and thinking) directly impact the rear wheels (feelings and physiology). Wherever the front wheels go, the rear wheels follow.

Applying this metaphor to real life, a depressed client can change their emotions and get symptomatic relief from depression by choosing a positive, healthy behaviour (e.g., playing golf with a friend). Glasser (2000) emphasizes that the healthy actions will positively impact emotions. He believes self-control starts by accepting responsibility for present behaviour and thinking.

Therapy Overview

Reality Therapy is the clinical application of Choice Theory. Glasser developed Reality Therapy in the early 1960s. Then he authored Choice Theory (formerly called Control Theory) in 1984 because he realized that in order for his counselling process to be accepted in the mainstream, it needed to be grounded in an effective theory explaining the 'whys' and 'hows' of human behaviour.

Reality Therapy is taught in a linear process that weaves among three components. The first component is called *setting the counselling environment.* Glasser (2000) insists that a comfortable therapeutic environment creates an opportunity for the client to learn that the counsellor can be of value and not a threat. This trust is critical for counselling rapport and is the foundation for successful counselling. The second component is called the *procedures that lead to change.* This phase of therapy represents the main body of counselling and consists of four strategic questioning areas used to understand the client's present situation:

- Ask the client how they are presently meeting their five basic needs. How are they determining those needs are not being fulfilled?
- Ask the client what their wants are to learn what they believe will improve their present situation.
- Dialogue with the client to define what they are presently doing to get what they want, and how these choices are impacting their total behaviour. The goal of this questioning is to increase the client's awareness of the effectiveness of their actions or inactions.
- Evaluate the client's choices and how they perceive those choices are helping them get what they want. Then determine what they are willing to do to get what they want. In this section of questioning, the counsellor usually explores concepts from Choice Theory.

The final component of Reality Theory is *planning, measuring, and follow up.* In this straightforward process, the counsellor assists the client to develop a client-centered action plan; that is, a plan based on what the client can control and realistically do on their own. It is important that the client determine clear measures of progress. Glasser (2000) believes that after a plan is developed, it is important to spend time challenging it to ensure that the client and the counsellor have effectively explored potential risks, determined needed core competencies, and put in place relapse prevention strategies, in order to increase the client's chances of success.

Techniques Overview

The effectiveness of Reality Therapy is based on the counsellor's ability to ask effective questions based on the tenets of Choice Theory. One helpful process that many professionals trained in Reality Therapy use is WDEP Radio, a metaphor created by Robert Wubbolding (1988), as noted below:

W (Want) – According to Glasser (2000), self-evaluating questioning occurs throughout the counselling process, because the client's wants and needs change almost daily. Also, the more wants and needs are explored, the clearer the picture of what the client really wants becomes.

Sample questions:

- What do you want?
- What do you really want?
- If you had what you want, what would your life be like?
- What is it you do not want to happen?
- What do you know you need in your life to be happy?

D (Direction and Doing) – The goal of this line of questioning is to assist the client to discover how their present behaviour is or is not working.

Sample questions:

- What are you doing these days to get what you want?
- When you do that, what are you thinking?
- Is what you are doing helping or hurting you?
- When you are thinking that, what do you feel?
- How does your body feel when you are feeling this way?

E (Evaluation) – This line of questioning promotes the linkage between actions and self- responsibility.

Sample questions:

- Does your present behaviour have a reasonable chance of getting you what you want right now?
- Can these choices take you in the direction you want to go?
- Is what you are doing helping or hurting you?
- How is what you are presently doing helping you for the long term?
- Would you be interested in learning a new way of doing things?

P (Planning and Commitment) – This is where the therapeutic action plan is designed. Reality Therapy suggests that all actions need to be simple, measurable, on going, immediate, and client-centered (within the client's knowledge and skills). Finally, the plan must have the client's commitment.

When a plan does not work, the client and the counsellor work together to modify it. Reality Therapy promotes the mantra "never give up."

Sample questions:

- What is it you want to start doing?
- What do you see as a good plan?
- I have a few ideas. Would you be interested in them as a start?
- How will you measure your plan for success?
- What knowledge and skills do you need to achieve this plan?

RATIONAL EMOTIVE BEHAVIOUR THERAPY: ALBERT ELLIS

Rational Emotive Behaviour Therapy (REBT) is a method of psychotherapy that is intrinsically brief and that also aims to help the client achieve intensive, profoundly philosophical and emotional change. — (Albert Ellis, 1996, p. 1)

The author of 70 books and more than 700 articles that represent a major contribution to cognitive-behaviour theory, Albert Ellis is one of the most influential and prolific psychologists alive today. His therapeutic approach can be described as active-directive; that is, actively asking questions to prompt a client to evaluate their own thinking, with the goal of removing destructive thinking and behaviour. For nearly 50 years, through his Albert Ellis Institute (http://www.rebt.org/), Ellis has been active in writing and teaching his theory, as well as seeing clients on a regular basis.

Theory Overview

Ellis (1996) is committed to the belief that all human beings are born with the ability to determine what they want in their life. Rational Emotive Behaviour Therapy (REBT) is a direct and efficient problem-solving method, well suited to Ellis' personality. His self-assurance – some would even say arrogance – enables him to confront his clients about their beliefs and tell them what is rational and what is not (http://www.rebt. org/dr/ biography.asp).

REBT argues that individual preferences are impacted by the interconnection of culture, upbringing, social supports, and environment. In this matrix, Ellis determines that parenting and early child development are powerful influences of positive mental health. All clients, regardless of history or preferences, can think rationally as well as irrationally, and their thinking directly impacts how they exist or how they may self-destruct. REBT is grounded in the logic that emotional and behavioural consequences originate from an individual's belief system.

Ellis (2001) teaches that many life problems occur because of a client's self-created, negative and internally self-defeating thinking. REBT provides a vehicle for assisting the client to understand their thought process in order to eliminate irrational beliefs that have been leading them down a road of despair. The REBT hypothesis is that irrational beliefs come from the client's illogical set of attitudes and values that are not accurate or in synchrony with the real world.

Ellis (1997b) coined the term 'masturbatory thinking' to categorize inflexible and rigid thinking that originates from irrational beliefs. A client who is trapped in this thinking becomes caught in the illogical belief that they must always be successful and perfect, and ought to know better. When a client becomes trapped in this kind of loop, this faulty logic becomes automatic and will negatively impact their life.

Ellis (2001) purported that irrational beliefs can be observed in several different patterns of thinking. Following are examples of several common belief patterns that REBT resolves:

- *Low frustration tolerance* – a client believes that they can no longer cope with a particular situation and gets upset (e.g., child crying).
- *Self-criticism* – a belief system that turns inward and attacks (e.g., blames self for everything that goes wrong).
- *Over-generalizing* – global beliefs (e.g., everybody is angry).
- *All-or-nothing thinking* – defines the world in clear extremes (e.g., peer does not say hello, client assumes peer no longer likes them).
- *Self-labeling* – a self-proclaimed label (e.g., dummy).

REBT explains that invariably these kinds of irrational beliefs have been created without any evidence or facts. A major downside of irrational thinking is that, if left alone, these beliefs become the primary filter that influences how a client interprets the world. If this filter is not corrected, the client is at risk of developing mental health problems such as anxiety.

The foundation for REBT is based on what Ellis calls the ABCs: Activating events, Beliefs and Consequences (1962). This model identifies the sequence of illogical, self-validating, negative thinking: A peer raises her voice (Activating event) and upsets the client. The client responds based on some irrational belief (Belief), and reacts by yelling back at the peer in anger and feels hurt (Consequence). Ellis' point in this model is the client is often only aware of the A (activating event) and C (consequences). In counselling, the main outcome is to bring B (irrational beliefs) to the client's level of awareness.

Therapy Overview

In REBT, the counsellor is very active in the therapeutic process, and often will encourage the client to do work both in and out of counselling (Ellis, 1997a). REBT purports that it is critical for the counsellor to accept clients without judging, though that does not mean supporting or excusing negative behaviours. REBT does not stress the need for rapport and warm regard, like Carl Rogers and others.

In REBT, the ultimate goal of the therapeutic process is permanent cognitive change. REBT facilitates this change by teaching the client the correlation between internal beliefs and behaviours. Acknowledging this linkage impacts positively upon the client's perception filters, allowing them to live life autonomously and independently. Ellis (1997b) wants a client to know clearly that the intention of the therapeutic process is to help them change quickly, so that they can see immediate improvement. REBT often promotes this insight at the beginning of the counselling process, to motivate and encourage the client.

As previously mentioned, REBT is clearly grounded in exploring and analyzing illogical thinking, using the ABC model. Following is an overview. The first three letters (ABC) are the core theory, and all the letters after C represent the therapeutic process REBT follows to assist the client to overcome irrational beliefs:

A – Activating Events – People, places, or things that bring painful associations.

B – Beliefs – Client can create both rational and irrational beliefs. Faulty thinking and irrational beliefs lie at the core of human problems. Most of these beliefs are programmed, and over time become automatic. Irrational beliefs directly influence how a person operates and responds to their world.

C – Consequences – These are the self-defeating behaviours and disturbing emotions attached to beliefs, in response to an activating event.

D – Disputing – For a client to get out of their negative loops, irrational beliefs must be challenged in a safe manner. REBT teaches that for a client to move forward they first need to become aware of their irrational thinking. Several examples of how a counsellor can challenge and dispute irrational thinking are (Bishop, 2001):

- *Functional disputing* – a line of questioning to point out the practical realities of irrational thinking in real time (e.g., how is this kind of thinking presently helping you?).
- *Empirical disputing* – asking the client for evidence to demonstrate how irrational thinking may be misleading their behaviours and emotions (e.g., where does it say they have to treat you this way?).
- *Philosophical disputing* – exploring the client's internal model of the world to focus on worst case scenarios, to help them move on to evaluate their processing logic (e.g., if you lost your job, are you saying you would never find another?).
- *Disputing strategy* – This step assists the client to understand how their present irrational beliefs are not serving their best interests.

E- Effect – A clear awareness of the illogical thinking leads to the development of internal core competencies. The counsellor can choose from literally hundreds of cognitive behavioural techniques to teach the client to think more effectively to better cope with activating events.

F- Feeling – When the client overcomes irrational thinking and replaces it with new effective thinking, they are able to create new consequences that result in healthier behaviour choices and more positive feelings.

Techniques Overview

Ellis and his followers created many techniques to assist clients to learn how to think more effectively. Below are a few techniques that can be used with REBT to teach new core skills:

Continuum line – Provides the client with a baseline as to how their present thinking is impacting their life.

Humour – Use of appropriate humour can help a client make an internal shift to assess their present thinking. Ellis believes that humour is healthy and helps a client loosen up, as long as it is not offensive (Ellis, 2001).

Use of analogies or images to illustrate problems – The creative use of analogies or images to illustrate a problem in a different way can assist the client to take the focus off themselves and reframe a current situation from another perspective.

REBT self-help forms – Forms developed by Ellis to teach the ABC model (Howatt, 2000). Often the client is asked to complete these forms as homework to practice and incorporate the core concepts of the ABC model into their life. For more information on these forms, visit the Albert Ellis Institute website (www.rebt.org/).

COGNITIVE-BEHAVIOURAL THERAPY: AARON T. BECK

Cognitive therapy consists of all the approaches that alleviate psychological distress through a medium of correcting faulty conceptions and self-signals.
— (Beck, 1976, p. 214)

Aaron Beck, MD, was trained in neurology and independently developed his Cognitive-Behavioural Theory (CBT) in 1967, but acknowledges Albert Ellis' influence. Beck's approach can be described as goal-directed, structural, time-limited, and emphasizing internal locus of control. He generally defines all techniques that modify faulty thinking as being cognitive-behavioural.

Beck continues to contribute to the evolution of cognitive-behavioural therapy and is universally recognized for his commitment to quantitative and qualitative research in treating depression with CBT. CBT as an alternative to medication has been shown to be an effective and powerful treatment strategy for depression and other cognitive issues. Principal at the Beck Institute (www.beckinstitute.org), he has published 375 articles and 14 books.

Theory Overview

CBT considers that negative thinking sours one's experience of the world. Beck (1967) writes that a client's dysfunctional thinking often comes from internal processing errors, which he calls "systemic bias errors." These occur when the client takes information from the environment and internally processes and defines this information as pain, loss, and hurt. CBT identifies this kind of faulty processing (Figure 3-1 Beck's Cognitive Triad) as the driving force in the creation of many current mental health issues.

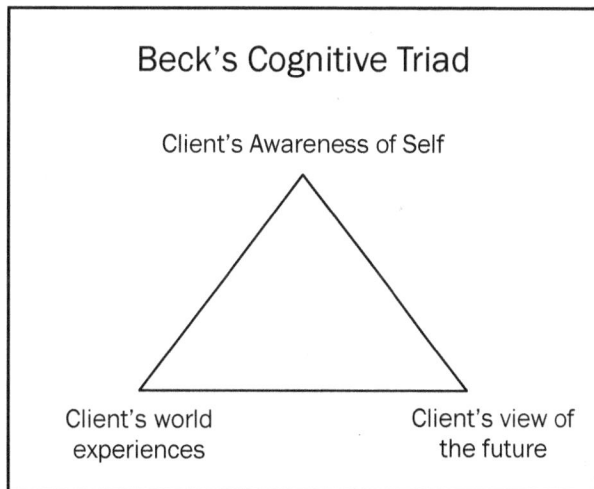

Beck's Cognitive Triad

Client's Awareness of Self

Client's world experiences

Client's view of the future

Figure 3-1 Beck's Cognitive Triad

Below are eight common CBT examples of systemic bias thinking (dysfunctional thinking):

- *Polarized thinking* – dichotomous thinking (black or white).
- *Over-generalization* – perceiving a situation in a particular way and applying the same thinking to all future situations.
- *Labeling and mislabeling* – using dysfunctional thinking from the past to define self and present reality.
- *Magnification and minimization* – reporting a particular situation more or less than it actually is.
- *Selective abstraction* – pushing aside the positive parts and focusing only on the negative.
- *Arbitrary interference* – forming conclusions without evidence.
- *Personalization* – connecting information to oneself from an external situation that has nothing directly to do with oneself, without any logical evidence for the connection.
- *Mind reading* – presuming what others are thinking, without proof.

Beck (1997) compares the client who interprets information from their environment to a scientist who bases results on a faulty experiment. The core of CBT is teaching the client to stop misinterpreting the world. This needs to occur before the client can take charge of their life. Beck (1999) expounds that personality is developed and shaped by the client's internal cognitive schemas.

Cognitive schemas are the drivers that influence personal views, beliefs, internal values, and life assumptions (Clark, Beck, and Alford, 1999). These cognitive schemas determine how a client interacts and processes stimuli in times of stress. Beck teaches that schemas can be either functional (supportive) or dysfunctional (non-supportive).

CBT explains that clients can develop many different kinds of schemas in either of these two categories. When a client lives by dysfunctional schemas (e.g., "I am dumb and will never be successful"), they negatively impact their view of the world and potentially their mental health.

To assist a client to discover how they view the world, Beck (1997) developed the cognitive triad. The triad is made up of three parts: client's views of themselves; client's view of their world experiences; and client's view of their future. The triad's purpose is to teach the client how their present cognitive schemas in each of the three areas are impacting them, and the connection to mental health issues such as depression.

Beck's Triad provides a visual interpretation of the different origins of dysfunctional thinking that can negatively impact a client's internal logic.

Therapy Overview

Beck (1995) believes that it is important for the counsellor to build a supportive relationship with the client in the early stages of counselling to dispel fears surrounding the helping process, so the client can derive the maximum benefits from counselling. The therapeutic process of CBT typically follows these stages:

1. Test the client's present reality.

2. Facilitate a reduction of the client's anxiety so that they are ready to grow

3. Teach the client how their beliefs and assumptions are having a negative impact on their present condition.

4. Create an action plan to develop the knowledge and skills needed for future success (Howatt, 2000).

The success of CBT depends on the client's internal commitment and motivation. For the client to achieve positive outcomes in counselling, they must be an active participant. CBT emphasizes the importance of the counsellor and client working together to challenge the sort of wrong-headed thinking that has undermined the client's well being.

Beck terms this process "collaborative empiricism" (Howatt, 2000). Beck asserts that the main outcome of counselling is to assist the client to discover how their problems originate from faulty thinking that leads them to misinterpret information received from their external environment (Beck, 1997).

To help the client uncover their dysfunctional thinking errors, CBT uses questions and conversational dialogues to gently bring these insights to the surface. A natural two-way conversation, called "Socratic dialogue" (i.e., questioning), accomplishes a natural cognitive reconstruction by providing the client with an opportunity to process and identify their systemic errors in thinking (Clark, Beck, and Alford, 1999).

Socratic dialogue provides an opportunity for the counsellor to question the validity of automatic thoughts. This process is often where cognitive shifts occur. Once the client becomes aware of how these thinking errors create automatic thoughts, fully accepted as facts, they can begin to take control of their thinking. These shifts allow the client to reframe negative cognitive schemas and recognize cognitive misrepresentations so that they can separate fact from opinion. When the client gets to this point, they are capable of positively interpreting and reframing their present life challenges.

Techniques Overview

Beck and his associates developed many different techniques to assist clients to process the world more effectively. Below are four samples of some commonly used cognitive-behavioural techniques:

Beck Inventories – Hopelessness, Suicidal Ideation, Depression and Anxiety. The counsellor uses one of the above diagnostic tools to assess the client's present mental health. The client's situation determines the appropriate inventory. This inventory taken at the beginning of counselling provides real time information for both the counsellor and client to track progress. For more information on this tool, visit Beck's website.

Redefine the Problem – The counsellor assists the client to redefine their life problems by reducing the perception of doom and failure and empowering the client to see their present situation in a different light.

Cognitive Restructuring – The client decides on realistic self-enhancing statements to promote problem-solving and/or effective actions and then practices this statement outside as homework.

Triple Column Technique – This provides the client with a visual representation and breakdown of their cognitive distortions. It teaches them to become more aware of their internal automatic thinking. The format is below:

Automatic Thought	*Cognitive Distortion*	*Rational Response*
I am "chicken"	I should be brave all the time.	I am human, and I do not have to be perfect all the time.

10 BEHAVIOURAL COUNSELLING STRATEGIES: PAVLOV, SKINNER, BANDURA

It is assumed that all behaviour is determined and that the variables determining it can be discovered and changed. (Todd and Bohart, 1994, p. 276)

The development, creation, and learning of new behaviours represents one common link between all behavioural theories (Wilson, 1989). Regardless of the model, the majority of counselling strategies used today for addictions counselling are designed to assist clients to overcome maladaptive behaviours. Based on an educational model for developing human behaviour, these strategies represent a significant commitment to scientific methodologies. This section briefly outlines three well-accepted behavioural strategies and 10 techniques commonly used in behavioural therapy.

CLASSICAL CONDITIONING: IVAN PAVLOV

Essentially only one thing in life is of real interest to us – our physical experience.
— (Girogian and Pavlov, 1974)

Ivan Pavlov's first major publication, *Work of the Digestive Glands*, was published in 1897. As a result of this work, in 1904 he became the first Russian physiologist to win the Nobel Prize. For the next 35 years, he devoted his energy to the study of conditioned reflex. His studies of the brain became the underpinning for classical conditioning. For more information, visit www.as.wvu.edu/~sbb/ comm221/chapters/pvlov.html.

Theory Overview

Classical conditioning is a process whereby a neutral stimulus (e.g., ringing a bell) is paired with an automatic response (e.g., salivation when food is seen or smelled). In Pavlov's famous experiment, Sam the dog became conditioned to salivate in response to the neutral stimulus (ringing a bell), without the stimulus of food (Pavlov, 1960). Figure 3-3 shows a model of classical conditioning.

Therapy Overview

When using concepts from classical conditioning, the following are important considerations for reinforcing or eliminating conditioning:

Step 1 Neutral Stimulus Needs a neutral stimulus, e.g., ringing of a bell.	Unconditioned Stimulus The sight or smell of food created an unlearned, automatic reflex that would activate salivation.	Unconditioned Response The response is salivation.
Step 2 – Over time (note: can happen with only one exposure), if Step 1 is repeated, the pairing of the neutral stimulus and the unconditioned stimulus can become as one. Neutral Stimulus + Unconditioned Stimulus = Unconditioned Response		
Step 3 – To test if the neutral stimulus has been conditioned, one only needs to activate the conditioned stimulus to determine whether it creates the unconditioned response: *Conditioned Stimulus = Conditioned Response*		

Figure 3-3 Classical Conditioning Model

- *Generalization* – something similar to a bell is sounded and triggers the conditioned response.
- *Discrimination* – opposite of generalization. For example, Sam the dog was able to discriminate between certain bell sounds, and only respond to the original stimulus.
- *Extinction* – occurs when the bell is sounded and no food follows on a number of occasions. In time, the dog will not salivate automatically. When this occurs, it is said that the bell has gone back to being a neutral stimulus.
- *Spontaneous Recovery* – if the bell is sounded and no food is presented, extinction will occur. But if at some time the bell sounds and food is presented, conditioning can spontaneously return.

OPERANT CONDITIONING: B. F. SKINNER

A response followed by a reinforcement stimulus is strengthened and therefore more likely to occur again. A response that is not followed by a reinforcing stimulus is weakened and therefore less likely to occur again. (Ormrod, 1974)

In the 1930s, B.F. Skinner became interested in how animals learned a concept he called Operant Response (Skinner, 1971). In 1948, he joined the faculty of Harvard University, where he was active as a teacher, writer, and researcher until his retirement. For more information, visit: www.indiana.edu/~edpsych/topics~/behaviour.html

Theory Overview

Operant response is defined as a response that can be modified positively or negatively by a consequence. To understand observable behaviour(s), Skinner measured and tracked rates of progress. This monitoring provided the information required to predict outcomes by determining how any given consequence impacted behaviour. Skinner noticed the impact of both positive and negative stimuli on animal behaviour and developed a formal model for conditioned learning. He used predictable sequences of conditioned learning for shaping behaviour (the desired behaviours become automatic).

Therapy Overview

Below is a brief overview of the four stages of learning as described by operant conditioning to shape new behaviour.

- *Goal* – To increase or decrease a chosen behaviour.
- *Voluntary Response* – The desired behaviour is voluntary and must be carried out at the learner's own will.
- *Emitted Response* – The behaviour must be acted out in the determined learning environment.
- *Consequence* – Once the behaviour is emitted, the desired conditioning begins.

Conditioning relies on the pre-determined consequences (positive or negative). To be effective the desired consequence must occur directly after the emitted behaviour. This begins the conditioning process. An important note: Skinner warned that if there is much delay in the contingent consequence, it might impact the accuracy of the conditioning, or lead to conditioning unwanted behaviours.

SOCIAL COGNITIVE LEARNING: ALBERT BANDURA

Self-belief does not necessarily ensure success, but self-disbelief assuredly spawns failure. — (Bandura, 1997, p. 77)

Albert Bandura was the first psychologist to advance the cognitive aspect of learning and, similar to Pavlov and Skinner, was a prolific writer and researcher. In 1973, Bandura became president of the American Psychology Association (APA) and in 1980 he received the APA's award for Distinguished Scientific Contributions. For more information, visit: www.ship.edu/~cgboerre/bandura.html.

Theory Overview

Bandura based his social cognitive learning theory on his research of how children learn aggression. Bandura (1986) taught that clients can learn from observing others, and that there does not always need to be an observable reward (positive or negative) for learning to occur.

Therapy Overview

Bandura's (1977) four stages of social cognitive learning:

- *Attention* – The client makes a conscious cognitive choice to observe the desired behaviour.
- *Memory* – The client recalls what they have observed from the modeling.

- *Imitation* – The client repeats the actions that they have observed.
- *Motivation* – The client must have some internal motivation for wanting to carry out the modeled behaviour.

When the client is motivated to repeat the behaviour, mastery can occur with practice. This process works differently for each client, and it is not easily predictable how long one client will take to learn a task compared to the next. The variable of previously learned skills impacts performance (Bandura, 1969).

10 BEHAVIOURAL COUNSELLING STRATEGIES

Techniques Overview

Following are 10 commonly practiced behavioural strategies, which provide a sampling of behavioural techniques used in the field of addictions.

- *Contingency Contract* – A contingency contract defines the desired behaviours, pre-determines rewards to be received; and specifies timeframes.

- *Journaling* – Journaling is a powerful tool for separating facts from opinions. "Using expressive writing reduces intrusive and avoidant thoughts about negative events and improves working memory," (Carpenter, 2001, p. 68).

- *Behaviour Modeling* – The client observes the counsellor or someone else performing a specific task, then attempts to imitate.

- *Behaviour Rehearsal* – New behaviours are practiced in a safe place (e.g., counselling).

- *Bibliotherapy* – The assignment of meaningful educational readings.

- *Goal Setting* – A process for brainstorming possible goals and implementation strategies, choosing specific goals and strategies, and then putting these strategies into a sequence with timeframes. The outcome of formal goal setting is to mobilize the client's resources and support them to get moving in the right direction.

- *Activity Scheduling* – Assigning and scheduling specific activities (e.g., work, AA meeting, hug children daily) to support mastery of desired behaviours.

- *Physical Exercise* – Monitor on Psychology, July/August 2002, reports exercise as being one of the best stress reduction techniques. A client with an addiction often needs to reduce stress levels. Ensure the client consults with their doctor before starting a new physical exercise program.

- *Self-Monitoring* – The client is assigned to monitor thoughts that can be potentially problematic and can lead to ineffective choices. The client records them for discussion in counselling sessions. The goal is to bring about a conscious awareness of automatic thoughts and the connection to unwanted behaviours.

- *Counter-conditioning* – A strategy for reducing anxiety. The client practices the opposite emotions of anxiety, such as relaxation. They can be trained in guided imagery (a visual relaxation technique), deep breathing, or listening to music.

CHAPTER 4

The Rubik's Cube of Addiction Counselling

This six-part series was originally published in Counsellor magazine. Each part is considered a core component for effective addiction counselling. This series uses the metaphor of a Rubik's Cube to interconnect the six parts.

PART I

SETTING THE STAGE FOR COUNSELLING

LAST Christmas I had the opportunity to shop in one of the world's most famous toy stores, FAO Swartz in New York. As I walked around in circles feeling overwhelmed by the choices, I maintained my resolve that I was not going to leave this store without one toy for each of my three children.

After searching high and low and considering many options, I realized that this shopping stuff is stressful. I was fearful of making a poor choice. Getting a gift was becoming a test and I was afraid I would not choose correctly. But being a counsellor I talked myself down and removed this irrational line of thinking. And after a bit more looking I bought a classic toy for each of my children: the Rubik's Cube.

On Christmas morning I watched with joy as my children started to play with their Rubik's Cubes. As they became frustrated, I discovered after some discussion with them that their frustration was due to not having a clear path to follow. I made this brilliant insight because they asked me for the cheat sheets. I asked, "What is a cheat sheet?" Clearly there is a generation difference, as my children are used to the video game world that apparently has cheat sheets for figuring out how to play a new game. I don't recall ever asking for this when I got my first Rubik's Cube as a kid. Somehow, after lots of effort and frustration I figured out how to put the cube back together.

As I reflected on this incident it dawned on me how my children's frustration is similar to that of my addiction counselling students who often are looking for a shortcut for becoming seasoned counsellors. My 2005-2006 class is a group of wonderful young professionals who are preparing to become addiction workers. I have 18 students in total, 12 of whom already having university degrees from some of the top schools in Canada.

These students are keen to learn. But the sheer volume of learning in this program is great as students have to navigate many courses and somehow pull them all together to become addictions counsellors – hence the Rubik's Cube of addiction counselling. The students need to process and understand addiction counselling theory, addiction counselling crisis intervention, prevention, addictive disorders, introduction to substance abuse, ethics, family counselling, group counselling, etc.

It is a real challenge for them to put all the pieces together. They ask me nearly every day to help them determine the right kinds of questions to ask, and get approval to find out if it is OK to say this or do that … all coming from the same place I was when I was trying to pick out the right toy for my children and fearful of not doing the right thing. I think this fear is healthy as it shows a clear consciousness of wanting to do the right thing. But in the end, even noble fear is fear, and fear can prevent growth and learning.

This is the first of a series of articles to provide both new and experienced addiction counsellors with what my son Tommy would call cheat sheets, but instead of playing a video game the stakes are higher; these are for addiction counselling. The focus here is to set the stage that prepares the client for the counselling process.

Setting the Stage

The seven steps for setting the stage for addiction counselling outline the stages that need to be addressed before the session can begin, but after the client has been screened formally or informally. The goal is to provide a cheat sheet that points out important elements to be in place before starting addiction counselling. But I make it clear to my students that the counselling process starts as soon as we engage the client. This model has been created for working with a person face to face, but some of it would also be applicable for telephone counselling.

If you have ever tried a Rubik's Cube you know that it must be well put together and functional before you can start to figure out the right pattern to solve the puzzle. Similarly, addiction counselling needs a solid foundation that is functional for both the counsellor and client. The counselling environment and trust are built on the steps outlined below. Throughout the process the counsellor will tune into core addiction counselling skills such as empathy, being non-judgmental, listening, and positive body language to help move the client through each step

Step 1. Preparation for New Client – From the time an addiction counsellor sees the client in person and starts to communicate both client and counsellor are forming a set of first impressions.

To help my students understand self-awareness and the impact of their behaviour on the counselling process, I teach the below points. I coach my students to be aware of the kinds of details to help them get ready mentally for each new client. The steps are an example of a road map that can be used to get the counselling process underway.

Internal preparation – Before meeting any new client it is important to prepare by changing channels and getting oriented from what you are thinking about. Every client is important and deserves your best. Also, most clients to some degree are counting on you to help them find a new path, so it is critical for you to be mentally tuned into and ready for each client before you proceed. Internal preparation needs to be done consciously to ensure your mind is cleared of issues and ideas that are not relevant to the next client. The first step is to acknowledge the value and importance of cleaning your mind and getting your energy lined up and ready. Clients are intuitive and they know if you are mentally in the room or not.

Body language and facial expression – From first eye contact with a client, it is important to start assessing their body language and facial expressions. In addition, you must be mindful of yours. What the client sees will influence how comfortable they feel. Skilled addiction counsellors understand the impact of body language and facial expressions.

Monitor Safety – From the first time you approach a client, it is valuable to analyze and assess for potential safety or risk factors, such as, does the client have any obvious medical issues (e.g., open sores); do they appear functional (e.g., neurologically oriented in time and space); are there any obvious physical or mental concerns; and does the client appear to be healthy and groomed. Addiction counsellors cannot be blind to potential danger to the client or themselves. Addictions can lead to high-risk behaviours, thus it is paramount not to be naive. As my old football coach told me "keep your head on a swivel and pay attention."

Moving Towards a New Client – For safety, it is advisable to not walk straight on to a client. Angles are helpful for safety and positioning for salutation. Since most people shake right-handed, when moving towards the client keep your right eye lined up with their right eye. This creates an offset angle for moving out of the way quickly if you need to. I recall how I learned this. I used to walk straight towards my clients, often with a smile and my arm extended to shake hands. Until one day a rather large client came into my office and as I got up and walked towards him I heard someone behind him saying, "Please stop and turn around slowly, sir." The person making the request was a police officer who was there to arrest the client for a parole violation. How he knew the client was in my office is still a mystery, but when the client got the direction, he started running forward while looking backwards, and I was knocked to the wall.

Meeting A New Client – When approaching a new client, my first task in a busy waiting room that I share with several other professional helpers is to find the right person. I am not a fan of yelling out names, for obvious confidentiality reasons. Once I get a sense from eye contact who my client could be, I walk towards them and around 6-8 feet away, I say the client's first name to see if they are the right person. Once I have done the informal salutation, I move forward a foot or two more and stop around 4 feet for a more formal salutation. I do the following to empower the client and to ensure it is OK to shake their hand. I do not assume it is OK, so I ask a permission question, such as "would you like to shake hands?" Amazingly, most clients are neutral and nod and shake hands. Once I get permission I stabilize myself to shake hands by using a T-stance to create a nice strong base, which provides me a good center of balance. A firm, confident, short handshake ensures I keep my hand parallel with my thumb straight up so it is neutral, safe, and professional. A top hand turned down is a controlling handshake and palm up is a passive handshake.

Giving Directions to the Office – After the handshake I step to the right and back out of the way and encourage the client to walk past as I give directions to my office. I follow the client, staying a full body to the left or right, but never directly behind. I direct them verbally to where they need to go. This is a good opportunity to study the client's gait. Since neurological damage can negatively influence how a person moves, it is useful to notice events that are outside the realm of normal.

Offering a Seat – Once we are both in the office, I encourage the client to sit first and ensure the chair I am offering is at least as nice as mine or better, and farthest from the door. Before sitting myself, I check to see if they need anything or if I can get something for them, such as a glass of water, before we begin.

Step 2. Building Rapport – The art of communication is important for a counsellor to understand. I teach all my students a communication model; I do not assume they have strong communication skills. We work on developing both intrapersonal and interpersonal skills as well as their own communication model so they are equipped with conversational skills to build rapport with a client. Rapport is in essence helping a client see you are human and trustworthy. A client must feel safe, trust you as a counsellor, and not see you as a threat. The objective of rapport building is to find some common ground, to assist the client's transition, and to help them feel comfortable to talk about their problems. Another goal of rapport is to provide an environment that supports the client so they feel they are not being judged and comfortable to consider the situation. Finally, rapport provides an opportunity for the client to lower their anxiety so they can move forward positively.

Step 3. Client Matching – Much like after you have been checked at an airport gate, been sent to your plane, and checked once again to ensure you are on the right flight, you must check whether your client is in the right place. If the client is not in the right place, out of professional courtesy, provide meaningful direction to help them find the right service. Whenever in this position and it is appropriate, provide a referral and/or recommendation. Then ensure the client is aware of what your current facility or organization does and what your role is, as well as how long you normally work with clients. This helps promote the end of the process and that the goal of treatment is to help the client graduate to the next level of independence. Once they are clear of everything you have said, ensure it all makes sense to them. Also, for the client's safety and treatment success, as well as your safety, this step ensures you are comfortable with the level of interaction thus far. The kinds of questions you want to consider are: Is the client currently on chemicals and if so are they functional; is the client in crisis and if so what is their current level of equilibrium (emotional stability).

Step 4. Disclosing Professional Education and Competencies – With every new client, it is important to disclose your professional education and competencies so that they are aware of the level of training and the function of the professional they have in front of them. Clients often do not know or fully understand the various levels of addiction counsellors (e.g., one trained in a community college and one who is trained in a masters program). This is often an excellent education frame for the client to understand the hierarchy and where you fall in this hierarchy. It is important for them to be aware of your role in the care continuum.

<u>Step 5. Confidentiality Statements and Other Paperwork</u> – Once the client and you are confident and comfortable that the client is in the right spot, the next actions that need to be addressed are the limitation of confidentiality and the pre-assessment paperwork, such as release of information and confidentiality form. This is a major administrative part of the addiction counselling process. In addition, in this section I ensure the client is aware of all formal or informal ground rules that are relevant to the situation.

<u>Step 6. Consent</u> – After the client understands the limitations of confidentiality and has completed all the pertinent paperwork, it is important to do one more efficacy check: getting permission to continue with the needs assessment that will outline the primary and secondary issues that need to be addressed in the treatment plan. The treatment plan is the addiction counsellor's blueprint for determining the kinds of recovery tools and addiction counselling strategies that will be employed to assist the client move forward and take control of their life.

<u>Step 7. Needs Assessment</u> – Everything that has been done to this point has cleared the way for the addiction counsellor to do a needs assessment to determine their individual needs and wants, as well as how motivated they are to take action. All these variables come into play to determine the client's treatment plan.

The above seven steps outline some cheat sheet material for assisting counsellors to set the stage for addiction counselling. I often wish I had been provided with this kind of information and level of detail before I started work as an addiction counsellor and I encourage you to write out your own cheat sheet.

The first article focused on the first side of the Rubik's Cube of addiction counselling – orientation. Part two offers a cheat sheet for completing the second, more difficult, side, helping assess if they have an addictive disorder. It provides a cheat sheet of five best practices that I teach my addiction counselling students to follow when doing an assessment. All of these have application in any counselling agency or with any assessment tools or model a counsellor is using.

PART II

FIVE BEST PRACTICES FOR ASSESSING ADDICTIVE DISORDERS

Part I of *The Rubik's Cube of Addiction Counselling* series explored the process of getting a client oriented and to the point of consenting to treatment. Like the TV show *24*, part two is still in the same day, following the first 15-20 minutes of the counselling session.

Framing Assessment Best Practices

The goal of any assessment is to work with the client to determine the most prudent and appropriate action plan to address their current situation. The best practices presented here do not outline step-by-step guides for doing an addiction assessment; they point out what the assessor needs to evaluate.

Though it may appear the assessment starts after consent, it actually begins at first contact. An addiction counsellor must project a caring and supportive position at first contact for a client to feel safe, as well as to start to observe and assess their behaviour.

In all first sessions, what happens after consent influences whether the client will continue in treatment. Statistically, a large percentage of clients drop out of addiction counselling in the first three or four sessions.

The very word 'assessment' can be intimidating and create fear and shame for a client. Who really wants to be assessed? Who really wants to admit they have messed up their life? It is important to never forget the amount of courage it takes any human being to ask for help. The assessment process is one of discovery and is for assisting the client to get aligned with the right resources in the right order.

I impress upon young addiction counsellors the importance of not falling into a robotic state when doing an assessment. The assessment process is no different than counselling. It must be engaging, interactive, and compelling. I point out how all the new neat and powerful assessment tools will never replace an addiction counsellor's critical thinking.

Anyone can ask 20 questions to explore a client's history and addictive behaviour over the last 12 months. The best assessors want the facts, adhere to rigor and protocols, and do not accept shortcuts.

Three important milestones in an addiction counsellor's development of effective assessment skills are: 1) *Clinical skills* – must have an understanding of addiction counselling theories, models, drug classifications, addiction disorders, assessment skills, crisis intervention, etc; 2) *Clinical experience* –

acquired practical and supervision experience to develop sound clinical judgment; and 3) *Clinical instinct* – development of decision making skills that evolve from considering the facts and learning to trust gut instincts.

Assessment of addictive disorders is a science and an art. No assessment tool or clinical measure alone can make a diagnosis. Addiction counsellors must continue the quest of continuous improvement and development.

Five Assessment Best Practices

The five assessment best practices below begin with the client at first observation. However, the detailed assessment questions are not asked until after consent is given.

The assessment process has two basic structures. One we will call informal is where the counsellor begins to interview the client without following a standard procedure. This practice relies on the clinical expertise of the counsellor to interact with the client to discover the client's needs and wants and to help them make an action plan.

The other assessment option we will call formal. This is where the addiction counsellor follows a predetermined protocol with every client. For example, each client is given the same structured clinical interview, using a set of predetermined questions. My students are trained to do formal assessment using a biopsychosocial, structured clinical assessment tool.

One common strategy in formal structures is for administrations to predetermine clinical measures and screening tools to assess risk that every client completes. This is followed by a second round of clinical measures that is more specific to the addictive disorder and that appears to be aligned to the client's current situation based on the results of the first round.

This helps provide more collaboration and discover potential addictive disorders and risk. It includes a set format for treatment plans and recovery contracts, making it easier for new addiction counsellors to follow a formal assessment process and develop clinical skills and experience.

I teach my students to use these five best practices, whether the assessment is formal or informal. Adding these to a counsellor's assessment practice will increase the likelihood that a client will get off to the right start. These best practices are not listed in order of importance as each has its own merit.

Assessment Best Practices

Assessment of client's current level of safety – From the beginning of the assessment, the addiction counsellor needs to constantly assess the client's degree of safety and whether there is any potential risk. Every client who comes to an addiction counsellor may be at risk of harming themselves or someone else. They may be at risk of not telling the truth of their current situation for many reasons, such as shame and guilt.

The addiction counsellor needs to determine the client's current degree of safety, whether any pending crisis or risks could negatively impact their quality of life and their ability to receive treatment. Before a client can deal with their addiction crisis, it is important to help them develop an action plan to mitigate any additional crisis as soon as possible.

The more crises a client is in, the more distractions, anxiety, and stress they experience. Many crises can disrupt a treatment success. A woman terrified of her abusive husband or a gambler on the run from a loan shark are examples of external drivers that can negatively impact a client's level of functioning, safety, and ability to focus on the addiction crisis.

In addition to external crisis, a client also may be experiencing some internal turmoil such as a medical issue that requires attention. For instance, a needle user may have several abscesses in their neck from broken needle tips.

The following questions are helpful for uncovering current crises. Each question does not have to be asked directly but in the course of questioning needs to be explored.

- Is the client in any immediate crisis in addition to their addictive disorder?
- Is the client at risk of harming themselves?
- Is the client at risk of harming someone else?
- Is there a need for medical attention?
- What action plan needs to be taken to help the client deal with the current crisis?

Assessment of client's current level of functioning – Three levels of functioning must be screened for throughout the assessment. Notice I used the word 'screened.' Most addiction counsellors are not trained to treat or assess all levels of functioning, but they can be trained to refer and bring in other professionals to support the multidisciplinary treatment team.

Addiction counsellors must have some basic knowledge and skills in three areas to be effective in doing an assessment: 1) *Ability to evaluate the client's current level of cognitive functioning.* While interacting with the client, it is important for the counsellor to observe the client's orientation to time and space, recall, verbal skills, cognitive ability, and physical appearance. Alcohol and other drugs can negatively impact a person's cognitive ability. Some clients may require neurological testing if the addiction counsellor perceives potential cognitive issues; 2) *Ability to recognize mental health risks.* A client's appearance and behaviour in the assessment may indicate some form of a personality disorder such as schizoid or borderline personality disorders that, if extreme, may need to be referred to a mental health practitioner. Addiction counsellors need to be aware of the different personality clusters and understand their professional competencies when dealing with this population. Another mental health issue that must be referred is a client with a complex dual diagnosis such as schizophrenia and THC who has gone off their medication and is having auditory hallucinations. A large percentage of people with addictive disorders have a dual diagnosis (mental health disorder with an addictive disorder), so counsellors must be clear of their professional competencies for treatment; 3) *Ability to assess whether a client is able to function in a counselling environment.* A client may be too impaired to function safely in a counselling environment. The addiction counsellor must pay attention to the level of functioning to ensure the client is able to comprehend what is happening in the assessment process and to ensure both the client and counsellor are safe. Security or police may have to be called to prevent a person from driving home impaired.

When assessing levels of functioning, the Client Placement Criteria from the American Society of Addiction Medicine (see next page) provide a detailed breakdown for what they purport all clients must be assessed for constantly in the following six dimensions (Coombs & Howatt, 2005) that augment and support the five best practices being discussed in this article.

Assessing client's level of motivation – The addiction counsellor must constantly assess the client's level of motivation, and if needed, introduce appropriate motivating strategies to move the client up a motivational level. The action plans for the day must be aligned to the client's current level. No two clients are alike, and counsellors cannot assume all clients are at the same level of motivation. Often in the assessment stage the benchmark for assessing motivation has been set by the stages of motivation identified by Prochaska, DiClemente, and Norcross (1992). The goal of the assessment is to move the client to preparation and get them ready to take action. Motivational interviewing is a powerful process for helping move a client along the stages of motivation:

- *Precontemplation –* The individual is not intending to take action in regard to their substance abuse problem in the foreseeable future.

- *Contemplation –* The individual intends to take action within the next six months.

- *Preparation –* The individual intends to take action in the next month.

1. **Acute intoxication and/or Withdrawal Complications.**
   A. What risk is associated with the client's current level of intoxication?
   B. Is there significant risk of severe withdrawal symptoms, based on the client's previous withdrawal history, amount, frequency, and recency of discontinuation of chemical use?
   C. Is the client currently in withdrawal? To measure withdrawal, use The Clinical Institute Withdrawal Assessment of Alcohol Scale (CIWA).
   D. Does the client have the supports necessary to assist in ambulatory detoxification, if medically safe?

2. **Biomedical Conditions or Complications.**
   A. Are there current physical illnesses, other than withdrawal, that may need to be addressed, or that may complicate treatment?
   B. Are there chronic conditions that may affect treatment?

3. **Emotional Behavioural Complications.**
   A. Are there current psychiatric illnesses or psychological, emotional or behavioural problems that need treatment or may complicate treatment?
   B. Are there chronic psychiatric problems that affect treatment?

4. **Treatment Acceptance or Resistance.**
   A. Is the client objecting to treatment?
   B. Does the client feel coerced into coming to treatment?
   C. Does the client appear to be complying with treatment only to avoid a negative consequence, or does he or she appear to be self-motivated?

5. **Relapse Potential.**
   A. Is the client in immediate danger of continued use?
   B. Does the client have any recognition of, understanding of, or skills with which he or she can cope with his or her addiction problems in order to prevent continued use?
   C. What problems will potentially continue to distress the client if the client is not successfully engaged in treatment at this time?
   D. How aware is the client of relapse triggers, ways to cope with cravings, and skills to control impulses to use?

6. **Recovery/Living Environment.**
   A. Are there any dangerous family members, significant others, living situations, or school/working situations that pose a threat to treatment success?
   B. Does the client have supportive friendships, financial resources, educational or vocational resources that can increase the likelihood of treatment success?
   C. Are there legal, vocational, social service agencies or criminal justice mandates that may enhance the client's motivation for treatment?

Note: The above come from the American Society of Addiction Medicine, *Client Placement Criteria for the Treatment of Psychoactive Substance Use Disorders, Second Edition, 1998 (PPC-2)*. A copy of the criteria can be obtained by contacting The American Society of Addiction Medicine, Inc., 4601 North Park Ave., Upper Arcade, Suite 101, Chevy Chase, Maryland 20815.

- *Action* – The individual has made overt attempts to modify their lifestyle. The person is working on a recovery plan and attempting to prevent relapse.

In order to help motivate clients to progress from one stage to the next, it is necessary to observe the below principles (Prochaska & DiClemente, 1983) and to keep them in mind throughout the assessment process:

- *Principle 1:* The rewards for changing must increase if clients are to move beyond precontemplation.
- *Principle 2:* The "cons" of changing must decrease if clients are to progress from contemplation to action.
- *Principle 3:* The relative weight assigned to benefits and costs must cross over before a client will be prepared to take action.
- *Principle 4:* The strong principle of progress holds that to progress from precontemplation to action, the rewards for changing must increase by one standard deviation.
- *Principle 5:* The weak principle of progress holds that, to progress from contemplation to action, the perceived costs of changing must decrease by one-half standard deviation.
- *Principle 6:* It is important to match particular processes of change with specific stages of change.

Assessing and discovering why client wants help now and their available resources – Most of the population with an active addiction have thought about stopping many times before they come to counselling. As an addiction counselor, it is important to identify some of the motivation drivers as well as some of the available and accessible resources.

- What influenced the decision to come for help today? What are the most obvious internal (e.g., emotions) and external (e.g., relationships) reasons that have motivated or influenced the client to come for help? This will help determine if the client is being internally or externally motivated, as well as their current locus of control and choice about wanting help. This is important information when considering a stay-safe or relapse prevention plan.
- Determine the client's current resources. Be clear of what support systems are in place as this can influence the decision making around placement.
  - ◊ Have they been able to stop before on their own?
  - ◊ If they have stopped before, how did they do it? What worked and what did they do?
  - ◊ Do they have safe shelter and food?

◊   What is their current economic situation?
◊   What peer support and relationship support systems are in place?
◊   What support systems do they currently have that are safe and
      willing to support them?

Assessing the best treatment placement and intervention for the client – After completion of the assessment, the one important goal is to determine where the client will most likely be able to achieve the outcomes that have been determined from the formal or informal assessment. Dr. Robert Perkinson (2004) reports standards for selecting the right placement for a client in need in the United States. These are outlined in the table on the following page.

Closing

The above five best practices will assist when assessing a client, whether the addiction counsellor is using a formal or informal assessment strategy. Part three of this series will look at the next side of the Rubik's Cube of addiction counselling: aligning treatment plans, recovery tools, and recovery contracts for measurable outcomes.

Level 0.5 Early Interventions

These are organized services delivered in a wide variety of settings. Early intervention is designed to explore and address problems or risk factors that are related to substance use and to assist the individual in recognizing the harmful consequences of inappropriate substance use. Clients who need early intervention do not meet the diagnostic criteria of either chemical abuse or chemical dependency, but they have significant problems with substances. The rest of the treatment levels include clients who meet the criteria for psychoactive substance abuse or dependency.

Level I: Out client Treatment

Out client treatment takes place in a nonresidential facility or an office run by addiction professionals. The client comes in for individual or group therapy sessions, usually fewer than nine hours per week.

Level II: Intensive Out client / Partial Hospitalization

Level II.1: Intensive Out client Treatment. This program is a structured day or evening program with nine or more hours of programming per week. These programs have the capacity to refer clients for their medical, psychological or pharmacological needs.

Level II.5: Partial Hospitalization. Partial hospitalization generally includes twenty or more hours of intense programming per week. These programs have ready access to psychiatric, medical, and laboratory services.

Level III: Residential / In client Services

Level III.1: Clinically-Managed Low-Intensity Residential Services. This is a halfway house.

Level III.3: Clinically-Managed Medium-Intensity Residential Services. This is an extended care program oriented around long-term management.

Level III.5: Clinically-Managed High-Intensity Residential Services. This is a therapeutic community designed to maintain recovery.

Level III.7: Medically Monitored Intensive In client Treatment. This is a residential facility that provides a 24-hour, daily structured treatment. This program is monitored by a physician and is able to manage the psychiatric, physical, and pharmacological needs of clients.

Level IV: Medically Managed Intensive In client Treatment.

This facility is a 24-hour program that has the resources of a hospital. Physicians provide daily medical management.

Part III

Aligning Treatment Planning, Recovery Tools, and Recovery Contracts

The first part of this series explored setting the stage and orienting the client to addiction counselling. The second outlined considerations for screening and assessing to help them determine their options. This part explores strategies and considerations for aligning treatment planning, recovery tools, and recovery contracts based on the client's needs and readiness.

Parts I and II set the stage for this part of the process that often occurs in the first session. Intake, screening, and assessment of persons with a potential addictive disorder need to balance rigor and action to get them moving in the right direction as quickly as it makes sense. Rarely is it of value to have a client go through hours and hours of clinical measures and assessment.

Clinical measures and assessment tools need to facilitate the process, not dominate it. Our goal is to get a client engaged in an action plan that meets their needs and wants.

Addiction counsellors use clinical measures and screening tools to ensure the assessment conclusions have efficacy. Different agencies and providers navigate assessment processes differently. I teach my students that we want to get to action planning as soon as possible so the client is focused on new actions to instill the confidence they can make a change and take charge of their life.

The treatment plan evolves from the formal or informal assessment. It is aimed at defining the goal and objectives and determines the kinds of addiction recovery tools that will be used to guide the client along the change continuum.

Our role as addiction counsellors in the treatment planning process is to help the client discover opportunities. Often in the early stages of treatment, especially during the assessment and treatment planning phase, our role may require us to help the client to take actions. In these situations, clients benefit from the use of Motivational Interviewing. (For more information on this recovery tool go to http://www.motivationalinterview.org/.)

Regardless of the methodology, the goal of the assessment process is the same: to facilitate the development of the client's treatment plan by setting priorities and actions. Before developing the treatment plan, the counsellor must keep in mind all actions must be aligned with the client's current level of motivation and capabilities. For example, Ries (1994) reports that nearly one-third of patients with psychiatric disorders experience substance abuse and more than one-half of substance-abusing clients have met the diagnostic criteria for a psychiatric disorder. A dual diagnosis may influence a client's capabilities.

Being in tune with the client's level of motivation helps reduce the risk of false compliance, which is when a client agrees to a treatment plan but has no intention of really following it (Craig, 2004). For treatment to be successful, the client must not only agree with their treatment plan, they must be committed to the actions that go with it. An impressive, well thought out treatment plan is of little value if the counsellor is the only one excited about it. All treatment plans must be aligned to the client's level of motivation and capabilities (e.g., level of functioning).

Miller and Rollnick (2002, pp. 201-216) point out examples of interventions that can be used, depending on the client's level of motivation.

Stage of Change	Goal	Intervention
Pre-contemplative	Increase awareness; focus on cognitions rather than behaviour	• Acknowledge/support client's feelings • Explore self-concept • Reinforce client's internal locus of control • Suggest self-monitoring tasks • Provide objective feedback
Contemplative	Work through ambivalence	• Decisional Balance process • Self-monitoring
Preparation	Assist client to formulate their treatment goal and match the need with appropriate treatment	• Identify strengths/coping supports • Select appropriate recovery tools (e.g., individual counselling)
Action	Assist client in the treatment process	• Assign recovery tools and put into client recovery contract.
Maintenance	Assist client in maintaining treatment	• Relapse prevention and preparing for the future (e.g., developing new skills).
Relapse	Assist client in returning to change strategies	• Assess motivation and focus on getting back on track and aligned to a treatment plan.

Developing the Treatment Plan

Once the counsellor has rapport and client agreement as to critical areas, and defines the current level of motivation and capabilities, the counsellor and client work collaboratively to develop the treatment plan.

Like solving a Rubik's Cube, it often takes patience and creativity to find the right treatment plan for a client. Treatment planning matching (selecting an intervention to help the client make a change) never follows the rule that one size fits all. The treatment must match the client's current needs or the result is like trying to put a square peg into a round hole.

There are many wonderful and proven recovery tools that have helped millions but may not be appropriate for every client. Counsellors need to be careful not to try to fit every client into the same treatment plan. Every client's treatment plan needs to be designed and aligned to their individual needs and situation. Counsellors need to be open to the fact there is more than one road to recovery and their role is to help the client draw the map for their journey.

An exception to when the treatment planning process is not a collaborative one is when the client is threatening suicide and/or homicide. If you believe a client is a danger to themselves or others, you need to take action and report this risk to appropriate authorities and persons involved. I teach my students to err on the side of caution and whenever in doubt to get a second objective opinion from a peer or supervisor. Saying, "I did not think this was a real threat" is not defensible. You must be able to defend all your actions, and remember that taking no action is no defense.

Treatment Planning

The *ATTC National Curriculum Committee* (1998) points out that the main goal of a treatment plan is to help the client overcome their addiction disorder. The plan addresses areas of the client's life that need to be put back in order, such as family, employment, health, and money.

Addiction counsellors who are doing treatment planning may review the *Addiction Counselling Competencies: The Knowledge, Skills, and Attitudes of Professional Practice* document at http://www.nfattc.org/uploads/TAP%2021.pdf. This publication was prepared under the Addiction Technology Transfer Center's cooperative agreement from the Center for Substance Abuse Treatment (CSAT) of the Substance Abuse and Mental Health Services Administration (SAMHSA). I recommend you go to this site and read pages 36-42 on treatment planning.

All treatment plans need to include long-term goals in order of priority (primary, secondary, and tertiary) with short-term action steps for achieving each goal. It is important to include the following three elements for all action steps:

- *Interventions* – defined recovery tools
- *Timeframe* – defined period of time
- *Measurement Devices* – defined criteria for success

Short-term action steps need to be SIMPLE – meaning the client has the **S**kills to implement them on their own; **I**mmediate action can be taken; they are **M**easurable; they are **P**lausible, so the client's chance of success is positive; and they are **L**egal and **E**thical.

To review 13 core principles for treatment planning that have been set out by the National Institute on Drug Abuse research, go to http://www.nida.nih.gov/PODAT/PODAT1.html

I highly recommend the John Wiley's Treatment Addiction Planner (hard copy and electronic treatment planning tools), progress notes, and treatment planning homework resources. This tool may be viewed at http://ca.wiley.com/WileyCDA/WileyTitle/productCd-0471725447.html

Recovery Tools

Recovery tools are strategies that an addiction counsellor can draw upon to facilitate treatment plan success and reduce relapse. Each tool is independent of the other; however, the tools may be used interchangeably (e.g., disease model and peers support programs).

The purpose of all recovery tools is to provide the client with a path to obtain new knowledge and skills. The tool chosen must be aligned to the treatment plan with a definable and measurable outcome.

The more tools the addiction counsellor researches and knows, the more opportunities they can offer the client. Recovery tools include:

- Detoxification – the process of eliminating drugs from the body.
- Drug testing – an effective strategy for determining the levels of drugs in a person and for promoting internal accountability, measurement of success, and compliance.
- Family intervention – an attempt to assist a family member to address an addiction.
- Group therapy – a strategy for helping a group of people with a common concern.
- Individual therapy – a one-on-one process in which the counsellor is able to work with the client to help them achieve desired goals.
- Motivational interviewing – a strategy for motivating a person with an addictive disorder to take action.

- Nutritional counselling – teaches clients how to live more effective and healthier lives by following a healthy diet.
- Peers helping peers – the most effective recovery tool.

A current resource providing an overview of many of the recovery tools that addiction professionals are using is *Addiction Recovery Tools,* edited by R. H. Coombs and published by Sage Productions Inc., Thousand Oaks, CA.

Recovery Contract

A written recovery contract is a strategy for helping clients develop owner-ship and responsibility for their treatment plan. This is a measurable and definable agreement that outlines the actions and commitment of a client over a determined period of time.

The recovery contract outlines the step-by-step actions that have been defined by the treatment plan, including times and dates for actions, sup-port systems, progression of goals, and how progress will be measured. This enables the client to decide what they will and will not do, so that each day they have a clear direction. Many of my clients report that a recovery con-tract acts like a lighthouse that provides direction.

The recovery contract must also include agreements such as do no harm to self, crisis management plans, and relapse prevention plans.

The recovery contract can be as simple as a one-page summary attached to a weekly timetable that a client can put on their fridge so they know each day what meetings and tasks they have.

This contract must be reviewed and updated on a regular basis through-out treatment to integrate factors such as risk management and relapse pre-vention to ensure it is current.

Recovery contracts can be used effectively in intensive outpatient, pri-mary inpatient, and continuing care settings. They are most effective when the client's support systems are involved, know the specifics, and are sup-porters of its success.

The last step is to do a detailed review to ensure the client understands the contract and is motivated to honor it. Have the client sign the contract and give them a copy. Let them know this is not a legal agreement and what will happen if it is broken. It is important that the client know that, if they break the contract, they can feel safe to come back to you to pick up the plan and refocus.

The Drug Addiction website provides information on recovery contracts at: http://www.drug-addiction-information.com/drug-addiction/.

In Summary

The addiction counselling treatment process is like solving a Rubik's Cube; it is done one side or one step at a time. So far we have explored the importance of orienting the client to counselling and assessment and using this information to build the treatment plan, which is supported by addiction recovery tools.

The recovery contract aligns all the actions into a definable road map for the client to follow. However, just because the client is motivated, has a great plan, has excellent support strategies in place, and is following their recovery contract is no guarantee they will not end up in a crisis.

The next article in this series will review important considerations for managing risk, such as safety, relapse, and crisis.

PART IV

RISK MANAGEMENT CONSIDERATIONS IN ADDICTION COUNSELLING

As we turn the Rubik's Cube of addiction counselling once again, we see the fourth side is as important as the first three, as it deals with managing risk when dealing with a client. The first three sides provided color and structure for getting the client ready for counselling, intake, assessment, designing and developing a treatment plan, and implementing a recovery contract.

Traditionally, once the recovery contract is in place, the client has defined the first step in their journey to recovery. However, like any journey there can be bumps and sharp turns along the way. This side of the Rubik's cube discusses the aspect of risk management, where the goal is to prepare for events that may put the client's journey at risk.

This part introduces five core questions that build a framework for managing the kinds of risks that could disrupt a client's journey. A client's resiliency develops each day they are able to achieve milestones set out in their treatment plan and recovery contract.

In the early stages of recovery, a client's resiliency may not have developed or is fragile; events and perceptions may put them at risk. Addiction counsellors need to learn to anticipate the kinds of events and perceptions that can negatively impact a client. The five questions discussed here are intended to get the addiction counsellor thinking about some of the kinds of risks that may impact a client. At the end of this article, ask yourself what other questions you could ask in preparation.

6 Risk Management Considerations:

1. Do I have a crisis intervention model ready?

Crisis often comes without notice, thus having a crisis intervention model ready and in place to support a client who perceives they are in a crisis is critical for their safety. One of the first rules for managing a crisis is to be aware that what may be a crisis for one person may not be a crisis for another. The person who is experiencing the crisis defines crisis. The role of an addiction counsellor, when they have a client in crisis, is to support them to get past it. The treatment plan is not the priority when a person is in crisis; the crisis is. Once the crisis is resolved, the person will have the capacity and opportunity to continue with their treatment plan and recovery contract.

A few common examples of the kinds of crisis a person may need to deal with are: personal safety issues (e.g., have an abusive husband), financial challenges (e.g., lost their job), no safe shelter, no means to feed themselves, coping with anger management issues (e.g., in trouble with their employer), or stopped psychiatric medications on their own and are now suffering the consequences. One common factor in all these examples is that these events can become all-consuming and paralyze a client. They can flood the client's ability to cope and disrupt their journey, and each will need a crisis intervention.

The *Six-Step Intervention* developed by James and Gilliland (2005) is a proven and effective crisis intervention model that can be added to the addiction counsellor's toolbox. The number one consideration in crisis is the *preservation of life and to prevent the crisis from escalating out of control.* The below model provides a structured process for managing general crisis situations:

Step 1 – Define the problem. The client's functioning ability determines how directive the counsellor will need to be. It is important to be mindful of the *intensity, duration, and degree* of the crisis. This will help the addiction counsellor calibrate the potential extent and damage to the person(s) involved in the crisis. The lower their functioning, the more directive the counsellor will be, especially if safety is an issue. One of the telling signs of recovering is when a person is able to make decisions that are cognitively sound, and is able to be part of the collaborative process. This is a sign that the counsellor can be more non-directive.

Step 2 – Ensure personal safety. Safety is a major concern and the first goal. The outcome is to get the client to a safe place. However, the counsellor must be careful not to put themselves within arm's length of danger.

Step 3 – Provide support. Rapport, trust, empathy, and compassion are all-important to a person in crisis. Their body may not be injured, but crisis can injure their mind and soul. Clients need this security band-aid to help them gain control of emotional bleeding that may be occurring.

Step 4 – Explore options and alternatives. What are the options, and what needs to be done? This needs to involve the person as much as possible. The counsellor has a role in crisis situations to offer suggestions when the client is lost for direction or is not making safe and healthy decisions.

Step 5 – Make a plan. Develop a plan that is realistic and action oriented that gets the client on track to solve the crisis, keeping in mind the importance of their recovery and how the plan can be aligned with the journey as much as possible.

Step 6 – Get a commitment. Be mindful of the client's motivation and commitment to the plan. The goal is to get a commitment to take action and move forward in a set time with follow up and support.

2. Do I have a strategy for reducing the risk of suicide & homicide?

In addition to using the six-step model, having a framework to prevent suicide and homicide is important. James and Gilliland (2005) suggest professionals be aware and monitor the following three points:

- *Risk factors:* (Has this person attempted suicide before? What kind of stressful or traumatic events have recently been going on in their life? Do they have a plan and a means for suicide?)
- *Suicidal/homicidal clues:* (Do they say they want to die, or are going to kill themselves? Do they make comments like, "There's no point in going on any more"?)
  - ◊ *Verbal clues:* Spoken or written statements that can be either direct ("I'm gonna do it this time.") or indirect ("I'm of no use to anyone anymore.").
  - ◊ *Behavioural clues:* Purchasing a grave marker for oneself, or slashing one's wrist as a practice run.
  - ◊ *Situational clues:* May include concerns over a wide variety of conditions, (e.g., death of a spouse, divorce, a painful physical injury or terminal illness, sudden bankruptcy, preoccupation with a loved one's death anniversary).

◊ *Syndromatic clues:* Include symptoms such as severe depression, loneliness, hopelessness, dependence, and dissatisfaction with life.

- *Cries for help:* (The fact that they are even talking to someone about it is a sign that they're feeling ambivalent.)

When dealing with a potential threat of suicide or homicide, it is important to ask direct questions, such as:

- Are you thinking about killing yourself?
- Are you thinking about killing someone else?
- Have you tried before to kill yourself?
- Do you have a plan as to how you would kill yourself?
- Do you have the means to kill yourself today?

In the above five questions, the more the person responds with a yes, the greater the risk. However, answering the first one as a yes and the rest no, the person may still be at risk, and it is important to use the six-step crisis intervention model to assist them to feel they are in control again and safe.

Finally, legal and ethical questions of action are defined by professional codes of ethics and legislation. It is the counsellor's responsibility to be aware of reporting procedures whenever suicide or homicide have been threatened, regardless of how effective the intervention.

3. Do I have a relapse prevention strategy in place?

There are many triggers, such as person, place, thing, smell, thought, or taste that may spark a person to return to an old behaviour. We know in treating clients with addictive disorders that relapse is going to happen and this may become a major event that gets the client off their journey. Effective crisis prevention is the implementation of a well thought out relapse prevention plan.

Two of the most widely used models today are:

- Allan Marlatt and Judith Gordon's RP relapse model that is rooted in social learning theory and cognitive psychology. This model operates from a biopsychosocial perspective. Visit http://www.niaaa. nih.gov/publications/arh23-2/151-160.pdf for a full overview of this model.
- Terrance Gorski's CENAPS (Center for Applied Sciences) relapse prevention model that is grounded in cognitive-behavioural psychology. For more information, visit http://www.cenaps.com.

Two mnemonics developed by Gorski teach clients a strategy for how to stay aware and avoid relapse. ESCAPE points out the kinds of behaviours and triggers that may lead to relapse, and RADAR is an action plan when faced with ESCAPE situations.

Gorski's Mnemonics

RADAR	ESCAPE
R = Recognize	E = Evade + Denies
A = Accept	S = Stress
D = Detach	C = Crisis building and/or compulsive behaviour
A = Ask for Help	A = Avoid
R = Response	P = Problems
	E = Evade + Denies

4. Do I monitor the client's self-esteem?

Self-esteem is critical for developing one's resiliency that is needed for recovery. The amount of self-esteem a client has defines the perception of their value and belief in their current and potential abilities. Self-esteem can be defined as one's internal belief and abilities for coping with the challenges of life. One core life task for each client is learning how to develop happiness from within. Two components of self-esteem that are important for recovery are:

- *Self-efficacy* – confidence in the ability to think, understand, learn, choose, and make decisions. The experience of self-efficacy generates the sense of control over one's life.

- *Self-respect* – belief in one's value, right to live and to be happy, comfort in appropriately asserting thoughts, wants, and needs. The experience of self-respect makes it possible for a person to become aware of the importance of taking care of oneself and of making healthy choices.

Strategies for increasing self-esteem are important to have in the counsellor's toolbox. Some examples are:

- Work with the client to define the kinds of events and perceptions that impact their self-esteem, then develop an action plan for coping with these challenging situations. Role playing can help the client develop their competency.

- Define with the client where they have healthy and safe emotional support and social approval. Clients benefit in their recovery from having healthy relationships to feel valued and accepted. Peer groups are potential sources for this kind of support.

- The client can make a daily recording of personal achievements and success. Journaling is a powerful tool for helping clients process and cope with events of the day, but it also is a great strategy for creating a living document that defines a person's success and self-esteem levels (e.g., track perceived highs and lows then explore the root causes of the lows and what alternatives the client has).

The client's primary problem may not be reported as low self-esteem, however, it is recommended to monitor their self-efficacy and self-respect as a risk management strategy.

5.   Do I have a process to deal with a grieving client?

One challenge for many clients in the early and middle stages of recovery is to process losses that have occurred because of the addictive disorder. These might include a gambler's loss of his house, or a drug addict's loss of her husband and children. Grief comes at different intensities and at different times for clients. Some may appear to be fine but three months into their recovery they become overwhelmed with grief. This grief may lead to depression, anger, self-hate, anxiety, or loss of hope, the kinds of emotions that can damage the client's resiliency. Addiction counsellors need to be aware of the grieving process and how to support their client.

Schneider Model

Stage 1: Initial Awareness of Loss. The client feels out of balance because of emotions such as feelings of shock, detachment, disbelief, disorientation, numbness, and confusion.

Stage 2: Attempts at Limiting Awareness by Holding On. The client tries to hold on to an experience as a way to cope and deal with the current situation, with the hope that it will go away. This kind of avoidance is normal.

Stage 3: Attempts at Limiting Awareness by Letting Go. This is when the client gives up on holding on, and accepts the situation has occurred and is real. Powerful emotions such as guilt, anger, and shame are likely to come up.

Stage 4: Awareness of Extent of Loss. This is traditionally called the mourning phase, and it is normal for a client to be flooded with conscious thinking about meaning and future direction.

Stage 5: Gaining Perspective on the Loss. The person is gaining their perspective, and organizing the loss in a way that is less draining on them mentally and emotionally.

Stage 6: Resolving Loss. This is the time to say good-bye, do unfinished business, and move forward.

Stage 7: Reformulating Loss in a Context of Growth. Out of the grief comes the will to want to grow, and move on with motivation for personal growth and discovery.

Stage 8: Transforming Loss into New Levels of Attachment. This is the stage where the person has transformed, and is now releasing the pain of the past fully as they are on a new plan of acceptance, awareness of the structure of life, and what it is to be a human being.

6. *Do I have a strategy to help a client manage Stress?*

Stress is real and can immobilize a client. Not taking action when stressed increases a person's risk of being negatively impacted. For example, the client's physical response to stress will lead to the release of the neurotransmitter epinephrine (adrenalin). Adrenalin is mainly responsible for the flight or fight response that was originally designed to keep humans alive and survive in the wild kingdom. It mobilizes sugars providing the body with increased strength, stamina, and energy to respond to a physical or emotional threat. Today this defense mechanism continues at the same levels as it did to help humans have fear and learn how to get to the top of the food chain. This response is often counter productive to our survival. For example, having a full chemical dump because someone left a door open in the house is an overreaction and puts hormones in the body that are not needed and that weaken the immune system. Many clients with addictive disorders have weakened systems because of the abuse they put their body through. It is important that they learn how to manage stress so it does not manage them.

Counsellors need to have a toolbox of strategies ready to assist in reducing and preventing stress. Below are four examples:

- Continue to review how the client is dealing with their recovery contract commitments to ensure they are coping with and managing the demands. Sometimes a client's recovery plan can be overprogrammed and become a major stressor.
- Teach the person normal signs and symptoms of stress overload, such as:
  ◊ Irritability – becoming overly critical and annoyed by little things.
  ◊ Insomnia – trouble falling or staying asleep.
  ◊ Fatigue – feeling weary for no apparent reason, having odd aches and pains, especially in the head, neck, or back.

◊ Weight changes – significant gain or loss.

◊ Respiration problems – shortness of breath or hyperventilation without much physical exertion.

◊ Psychological upsets – feeling of depression and anxiety.

Most important, coach the client, that when they feel stress, it is a normal response; they have some control over what they can do to manage it; and if it becomes unmanageable to report it to you and their doctor.

- Promote the value and benefits of exercise 20 to 30 minutes, several times a week once they have medical permission to exercise.

- Promote the importance of a healthy and balanced diet. Include high-octane nutrients, such as fruits and vegetables. Limit sugar, salt, and caffeine intake.

- Promote the value of life balance: how to manage work and home. Teach strategies to prevent and manage stress (e.g., meditation, music therapy, healthy activities, walking, guided imagery, and progressive muscle relaxation).

- Some or all of the above elements may end up in the client's treatment plan and recovery contract. It is important to monitor the ones that do not end up as primary or secondary issues as a part of client management. In addition, it is important to anticipate other kinds of risks for which you may need to prepare.

The next article in this series will introduce the fifth side of the Rubik's cube of addiction counselling and provide the framework for a problem solving approach to working with a client one-on-one.

PART V

HOWATT'S 6-STEP COUNSELLING ADDICTION MODEL

When most people think of addiction counselling, intervention is what jumps out as the most visible aspect. Perhaps it's because intervention is where "the rubber hits the road" and visible progress starts to be made in a client's recovery.

Intervention follows the foundation stages of orientation, screening and assessing, reviewing treatment planning and recovery tools, and managing crisis situations. These four early stages were examined in this series likening the successful treatment of addictive disorders to solving a Rubik's Cube.

Part I explored setting the stage and orienting clients to addiction counselling; the second outlined considerations for screening and assessing to help clients determine their options; the third reviewed treatment planning and recovery tools; and the fourth explored managing crisis situations.

Those first four sections provided addiction counsellors with a road map of the actions that need to be considered and in place prior to formal addiction counselling.

This section examines the fifth side of the Rubik's Cube, which represents intervention, and introduces Counselling Addiction Intervention, a six-step integrative model for helping clients in formal individual counselling. One of the biggest power tools in addiction recovery, it focuses on helping clients solve problems, make new choices, and take new actions in a one-on-one setting.

One of the core outcomes of addiction counselling is to provide clients with new information that acts as a conduit to new opportunities. It is important to note that in the first four parts of the Rubik's Cube series, a counsellor would need to already have in place their counselling micro skills (e.g., active listening), addiction theory, counselling theory, motivation theory, and recovery tools. However, my 18 years experience in the field indicates that the actual persona of the addiction counselor, in regard to their attitude towards the counselling relationship, authentic willingness to help, and their belief in a person's potential, may be the single biggest skill they can bring to addiction counselling.

While Corey (1996) states, ". . . no single theory is comprehensive enough to account for the complexities of human behaviours, especially when the range of client types and specific problems are taken into consideration" (p. 447), there may in fact be no one counselling model to deal with every potential problem that may arise. However, addiction counsellors must have a process that is proven to be safe, has clinical efficacy when helping people change, and is definable and measurable.

And all strategies in this business need to be built on continuous improvement platforms because they evolve as the counsellor develops more skills, experience, and expertise. This field is evolving and growing every day, so all addiction counsellors need to continue to grow, be committed to learning, and take professional development courses to stay current.

A well thought out counselling strategy will have a clear beginning, middle, and end. Since most addiction counselling sessions take about an hour to achieve effective results, having a strategy that is focused on learning new behaviours is beneficial. The outcome is to provide the counsellor with clear specifics as to where they are in the strategy at all times so they can maintain a clear focus and intention.

Too often I see young counsellors looping and asking questions without direction or a clear strategy. To be an effective addiction counselor, it is important to develop a counselling orientation that can be defined and measured. The Counselling Addiction Intervention provides a platform to build a counselling orientation.

The section below introduces the six steps of this intervention. It is important to note that, before a counsellor can ever engage in addiction counseling, they must be fully aware and adhere to their professional codes of ethics.

Step 1. Build Rapport

The first step is critical. People need to feel safe, learn to trust their counsellors, and feel they have common ground to be open and willing to engage in the kinds of conversations needed to facilitate change. The majority of clients have some relationship challenges in their lives (e.g., family), thus relationship building is often a first hurdle to cross in the counselling process. The counsellor must first develop a safe and healthy relationship in order to help a client.

What can the counsellor do to facilitate a healthy relationship? Corey (1996) teaches that the following characteristics, from a Rogerian Person-Centered Model, must be present to foster the development of a healthy relationship with a client:

- Two people must be in psychological contact.
- One person is experiencing incongruent behaviour.
- One person is demonstrating congruent behaviour.

- One person (the helper) is really concerned about the individual asking for help (the helpee).
- The helper demonstrates an understanding of the internal frame of reference of the helpee.
- The helpee is able to receive communication from the helper, and identify it as being empathetic and genuine.   (p.205)

Developing a healthy relationship with a client requires starting with simply discovering common interest. Common interest, in choice theory language, is the sharing of quality world pictures (Glasser, 1998). Glasser also teaches sharing common interest, such as sports, music, or other hobbies helps the client see similarities, and these simple, common building blocks can be the foundation for building a trusting relationship.

Building a healthy relationship really starts the first time a counsellor meets a client, as outlined in Part I. The Counselling Addiction Intervention approach to building rapport is more intentional.

In this rapport building stage it is important to be mindful that most clients, in addition to having an addictive disorder, have some deep regret and life challenges. Adler (1958) reported that when a person does not feel they are fitting in to the social interest (e.g., peer groups) they often become discouraged and end up in some addictive disorders. Adler (1963) taught all human behaviour is influenced by the client's personal life script (how they see their future) and who they are (their worth), which is based on their interpretation of private logic (view of themselves).

When clients feel discouraged, they are in a position of what Adler (1964) called Inferiority. Adler (1963) taught that all human behaviour is motivated to move from this position of inferiority toward Superiority. This superiority is not over others; it is over oneself, to be able to fit into the social interest (relationship with others). All behaviour the client creates is referred to by Adler as compensatory behaviour (e.g., addictive disorders). This behaviour may not appear to be effective by some standards; however, to the individual it is a way to move away from the anxiety and pain of feeling inferior.

Howatt (2000) teaches that one of the main goals of counselling is to help people discover what life tasks need work and mastering the following five: building friendships; establishing intimacy; contributing to society; getting along with one's self; and spiritual tasks. Many times addiction counsellors work with clients who have not yet mastered these tasks. Adler (1963) suggested that when an individual displays resistance, it is only because the helper has not yet found common ground. Howatt (1997) teaches that resistance is a symptom of lack of trust and common ground. Clients often display resistance when:

- They do not trust the counsellor.
- They do not understand what the counsellor is doing.
- They do not want to give up the old behaviour because they cannot see any other potential options as being better.
- They feel helpless.

One of the outcomes of building rapport is learning about what life tasks the person may feel they have not yet achieved and the kinds of behaviours they have been using to compensate.

Looking at clients through this model can prevent a counsellor from prejudicing their behaviours. An effective paradigm to keep the focus on helping rather than on judging, is to look at a client who may appear to be resistant and not motivated to change as not being bad or irresponsible, but as discouraged.

Another foundation for building rapport is a safe and comfortable counselling environment. Thorne (1992) explained that Carl Rogers, founder of Humanistic Psychology, believed that a person's inner skills would be brought out by the helper's *basic optimism*. Rogers (1986) reported the core conditions a counsellor must provide a person so that they can become secure enough to trust their inner skills, are empathy, congruency, and non-judgment.

As the addiction counsellor does this, they not only develop rapport and insight into the client's world, they also help the client. This is what Adler (1964) called "Ah ha!" It provides profound insights that can drive positive change.

One final note for addiction counsellors to keep in mind as they enter a counselling relationship is to be aware of their own prejudices and professional limitations. For example, some may not be able to work with all clients (e.g., alcoholic child abusers). If this happens, it is appropriate to refer the client to a professional who can be more objective.

Step 2. Define the Problem

The primary objective of this stage is determining with the client the specific focus and outcome for the current counselling session. It is important to develop as clear a picture as possible of what the client wants and what they are willing to focus on.

The strategy to laser in on the focus (problem) for the day may not always be obvious and clear. This often is the case in a first counselling session, especially when there has been no formal, structured assessment completed. The following questions will help determine the focus for the session:

- What is the biggest challenge facing you over the next seven days?
- What is keeping you up at night, meaning, what are you worried about today?
- If you were to pick one area of your life and change it tomorrow, what would it be?
- What is the single biggest issue you suggest we need to focus on to-day?
- I have heard you, and I have a few ideas as to some challenges you may have and perhaps a strategy as to the order to address them. Would you be willing to explore those with me?

Now this is where the model becomes dynamic. If, through your questioning and use of your core micro and helping model skills, the client does not appear to be motivated to talk about a problem or pick one, this is a sign they are not comfortable yet or not are fully motivated to take action. If a focus theme does not come out, continue looping up to step 1 to build more rapport with the client and continue to discover an area of focus that can be addressed in counselling. The goal is to get the client to come back to counselling. Change will happen at the client's speed, not the counsellor's.

Step 3. Assess Motivation for Change

There are times when a client is not ready or prepared to do anything about their problem, even though they have identified it. If they are not prepared to address the issue, continue to loop back to steps 1 and 2 and add strategies and techniques from the recovery tool, Motivational Interviewing. See Miller, W. R., & Rollnick, S. (Eds.) (2002). *Motivational interviewing: Preparing people to change addictive behaviour (2nd ed.)* for more information.

The industry best practice in addiction for assessing motivation for change is the six-stage model for determining readiness to change developed by Prochaska, DiClemente, and Norcross (1992).

Their *Precontemplation Stage* is when clients refuse to believe they have any issues that require change, or to show a lack of motivation for change. This has been defined as the *Unwillingness to Change Stage*, where the client is not psychologically ready, nor motivated to address the presenting issue. They show an unwillingness to change their present position, or have had insufficient time to process the information, and do not yet see the value in a new behaviour.

The *Contemplation Stage* is when the client starts to have dialogue and show willingness for change. This has been defined as the *Exploration for Change Stage*, where the client starts to make inquiries to explore the "what ifs," the potential, and the effort required. They also consider the new skills, knowledge, and attitude they will need to achieve the desired change (e.g., peace). However, they are not yet willing to take action.

The *Preparation Stage* is what the authors call the point where the client is concentrating and focusing on making change. Defined as *Preparing for Change Stage*, this is where the counsellor's main function is to act as a resource and instructor to help the client develop the foundation skills necessary to be successful in learning new behaviours. Once a client is motivated to take action, the counsellor may determine they will need to do research for the appropriate interventions or strategies to help the client learn.

The *Action Stage* is what Prochaska, DiClemente, and Norcross (1992) define as the time when the client is finally ready to initiate change. It has also been defined as the *Procedures for Change Stage*. When the client gets to this point, they are usually highly motivated to set a specific goal to reduce their concern area. This willingness for action sets up the next step, but an important word of caution: A client's goals need to match their current motivation to address the problem. For example, if a client is contemplating addressing their relationship with their father, asking them to have a meeting with their father to talk about how they can make things better would not be effective. A counsellor's goals for change must match the client's level of change.

Step 4. Set Goals

The goal setting step could also be called the change step. The steps to this point have defined the need and desire; now it's time to determine goals and actions. If it were easy to set a few goals, counselling would be simple, but often a client does not have the knowledge or skills to reach a defined goal that both they and the counsellor see as important. Thus the counsellor must prepare the client to take action to achieve their goals outside of counselling, where the majority of the real work in treatment happens.

For the most part, defining goals, setting objectives, and identifying needed resources are straightforward. The client must determine the long-term goal and the short-term goals needed to achieve it. Most clients know they want to stop an addictive disorder as an end goal but often lack the skills to achieve the short-term goals in order to be successful.

What is not so straightforward is changing behaviour. For example, Jimmy wants to have a better relationship with his father (long-term goal) but he has a profound irrational belief around perfection that must first be overcome (defined short-term goal). Because Jimmy's irrational belief has negatively impacted his ability to approach his father in the past, without new skills to curb this irrational thinking, the likelihood of attaining the long-term goal is diminished. Jimmy will be more successful by having this irrational thought challenged and removed.

The counselling process in this step requires exploration, insight, and teaching to help the client not only define goals but also to gain the perspective, skills, and abilities to achieve them. Many clients know what needs to be done but fail because they lack the skills to be successful. Counsellors are trained to identify the skills and abilities clients could benefit from to achieve their personal goals and transfer this learning in a proactive and positive way in the counselling process.

This is why counsellors, before using this strategy to its full potential, must have their counselling toolbox in place with all four Ts listed below at their disposal:

Theory – An understanding of why human beings do what they do. Counselling theories by authors such as Adler, Glasser, Ellis, Beck, and Bandura are but a few to choose from.

Therapy – A strategy to influence and teach the core learnings from a theory that provides clients with insight and understanding as to potential and options. In the field of addiction treatment, cognitive-behavioural theories that teach and promote internal locus of control have been proven effective for persons with addictive disorders. Many addiction counsellors have had success using Albert Ellis' (1975) ABC theory as a technique for discovering and overcoming irrational thinking.

Technique – This encompasses the strategies that come from a counselling theory. Behavioural therapy has proven that journaling is a useful tool for self-monitoring and reflection outside the counselling session. Adler's Magic Wand technique is a strategy for assisting clients to discover what they really want in the session (Howatt, 2000). Most counsellors develop a set of techniques and have a clear frame of reference of when, where, and how to use each technique in the counselling process.

Tools – Many effective recovery tools can be drawn on in this stage to help a client learn skills to enable them to attain their desired goals. One such in-session tool is stress management around relaxation deep breathing that helps a client calm themselves so they can talk about what they want without being overwhelmed with anxiety. Outside-of-session strategies include peer helping groups.

Step 5. Formulate an Action Plan

In this step, the counsellor and the client negotiate the action steps (short-term goals) to which the client will commit. These will be influenced by the client's current motivation level, skills, ability, and support resources available outside of counselling. All action plans are to be specific, measurable, and time-limited. It is helpful to write them out to reduce confusion around expectations and accountabilities.

Action plans must not be overwhelming, as this reduces the chances of success. Start small, and build slowly. The research says most people will fail before they succeed. Though we do not promote them, we expect relapses and plan for them. This is why every plan must have a risk management element to ensure the client's safety has been addressed to prevent a major relapse or other risk. For example, a female who has an abusive husband must have a stay-safe action plan ready.

The client's level of functioning and risk determines how detailed this action plan needs to be. As mentioned in Part III, every action plan is to be tested against the acronym SIMPLE: Simple (plan matches the client's current functioning); Immediate (can be done now); Measurable (can observe and measure progress); Plausible (client can do by themselves); Legal, Ethical (to ensure all elements of the plan are congruent to these steps).

In addition, one important action step in planning is doing a final walk through and testing the plan by trouble shooting with the "what if" questions to increase success.

Step 6. Plan Follow-up and Feedback

One rule that a counsellor can never break is that all plans must be followed up. The client must come to trust that what you say you will do, you will do; and you do not make plans that drift into thin air. Clients need addiction counsellors to be thorough and detailed. One important detail is to track what a client is working on and to be ready at the start of every session to follow up and acknowledge their progress, success, and growth. When a client does not follow through on a plan, focus not on what did not happen but on what needs to happen to get the plan back on track.

Becoming frustrated and upset with a client who does not follow their plan will rarely, if ever, excite or motivate them to change; it may just discourage them from coming back to counselling. Do not own the client's plan; it is theirs. It is the responsibility of the client to work as hard as you to resolve their problems. When the counsellor is working harder than the client, they need to ask themselves if they are clear of their professional objectives; are they being manipulated; or perhaps are they creating a potential dependency issue.

In closing, the main outcome of this Counselling Addiction Intervention is to provide a road map for addiction counsellors to help clients solve problems and create new solutions and goals. This model has been designed so the counsellor knows where they are in the counselling process at all times, as it has a clear beginning, middle, and end. For a visual overview of this model, review the figure *6-Step Counselling Addiction Model*. How many times the client will need to go through this process will depend on how many issues they have; how they progress toward their goals; and when they think they are on track and have achieved their goals.

The next article in this series will introduce the sixth and final side of the Rubik's Cube of addiction counselling. It will link the stages of recovery with after care, relapse prevention, and new beginnings.

Howatt's 6-Step Counselling Addiction Model	
Steps	**Main Outcomes for each Step**
Step 1. Build Rapport	• Learn about the client's model of the world • Develop common groups • Help the client feel safe and build their trust
Step 2. Define the Problem	• Define the focus for the session • Discover what problem(s) the client wants help with • Ensure the client, not the counsellor, is defining the problem
Step 3. Assess Motivation for Change	• Determine the client's current level of motivation to take action and address their problems • If the client is not motivated, use motivational interviewing to help motivate them
Step 4. Set Goals	• Define goals, objectives, and resources needed to obtain actions • Counsellor relies on their counselling toolbox to offer strategies and solutions • The counsellor teaches core skills needed to attain goals
Step 5. Formulate an Action Plan	• Define action steps and milestones • Action steps need to be measurable • Build in a risk management strategy
Step 6. Plan Follow-up and Feedback	• Start with activities and outcomes from last session • Use collateral data whenever possible • Provide meaningful feedback and acknowledge success

PART VI

THE JOURNEY

The paradox of this series likening the treatment process of an addictive disorder to the solving of a Rubik's Cube is that the last side of the cube is the only one that really matters. And if we never get to this point in treatment the client's hope of a quality future is minimal.

The first five sides of the cube are similar to emergency room treatment for someone who has been injured in a car crash. In that case, their injuries must be treated and their condition stabilized, so they can proceed to physical rehabilitation and move forward with their life. In addiction counselling, the first goal of treatment is to get the person to stop their addictive behaviour. When their condition has been stabilized, they can move on to full recovery from their addiction.

Addiction counselling interventions are designed to assist a client to navigate their current situation and to get them to a point where they are healthy and strong enough to move forward with their life.

This last side in the Rubik's Cube series provides a new tool for addiction counsellors to help clients get on the right track for the new journeys they will need to take to move away from a life of addiction or risk of addictions taking over their lives.

Addictions are seldom the real problem. Often the addiction and all its distress are fueled by other core issues, such as money, career, relationships, self-worth, and health. This may not be readily apparent, especially when powerful chemicals that are physically addictive can take over a person's life after just one use.

Consider for a moment how it is possible that Jimmy uses meth socially a couple of times a year without developing a craving for the drug. But when his friend Mary used meth for the first time, she was not able to stop until eventually an overdose took her life. In a short meth run of six month she gave up her job, morals, values, health, and spirit, all to keep an addiction satisfied.

So why did meth take Mary and not Jimmy? We really do not know. What we do know is drugs like meth need only be used once to take hold of a person and become habit forming. This is why an active, addictive disorder is often a person's primary problem when they come for treatment.

Once an addictive disorder has been stopped, the work is far from done. If this were not true, why would so many people relapse? This speaks to my point that the addiction is often a dangerous symptom, not the core problem.

The challenge to recovering from addictive disorders is that they must be replaced by new habits that are not as risky and that also help a person resolve core issues. Getting someone to stop an addictive behaviour is a major milestone, but it only provides an opportunity to make the real change to help them realign and resolve core issues.

This article introduces an aftercare strategy I call *The Journey*. The application of an aftercare strategy is for clients who have moved beyond ER treatment, have been stabilized, are mentally and physically strong again, and are ready for the next phase of treatment.

The goal of *The Journey* is straightforward: to provide the client with a framework architecture and an action plan for formulating and implementing new, healthy habits. A core hypothesis of this strategy is if a person is able to learn and practice new, healthy habits, this will increase their capacity to meet and balance the five areas of money, career, relationship, self-worth, and health.

The outcome is that the person will be at less risk of returning to their addictive disorder or forming a new one. It requires new goals, motivation, practice, time, and learning for new habits to form and become incorporated into their life.

Before a client is ready for this aftercare strategy, they must have reached a few core milestones: stopped their addictive behaviour; have mentally and physically stabilized; are no longer in crisis; have an integrated relapse prevention plan in place; and have the motivation and resources to move further away from their addictive disorder.

Depending on the counsellor's orientation and school of thought, most aftercare interventions would not be put in place until 8-12 months after the addictive disorder has been stopped so the person has time to become stabilized and ready to move forward. With serious drug users, this may take 12-18 months.

This, of course, is really just a guess because addiction treatment is not a perfect science and is client centered. Aftercare strategy in terms of timing is driven by the client's situation, readiness, and capacity. *The Journey* is a strategy for addiction counsellors to have as an option to offer clients who are looking for aftercare support.

The Journey: New Habits for a New Future

The following nine-step model will move at different speeds, depending on the client's readiness and motivation. As with any aftercare strategy, it is important before starting to point out the long-term benefits to the client. In

The Journey, the client is taught that each step of the process is designed to create discussion, reflection, and opportunities for counselling.

The addiction counsellor is ultimately responsible to use their counselling skills to facilitate this process. Since no two people are the same, it is difficult to predict how fast a person will move through each step. The key is quality, not speed.

Step 1. Introduction to Five Components of Life Balance – When the client and counsellor have determined the client is ready to move beyond the nuts and bolts of treatment and has progressed to move on to build a foundation and new habits, they begin *The Journey.*

This strategy begins by having the client take a fresh look at their current competencies and gaps in each of their five core areas of money, career, relationships, self-worth, and health. One way to introduce this idea is to use a metaphor of how out of balance many people are, whether or not they have an addiction, and how it is important to spend time examining these as a beginning place.

I suggest to my clients, "Let's assume we all have only 10 brain units to get through a day and to balance the five core areas. Also, keep in mind that these five areas form a hierarchy, meaning if we do not have our money needs met we will have a hard time focusing on anything else. Think back before your addiction and take a guess at how many brain units you spent in a typical day focusing on money, career, relationships, self, and health."

After the client responds, the counsellor can do a bit of normalizing and coaching and teach that many people spend six or seven brain units a day just dealing with money and career. This is perhaps why so many people are getting divorced, have low self-esteem, are overweight, or have mental health issues such as anxiety and depression.

The normalizing point is that if, over time, important areas of a person's life, such as health, self, and relat,ionships, are ignored, they risk running out of resources to keep up with the grind of life. And for some, the way to cope with life is to use certain behaviours as a way to escape or accept some perceived gap in one of these five areas. These behaviours can become habit forming for some and lead to serious addictive disorders.

The client is asked if they can relate to this metaphor and if they see any relevance to their life. The goal of this first step is not to focus on the past but to understand how important it is to have life balance in these five areas. This helps to promote and teach the value of looking at these areas and self-evaluating not the past as much as looking at what gaps the person may have in each of the areas so they can be helped along on the right journey.

<u>Action</u> – Evaluate competencies and gaps in each of the five life balance areas. I have designed a Life Balance Measure that I use with my clients in this stage to help us map out where the gaps are and what competences the client needs to learn. At this stage of the process I have my clients who have reading and writing skills start a bibliotherapy program, which includes *My Personal Success Coach* and *My Personal Success Coach Journal*. The Life Balance Measure eventually is used to track and monitor goals, daily progress, and emotions.

Step 2. Creating The Journey One Positive Habit at a Time – The next step is to introduce a 30-day renewable action plan. Whether or not a person had an active addiction, life is challenging and always presents ups and downs. We do not expect failure but, in the design of this plan, it is important to anticipate the kinds of turbulence that can bump a person off their journey. Some examples of the kind of turbulence that may need to be addressed are limiting beliefs about one's potential, unrealistic expectations, low frustration tolerance, and automatic negative thinking.

One core element for long-term success is to develop the resources needed each day to feel healthy and happy and not to be in a rush for the ending. Life is about today, not always tomorrow. Clients need to learn how to celebrate today and understand that goals are important but the process of attaining them needs to be as rewarding as the goals themselves.

The journey is really never over for any of us as we are always learning and growing. If we can adopt this thinking, we can hold a course to develop the new habits we want to add to our life. New habits are developed and integrated into the self when the following concepts are in place:

- Knowledge and Skills: Insight and capacity to perform the habit.
- Core Values: Individual's higher principles.
- Passions: Fuel that drives the imprinting of positive daily habits.
- Clearly Defined Target Objectives: Targets.
- Motivation: Active, conscious choice.
- Internal Locus of Control: Internal ownership of strategy and implementation.
- Repetition: Mastery of the habit.
- Time: Measure of confidence and competence.
- Self-Tracking: Daily monitoring.

Too often people fail to achieve new habits because they look at them from the wrong point of view. Setting of long-term goals is too often an exercise in good intentions that seldom pays dividends.

Embracing a perceptual shift from focusing on long-term goals to focusing on short-term goals is less psychologically overwhelming. As we proceed, we will explore how focusing on positive habit formation provides individuals with an opportunity to avoid becoming weighed down by self-appointed long-term target objectives by taking charge of manageable new daily habits.

Taking a few well thought out daily actions that are attached to a short-term target objective will lead to creation of new habits that are the building blocks for long-term success.

Action – Establish commitment and motivation to start to build new daily habits. The goal of this step is to teach this aftercare program and is designed on a 30-day renewable plan. The rest of the steps in this strategy are intended to move the plan to action and ultimately a way of living life one day at a time.

Step 3. Exploring Current Positive Habit Inventory – The purpose of this step is to discover all the positive habits that the client currently has in place consciously and unconsciously and is actively using. Positive daily habits are pillars of our day-to-day life. These are the soldiers that we can leverage to help build new habits and day-to-day success. This activity helps the client acknowledge how many positive habits we take for granted but are critical for both short- and long-term success.

It is the counsellor's job to use creativity and skills to help the client discover and acknowledge these positive habits. They may appear trivial, but clients need to recognize the value of positive habits such as good hygiene, understanding and valuing the importance of family, being committed to kindness to others, and caring for the environment.

We want clients to be aware of what they are already doing and to help them understand the goal of *The Journey* is only to add new habits as they are needed and to keep the ones that are working. Most humans are incapable of totally changing but are capable of replacing old habits with new ones.

This reinforces the concept that most people unconsciously have positive habits in place but seldom acknowledge them. Research shows that 95% of all cognitions occur unconsciously. As a result, we often do not recognize our habits until we think about them. By recognizing our habits, we can harness the 5% of controlled conscious thinking to motivate the development of new habits.

Action – Have the client acknowledge three to five positive habits that they have been following for the last 30 days, both personally and, if appropriate, professionally (career/school). These are pillars and acknowledge the client's success to this point in their recovery.

Some of the most obvious habits seen are a client who has received their 12-month chip from AA, has not missed a day of work in three months, and has made improvements in their physical health. Some people naturally have a hard time acknowledging their success so this may end up being a core counselling theme to help them move to the next step of the process.

Step 4. Exploring Roadblocks – Roadblocks can emotionally, cognitively, and spiritually disrupt the client from trying to push themselves to achieving their full potential.

The purpose of this step is to identify what the client thinks are their top three professional and personal roadblocks at this point in their journey. This will help point out their current perceptions in more detail than step 1.

It is paramount to clearly define the emotions of the roadblock, how it impacts the client's thinking, and the costs. Costs refer to how roadblocks are influencing the client's perception about their potential.

Roadblocks, when identified, can ignite motivation to make new conscious choices as well as fear. It will ultimately be the client's choice to take action to overcome a roadblock. But with effective counseling, they can be supported to understand that these fears are normal and together with a sound plan, the roadblocks can be overcome.

Overcoming a roadblock begins with the client starting a new set of daily habits that will help them gain the capacity to overcome it. The next few steps are intended to explore concepts and considerations that will prepare the client to launch their 30-day renewable plan.

Action – With the client, explore their current roadblocks. This step is designed to help the client discover and increase their awareness of the kinds of emotional roadblocks that are running automatic programs in their head. The chart on the next page shows some of the kinds of roadblocks a client may perceive.

Step 5. Moving Beyond Regret – Regret is an emotion that fuels pain. Ironically, this pain is similar to roadblocks as it can bring up negative emotions, which inhibit motivation and action. Left unaddressed, regret can haunt a client and lead to self-destructive behaviour such as relapsing to an old addiction.

Like a toothache, regret can eat at an individual and over time kill hope and positive habit formation. At this point in the client's recovery it is im-

Professional	Personal	Roadblock	Describe how item is a roadblock	What is the cost of this roadblock?
		Attitude (e.g., negative)		
		Time (e.g., always rushing)		
		Energy (e.g., fatigue)		
		Fear (e.g., avoidance)		
		Stress (e.g., anxiety)		
		Relationships (e.g., co-workers)		
		Health (e.g., weight)		
		Emotions (e.g., angry)		
		Focus (e.g., too many priorities)		

portant to not assume they have resolved all their regrets, nor to suggest they should have some regrets.

The goal of this step is to screen for unresolved regrets that the client has and that they can use to motivate them for action, not to guilt them into despair. It is critical that the addiction counsellor be clear of the objective in this step and uses their counselling skills to move the client through this step safely.

If done with dignity, tuning in to regret and taking responsibility for past actions, regret can be leveraged as a powerful, motivating, and positive force in the journey of creating new habits. However, to do this, the client must be clear that they need to be focused on moving forward and are not being held in the past.

Regret is often painful at first, though with empathy and support a client can learn to process it, move forward, and learn from mistakes to create the right journey for themselves. There is no evidence that holding on to the past is helpful. Regret, when challenged, provides an opportunity to take charge of how one views the world, which starts the process of moving forward to attain new success.

Action – With the client, discuss their top two or three regrets and how they are impacting their life choices and actions. Work with the client to process the opportunity and learnings that they can obtain from this exploration and what decisions this discussion helps them re-enforce about the journey they want to continue.

Step 6. What Ending do You want? – This step is to get the client to think about the ending of their life and what story they want to include once they have achieved what they want to as a person. The counsellor helps the client look to the future and define a realistic ending.

The goal is not to define how much money or fame they will have; it is to start a discussion around how they want to be remembered and what they want their legacy to be. For example, "I want to be remembered as a loving and caring father."

The previous two steps explored fear and guilt. This step's goal is to look beyond these to the successful completion of the life the client wants to have lived. Facing our own mortality is a challenge for all of us. Who we are and want to become are often a mask that few really look at.

Action – To get clients to start thinking about *The Journey* and how it will end. The goal is to ask the client to answer the question, "How do you want to be remembered, both personally and professionally?"

This will help in the design of the daily habits that will be needed to attain this ending and to move beyond fear and regret so they can meet their five life balance needs.

Step 7. What are your Core Values? – Core values are deep-seated beliefs that serve as the internal laws a client holds in real-time and are non-negotiable. Core values are filters that are used to evaluate oneself and the world, based on new information.

To help a person attain their short-term goals and to incorporate the daily habits needed for the right journey, they must be clear about what is important to them about each of the five life balance areas. This helps ensure that their goals and expectations are realistic and avoids setting expectations that are too low.

Addiction counsellors must use their counselling skills to help the client determine the most important elements for each of the following questions and to provide a rationale as to the value and benefit of each response for their long-term success.

Action – In this step the client is asked to take responsibility for their beliefs and to answer the following questions.

- What is most important to you about money?
- What is most important to you about career?
- What is most important to you about relationships?
- What is most important to you about self?
- What is most important to you about health?

Step 8. Acknowledging Your Passion – Passion is the engine that excites, motivates, and drives us all, yet to harness this energy we must be aware and tuned in to our passions.

Passion can capture our attention both positively and negatively. It can be a double-edged-sword that if not monitored regularly can fuel ineffectual behaviours such as addictions as an escape from pain (e.g., regret about relationships).

When we are consciously aware of our passions, we can control and use them to motivate and drive new habits. Idle minds are empty minds. When people go to work each day the same as the previous day, feeling trapped and having no passion in their life, their soul soon becomes empty and life seems to have no real meaning.

The human spirit is simple: it needs a fire burning. The role of addiction counsellors in this stage is to help clients tune in to a passion they have, return to a passion they had, or create a new one.

<u>Action</u> – Define what the client's passions are or what they would like them to be and start to incorporate the passions into the plan.

Step 9. Designing A Renewable Plan –

Action 1: Select the top three target objectives for the next 30 days. Target objectives represent what the client has determined as important and meaningful, based on what they have discovered in the first eight steps of this process.

Target outcomes must be specific and clearly understood what life balance areas they are intended to improve. No more than three target objectives at one time are to be worked on each month. Of course, as a client obtains success in any target objective they can add a new one.

This process is designed to continue and evolve from one daily habit to another to the client obtaining their life ending. The question often asked by clients is how long does this 30-day renewable process last. My response is, "You will know. This is not a decision for today."

Once clients learn what I know they soon come to the understanding that there is no ending; it is just a way to live life and a path to getting the success and ending they want.

<u>Action 2</u> – Research target objectives: Based on target objectives selected for the next 30 days, the client and counsellor work together to determine what positive daily habits will assist in achieving those objectives.

There is a need for daily structure and consistency to convert target objectives into new habits. Most target objectives require the development of several new habits. For example, if one wants to lose five pounds as their target objective, the daily habits will be to drink eight glasses of water, not eat past 7:00 PM, eat three healthy meals a day, and exercise 20 minutes daily.

The goal in this step is to brainstorm and decide on what daily habits will need to be started to put the client on the right track toward the three selected target objectives. The theory of this model is when a client continues to focus on habits, the habits become automatic and help bring the client to their target objective. Once clients develop a new habit, they no longer have to think about it and are on the way to achieving a target objective as a stepping stone for *The Journey*.

<u>Action 3</u> – After the client has researched the daily habits for each of their three target objectives, they are ready to begin the 30-day renewable plan. The succession of new habits over time will get a client to where they want to be.

Have the client align the target objective to the core value and passion that are connected to the life ending they want. Sometimes a client will want to discover in the early stages what their passion and core values are and the result will be their first target objectives.

The goal of this 30-day renewable plan is to put the client on *The Journey* one new habit at a time. Success is the result of many little choices. Clients need a strategy that is not overwhelming and a process that makes sense to them at the time.

30-Day Renewable Plan Template			
Name:	Start Date:	End Date:	Note: *Update this template every 30 days.*
Target Objective for Life Balance	Habit 1	Habit 2	Habit 3
e.g.: Lose Weight	*Eat fruit in the AM*	*Run 3 miles a day*	*Drink 3 liters of water at work*

This last step of the Rubik's Cube is critical for the client's long-term success and health. The journey often takes time. The key to this aftercare process is the 30-day renewable plan's focus on daily habit activities. It is important to track and monitor progress daily and to ensure the Renewable Plan Template is updated every 30 days. As clients achieve target objectives, they support the foundation and success for having a long and healthy journey.

As the strategy title implies, aftercare means after the intense emergency care, the next part of the journey is to get on a course that puts great distance from the past. To do that requires a commitment to look forward, one choice at a time.

CHAPTER 5

Addiction Recovery Tools

This chapter introduces addiction recovery tools and their application to addiction counselling.

MOTIVATED clients, even when committed to treatment, require recovery tools designed to translate motivation into tangible learning strategies and new behavioural habits for managing their addictive disorders. Regardless of where a client rests on the treatment continuum, the counsellor who uses a cognitive-behavioural model explores learning strategies that guide the client's development and ignite a dynamic reeducation process.

This chapter introduces six cognitive-behavioural recovery tools — classical conditioning, contingency management, cue exposure treatment, contracts for recovery, coping skills, and charting daily habits. These recovery tools bring structured expectations to the treatment process. They focus on dealing with thoughts and behaviours in the present, rather than on uncovering underlying issues from the past.

Each of these recovery tools, while employing a distinct methodological approach, provides insight into the development of new behavioural habits that place clients in greater control of their lives and environment. Addictions appear as habits that, in some cases, provide clients with an illusion of control.

The common goal of each of these tools is to help clients replace addictive habits with new, healthy habits that support recovery by creating instruments of control.

Classical Conditioning

Because many addiction clients believe that their environment controls them, it can help to teach them how the relationships defined in classical conditioning apply to their specific addiction. Understanding this connection can help them modify their addictive behaviour by implementing strategies such as Aversion Therapy and Counter Conditioning (Davidson & Neale, 1994) to bring an addictive behaviour to extinction and create a more positive habit using the same principles. Ivan Pavlov defined classical conditioning as a process involving a neutral stimulus (e.g., a bell) paired with an unconditioned stimulus that triggers an automatic response that requires no learning (e.g., food). In this famous experiment, Sam the dog became conditioned to respond to the neutral stimulus (bell) without the unconditioned stimulus (food) (Pavlov, 1960). It is helpful for addiction counsellors to be aware of the parallels of Pavlov's construction and addictive behaviours. This awareness can guide the client toward extinguishing and replacing an addictive behaviour.

Pavlov's research revealed the following insights that define simultaneously the terms of the behaviour to be modified and the manner in which a new habit can be structured:

- Reinforcement creates a conditioned response (CR) that gradually disappears without reinforcement.

- Extinction occurs when the conditioned stimulus (CS) returns to a neutral stimulus (NS), i.e., occurs when the bell is rung and no food follows.

- Generalization occurs when a conditioned response is elicited by another similar neutral stimulus [the sight of an object that looks like a bell gets a similar response as the conditioned stimulus bell].

- Spontaneous Recovery occurs after there has been extinction and the neutral stimulus relapses to the original conditioned stimulus.

Four Steps to Extinction

Awareness is the desired outcome of this application. An example of applying Pavlov's theory to a clinical setting involves:

1. Explain and teach the tenets of classical conditioning using examples relevant to the client's current state of addiction.

2. Make a list of all the potential environmental triggers that may have become classically conditioned (e.g., a favorite perfume). Have the client explore his or her present addictive disorder(s) by exploring the

relationship between CS and CR. The client explores in detail all per-ceived pairings (NS + UCS = CS) and sorts them out in writing to visually see the linkages.

3. With the counsellor's help, the client identifies different behaviours, thinking and emotional consideration(s) for extinction. Then the cli-ent is asked to monitor daily behaviours for 90 days through the use of an extinction log, which the client brings to counselling for guid-ance and reinforcement.

4. In the 90-day critical debriefing, the counsellor and client evaluate the extinction log and measure progress. The counsellor and client revisit step 1 and make a decision if step 2 is to be repeated for an-other 90 days.

For more information on classical conditioning, see Corsini and Wedding (2000), Corey (2001), and *Better Mental Health through the Pavlovian Paradigm — Innovations* (n.d.).

Contingency Management

Early in life, most of us learn that our actions always have consequences. Addicted clients, blinded by the euphoria of addictions, are unable to see the negative consequences of their behaviour. Contingency management, influenced by the work of B.F. Skinner (1971), is a cognitive tool that fo-cuses on changing maladaptive behaviours by controlling consequences. Known as behaviour modification, this process makes use of positive rein-forcement (rewards for appropriate behaviour), and punishment (negative consequences for maladaptive behaviour). Regarding punishment, the ob-jective is to develop predetermined consequences for addictive behaviour.

For example, if the desired behaviour(s) are not achieved, the desired reward is withheld (e.g., no Friday night movie). It is important to under-stand that punishment is not to be damaging to the client but rather serves as a motivator that stresses accountability in the treatment process. Contin-gency management promotes the application of positive rewards for short-term goal success. Research points out that rewards can become primary drivers for motivating learning (Friedman & Schustack, 2003). Budney, Sigmon, and Higgins (2001) explain that "controlled clinical studies have shown that contingency management interventions can enhance therapeu-tic outcomes across a wide range of substance abuse treatment populations" (p. 149).

The counsellor who uses contingency management as a treatment tool must, as a result, work with clients to determine positive rewards. For example, a client who is trying to cut down weekend alcohol consumption, using a harm-reduction orientation, makes the contract: if he goes for two weeks without a drink, he will allow himself to enjoy two drinks maximum when he goes for supper at a pub. If he does not comply, he withholds the reward of going out, this being the predetermined consequence. When implementing this treatment strategy, it is important for the counsellor to be aware of the steps that define the contingency management. Steps for developing contingency management plans:

1. Define the desired target outcome and the criteria used to measure success (e.g., urine test weekly). These determinants will come out of the treatment-planning process.

2. Make sure the contract clearly defines the expectations and agreements and is congruent with the treatment program. Both positive rewards and consequences can be chosen to reinforce behaviour.

3. Specify the following items in detail: dates, times, frequency, duration, measurements, monitoring of specific processes, risk management issues, relapse prevention, positive reinforcements, and punishments.

4. Put the contract in writing with the above criteria and have the client sign and date it.

For additional information on contingency management plans, see Higgins, Wong, Badger, Ogden, and Dantona (2000) as well as Kirby, Amass, and McLellan (1999).

Cue Exposure Treatment

Cue exposure is therapy designed to reduce relapse in addictive behaviour by tempting clients with stimuli that induce cravings to drink/consume while preventing the client from actually participating/satisfying the craving. Cue exposure is a relatively new recovery tool that considers tolerance, withdrawal, and cravings for drugs/alcohol as conditioned states that are amenable to change or extinction (Eliany & Rush, 1992). This exposure allows the client to create habits of resistance and refutation of the temptation.

Cues are specific to the addiction. For example, an alcoholic may find a cue in the sight or smell of a favorite beverage, in the mood states or situations in which drinking previously occurred, or in the people, places, times, and objects that had previously been associated with alcohol's pleasurable effects. While cue exposure is seen as a realistic treatment tool that increases self-efficacy and reduces desire, it is not without risk. The very stimuli that trigger a client's addictive behaviour are used to create the habits of resistance. Cue exposure approaches require the addiction counsellor to be trained and supervised both to mitigate risk and manage the intensity of the session. Thus this article does not provide an application outline for cue exposure; the goal is only to introduce you to this concept for your consideration.

The rationale for this treatment approach stems from clinical studies, which have found that many patients retain cue reactivity (cravings) after treatment (Chiauzzi & Liljegren, 1993). For example, Childress, McLellan, Ehrman, and O'Brien (1988) found that opiate-addicted individuals who achieved abstinence in treatment still presented physiological arousal to drug cues 30 days after treatment completion. Similar results have been found with cocaine (Washton, 1989) and alcohol users (Cooney et al., 1987). Given that cues augment relapse potential (Niaura et al., 1988), it has been argued that treatment can become an exercise in futility when the addicted person is re-exposed to relapse cues in his or her natural environment over a period of time.

For more information on cue exposure treatment, see Bouton (2000) and Drummond, Glautier, and Remington (1995).

Contract for Recovery

Even motivated clients need a highly structured treatment environment and will benefit from using contracts in the recovery process (Talbott & Crosby, 2001). A recovery contract is an action plan that defines the milestones (e.g., an AA 30-day clean chip or predetermined physician examinations) that must be achieved to result in positive treatment outcomes. The addiction counsellor works with the client to develop a specific step-by-step recovery contract based on the mutually agreed upon treatment plan. Updated on a regular basis throughout treatment to integrate factors that are prone to change (e.g., risk management and relapse prevention), recovery contracts should be considered a unifying treatment document by including details such as: exact time and dates for actions, support systems, progression of goals, and measurement of progress.

A recovery contract takes time, effort, and focus to create and implement because its goal is to outline the behaviours essential for a successful recovery. A well-conceived recovery contract will help fuel a client's motivation as well serve as a practical guide for day-to-day living. This structure helps the client deal with daily life stress and decision-making, and avoid distractions. This tool can be effectively used in intensive outpatient, primary inpatient, and continuing care settings. Recovery contracts are most effective when the client's support systems (e.g., family) are involved in the process and are aware of the contract specifics.

Four steps for creating a contract for recovery

1. The client and the counsellor develop a recovery contract (not legally binding) based on the client's treatment plan. Its purpose is to remove distractions and keep the client focused on a plan with well-thought out action steps. Establish expectations by taking a seven-day calendar and defining the action steps the client will be taking in the morning through the evening every day until "completion." Clearly outline the consequence for breach of contract.

2. Establish a recovery contract support team. The client will need to sign a release of information document before the counsellor can work with the support team directly. However, involving caring family members and peers supports the treatment efficacy of the contract.

3. Develop an emergency action plan outlining clear action steps in the case of a relapse. These steps must be included.

4. Present the final recovery contract to the client, who signs and dates it. The most effective contracts tend to be no more than one page, so as not to overwhelm the client. It is important to review the contract in detail to ensure client comprehension. The recovery contract team receives a copy of the contract so that accountability can be determined. Finally, set the reporting plan.

For more information about recovery contracts, see Talbott and Crosby (2001) and Talbott (1995).

Coping Skills Training

Coping skills (also called affect-regulation) is a strategy for helping clients to effectively manage stress, anxiety, anger, or frustration without resorting to their addictive disorder (Lazarus & Launier, 1978). "Affect-regulation training seeks to help addicts develop an internal rather than external locus of self-control, facilitating acceptance of personal responsibility for change so they can reap the emotional benefits of their efforts" (Scott, Kern, & Coombs, 2001, p. 192). Addicts tend to be "compulsive and ritualistic, relying on alcohol and other psychoactive drugs to help maintain their mood, energy and or arousal levels" (p. 192). The realization that external forces do not control them can help clients displace motivations and feelings that come from active addictive disorders. Coping skills can assist clients to tune into internal motivations.

Coping skills are specific to the experiences, fears, and commitment of the particular client. Coping skills techniques must be supportive of the client's treatment needs. The client's mastery of coping skills does not happen overnight. There is a transition phase in which the client will need support to cope with the uncomfortable emotions and feelings. Coping skills are instrumental in affording the client the respite from uncomfortable circumstances that can be potentially devastating to recovery. When integrating coping skills into the treatment environment, consider the following four-step model.

Four-step coping skills model

1. *Set the environment.* The client needs to feel that the counselling environment is a safe place to learn coping skills. The counsellor's first role is to build rapport and trust.

2. *Evaluate the client's core coping skills informally.* The core coping skills that the counsellor will explore through general open questions are related to emotions and/or environments that are associated with the client's addictive behaviour.

3. *Create an action plan* with the client to learn core coping skills using a variety of strategies: support groups, bibliotherapy (e.g., assigning Daniel Goleman's Emotional Intelligence or David Burn's Feeling Good Handbook) or specific psychosocial workshops (self-esteem). Once the coping skill design is developed, it needs to be put into a formal format so that the client is clear of the actions and desired outcomes.

4. *Follow up* by reviewing with the client on regular basis his or her progress in general and his or her progress in the area of coping-skill development. For additional coping skills resources, see Goleman (1995), Monti (1989), and Scott, Kern and Coombs (2001).

Charting Daily Habits

Progress in counselling can be difficult to qualify. Engaging a client in proactively charting daily habits creates a cognitive process that monitors and regulates daily behaviour (Bandura, 1978). In essence, identifying desired new habits and developing a charting program to implement those habits provides the client with a tangible tool to reinforce and measure progress.

The habit chart is a tool that promotes self-awareness by making concrete the expectations, thoughts, goals, and plans that will directly impact the client's behaviour and learning. As Bandura (1997) explains, reinforcing a behaviour that was positive in the past will assist the client to repeat the habit in the present.

This tool is influenced by Benjamin Franklin, who developed habit charting before psychology or addiction counselling was established (Friedman & Schustack, 2003). Franklin's chart listed 13 core competencies that he wanted to focus on each day, including moderation, resolution, and order. This pragmatic self-help approach provides insight into the residual value of the quest for perfection: Franklin did not believe it was possible to attain such lofty goals; however, he owned the insight that daily focus helped him to be a better and happier person. His approach reduced the behaviours and actions of success into smaller manageable activities. By simplifying the tenets of success, he invented a tool to create positive habits that still carries considerable value today.

Four steps for developing habit charts

1. The client first determines what habits he or she wants to reinforce daily, up to a maximum of five. With progress the client can add to the list; yet the counsellor must not overwhelm the client in the early stages with excessive habits.

2. The client clearly defines what each habit is and the activities associated with that behaviour (e.g., honesty and non-judgmental activities). This often takes time, but is an excellent process for teaching normalizing social standards.

3. The counsellor and client build a weekly habit chart template, ensuring there are several copies and a master. The goal is to use the habit chart for 30 days before a critical assessment.

4. The client starts a daily habit chart, each day checking a box (3) that represents the successful completion of the daily habit. Failure to complete the habit results in an X, which is a reminder that the client has the opportunity the next day to focus on the assigned habit. If the client continues to see X's, it may be an indication that the client lacks a core competency and needs further reevaluation of needs and wants. Many times, clients are not aware of microskills needed to achieve daily success. This process helps them start to focus on the mechanisms involved in developing new habits.

For additional habit-charting resources, see Covey (1990).

Creating New Habits

When clients confront the challenges of learning new habits, they are able to manage expectations and recognize that stressful conditions could easily prompt relapse.

An old adage says we must learn to walk before we run. This conception of learning applies to clients who seek the freedom earned in the creation of new habits. Creating new habits helps clients reeducate themselves through a variety of techniques that facilitate changes in thoughts, perceptions, beliefs, and reactions to events. In effect, clients learn to replace the distorted or false cognitions that contributed to their addictions with more adaptive or realistic ones.

PSYCHOSOCIAL RECOVERY TOOLS FOR ADDICTIVE DISORDERS

Psychosocial tools include lifestyle planning and monitoring, individual therapy, group therapy, peer support, and family treatment (Coombs, 2001, xii). The purpose of this article is to introduce six psychosocial recovery tools that have been proven effective in assisting addicted clients. Although, as with any recovery tool, the addictions counsellor must first establish a baseline assessment to determine client need(s).

Blueprint for Life/Work Designs

The Blueprint for Life/Work Designs is the product of 10 years of research and development involving thousands of career practitioners and educators across the United States. The program is sponsored by the National Career Development Guidelines, through a partnership with the U.S. Government and America's Career Resource Network (www.acrna.net), National Life/Work Centre, Canada Career Information Partnership, and Human Resources Development Canada.

Used by addictions counsellors, career counsellors, community services workers, educators, human resource specialists, and social workers, the Blueprint for Life/Work Designs provides an incremental strategy for acquiring critical skills that focus first on core life skills to prepare the person for reintegration into the workforce. Progressing through three developmental steps, the client develops critical core competencies to enhance effective living, including developing a rewarding career.

Personal Management: (1) Build and maintain a positive self-image; (2) Interact positively and effectively with others; (3) Change and grow throughout one's life.

Learning and Work Exploration: (4) Participate in life-long learning, supportive of life/work goals; (5) Locate and effectively use life/work information; (6) Understand the relationship between work and society/economy.

Life/Work Building: (7) Secure/create and maintain work; (8) Make life/work enhancing decisions; (9) Maintain balanced life and work roles; (10) Understand the changing nature of life/work roles; (11) Understand, engage, and manage one's own life/work building process. This entire model can be found online for your review and use. It is an exceptional resource for addiction counsellors: www.blueprint4life.ca.

Individual Therapy (Internal Locus of Control)

One major advantage of individual therapy is its ability to adapt and focus on the unique needs of the person's situations. Zweben (2001) purports that individual therapy enhances the quality of recovery through behaviour and lifestyle change based on the client's motivation level. Clients with addictive disorders often perceive the environment controlling them, leaving them feeling powerless. Internal Locus of Control taught in a one-on-one environment has proven to be an effective clinical tool in helping clients see the insight of choice. Internal Locus of Control is a personality construct, in which the client's perceptions of personal control are determined internally by ones own choices not external circumstances. Choice theory provides counsellors a user-friendly model for teaching Internal Locus of Control to their clients.

Choice theory, created by William Glasser, MD, uses metaphors that a client can easily relate to — such as a car to illustrate total behaviour (the connection of actions, thinking, feeling, and physiology) — from which the client learns why he does what he does (Glasser, 1998, 2000). This theory teaches clients how to demystify the whys of human behaviour and can open the door for accepting responsibility for self and actions. Choice theory purports that the environment only provides information and the client ultimately chooses how he will respond. In the field of addictive disorder, this power-of-choice construct can make the difference between recovery and relapse. Teaching the client choice theory can be an effective first step to owning this power.

Glasser's work is making a major impact in the fields of mental health, education, addictions, business, and justice, and is recognized in most modern counselling books that discuss counselling theory. For more information on choice theory, visit: www.wglasser.com.

Group Therapy (anger-management training)

"Group therapy provides an almost ideal forum for addressing core features of the addictive disorder: the person's inability to see and accept the reality that is plain to others, the lack of internal 'radar' needed to motivate and guide adaptive responses to the environment, the tendency to disown personal responsibility and focus instead on external solutions, and the overwhelming feelings of failure, guilt, and toxic shame that perpetuate the addictive cycle" (Washton, 2001, p. 240).

Group therapy is a powerful process for the development of a specific psychosocial theme, such as anger. Professionals who work in the addictions field commonly come across people who need to learn how to manage their anger. Research is very clear that anger hijacks clear thought. Clients in recovery need their best thinking to be successful. Optimally, group therapy is most effective when conducted by a professional with a strong background not only in the various kinds of addictive disorders represented in the group, but also in anger management.

Individuals on the road to recovery commonly report that anger is one of the most challenging emotions to overcome. An important aspect of anger management is teaching cognitive thinking strategies to the client. Research points out that anger-management problems tend to be related to thinking errors (Lochman, White, & Wayland, 1991). Group therapy provides an opportunity for each participant to learn to take control of anger from a variety of sources: peer group participants, the leader, and course handouts.

For example, leaders who teach participants cognitive-relaxation techniques can assist each participant individually and within the group dynamic to significantly reduce anger (Holloway, 2003). Regardless of the composition of the group, and whether it addresses guilt, anger, or relationships, a synergistic overlap of learning helps participants in group therapy to develop an awareness and quality of life through an understanding of the experiences of others.

For more information on anger management programs and group therapy with addicts, refer to: Kassinove, H., Tafrate, R. C. (2002). Anger management: the complete guidebook for practitioners. Atascadero, CA: Impact, www.growthgroups.com/anger-info.htm and Elder, I. R. (1990). *Conducting group therapy with addicts.* Brandenton, FL: Human Services Institute.

Peer-Support Programs

Peer support, essential to addiction recovery, is available in several programmatic formats. Alcoholics Anonymous, started in 1935 by "Dr. Bob" and Bill Wilson, is the largest and most successful recovery program in the world today (Kurtz, 2000). Over the last 67 years, AA, aligned with the disease model, continues to help millions achieve sobriety by creating a non-judgmental treatment environment. Miller reports that 80 percent achieve abstinence for one year with attendance at AA and an outpatient or inpatient treatment program (Miller, 2001). The AA format, which draws on the respect and understanding gained in dialoguing with others who can relate because they share similar experiences and addictions, has been used to help addicted individuals with a variety of substances and addictive disorders (sex, gambling, etc).

Six peer-support programs are:

1. Alcoholics Anonymous (AA) and other 12-step programs (e.g., Cocaine Anonymous, Debtors Anonymous, Narcotics Anonymous). This is a spiritual program based in the twelve steps and traditions that outline a protocol for recovery. For more information, see: www.alcoholics-anonymous.org and *Alcoholics Anonymous* (2001) (4th ed.). New York, NY: World Services Inc.

The following five alternative peer-support programs are relatively new:

2. Moderation Program — Unlike AA, this program is not for serious alcoholics. Audrey Kishline founded this program as an alternative to the twelve steps, because there are very few programs that specifically address the needs of beginning stage problem drinkers who are not yet alcohol dependent. For more information, visit: www.moderation.org.

3. Women for Sobriety — Like AA, this program encourages living 'one day at time' and abstention. Women For Sobriety is both an organization and a self-help program for women alcoholics. Jean Kirkpatrick, PhD, developed this program that has been recognized as the first national self-help program for women alcoholics. In 1975 the name of "New Life" was changed to "Women For Sobriety, Inc." and the program incorporated the Thirteen Statements of Acceptance of the New Life Program. For more information, visit: www.womenforsobriety.org/body.html.

4. Rational Recovery — Unlike AA, Rational Recovery does not promote the disease model. This program was founded by Jack and Louis Trimpey as an alternative for the twelve-step spiritual-based program. The goal of this program is teaching people how to achieve self-recovery. In addition, this program promotes the philosophy that the ultimate authority for all personal issues is the person. For more information visit: www.rational.org.

5. SMART Recovery® — Founder Dr. Simon Budman designed this program to help people find a meaningful life and a desire not to drink. SMART Recovery® has established four main goals: (1) enhance and maintain motivation to abstain; (2) cope with urges; (3) manage thoughts, feelings, and behaviours; (4) Balance momentary and enduring satisfactions. SMART Recovery® offers groups, publications, and an Internet e-mail list discussion group to help people learn how to achieve: motivation and lifestyle balance, as well as overcome urges and solve problems. For further information, visit: www.smartrecovery.org.

6. Humanistic Alternative Twelve Steps — A twelve-step program minus associations with "God," to include those who dislike a spiritual component. Religious underpinnings were replaced with Skinner's twelve behavioural steps. For more information, visit: www3.sympatco.ca/gdavidson/VariousVersions.htm.

For more information on peer recovery programs, visit: www.alcoholism. about.com.

Monitoring Treatment Plans Using Journaling

Addictive disorder treatments often are challenged with incidents of relapse that extinguish progress. What causes the addict to relapse? There are many theories as to why a person relapses. For example, recovery can be disrupted when a client stops their daily health recovery behaviours that make up the personal treatment plan. These might include attending AA meetings, healthy eating, and daily reading. Relapse often complicates recovery because of the emotions it breeds: shame, guilt, anger, frustration, and self-defeating thinking. In this example, one can infer that when a client sticks to the daily health recovery behaviours, the risk of relapse is reduced.

Keeping a daily journal provides the person with an interactive strategy to track and monitor personal progress. Through daily journaling, the client has a medium to process daily stress, separate facts from opinions and re-align goals. Journaling also helps the person slow down, allowing the client to put the day into perspective and think through and solve daily challenges. "Using expressive writing reduces intrusive and avoidant thoughts about negative events and improves working memory" (Carpenter, 2001).

To increase the benefit of journaling, the counsellor can determine each client's brain dominance and match the journal to the brain type. Brain dominance research suggests left-brained people often like journals that have structured measures and rigor (Howatt, 2001), where right-brained people respond better to less structure, similar to a traditional daily diary (Howatt, 2000). Regardless of the journal, for the process to be of value the client must be motivated and willing to journal. One final important consideration before recommending any journaling program is to ensure that the client is screened for functional literacy. For more information refer to: Neubauer, J. R. and Adams, K. (2000). *Complete Idiot's Guide to Journaling.* New York: New York: Macmillan USA.

Family Strengthening — A Cornerstone for Recovery

Addicted clients whose families participate in treatment have better outcomes than those treated alone. Treating clients as isolated entities is, as one observer noted, like taking the addicted client out of a dirty puddle, cleaning him up, and then tossing back him into the puddle (Coombs, 1997).

Family input is advantageous in gaining an accurate picture of the client's addictive disorder. And involving a client's family in the treatment process, especially spouses, can both enhance recovery and reduce relapse rates. Family education and counselling strategies that address issues of codependency and co-addiction, pathologies that reinforce addiction and undermine recovery, routinely include: multifamily group sessions, individual family therapy, couple therapy, and week-long family programs. These approaches use a variety of family strengthening techniques, such as psychodrama and family sculpturing, both powerful clinical tools that involve all family members in discussing and acting out dysfunctional family roles and behaviours. For example, Wegscheider (1981) defines four prominent roles in the alcoholic family: (1) the family hero; (2) the scapegoat; (3) the lost child; and (4) the mascot.

Family-oriented self-help programs such as Al-Anon (www.alanon. alateen.org) and Adult Children of Alcoholics (www.adultchildren.org) have a long history of making a significant therapeutic impact on addictive behaviours. For an excellent review of family assessment measures and family strengthening tools that can enhance recovery, see Schmidt and Brown (2001). In addition, visit the Strengthen American Families Web Site: www.strengtheningfamilies.org.

SCIENCE OF MANAGING RECOVERY:
THE LATEST ON DETOX, MEDS, AND DRUG TESTS

Despite the promise of 21st century scientific advances, chemical dependency continues to challenge and strain individual health, families, communities' safety, and the economy at large. "Drugs cost America 52,000 deaths a year and $110 billion. If left unchecked, illegal drugs will cost the United States 500,000 deaths and a trillion dollars over the next decade" (McCaffrey, 2000). As the cost of chemical dependency balloons, our society will need to pay more attention to the prevention and treatment of addictions.

Pharmaceutical and medical interventions comprise a core standard of addiction treatment. This article discusses three such recovery tools used today to tame and manage addictions. Addiction counsellors need to learn the mechanics of chemical detoxification, pharmaceutical medical interventions, and drug testing. Although addiction counsellors cannot prescribe medications or directly facilitate interventions that involve drug testing, clients receive the most efficacious treatment from addiction counsellors who understand the protocols and benefits of these treatment options.

Detoxification

Merriam-Webster's Dictionary defines "detoxify" as (1a) to remove a poison or toxin or the effect of such from; (1b) to render [a harmful substance] harmless; (2) to free [as a drug user or an alcoholic] from an intoxicating or an addictive substance in the body or from dependence on or addiction to such a substance. Scientific advancements offer three modes of detoxification, depending on the client's level of dependency. In traditional detoxification, a client may enter into a 5- to 15-day medically supervised detoxification program. Rapid chemical detoxification is achieved by placing the client in a comatose state while moving through phases of withdrawal. In outpatient detoxification programs, the client participates in medical intervention, but goes home each day.

Clients who are psychologically and physically addicted to chemicals will need to undergo detoxification as a component of therapy — the question is, how do we know which detox strategy is right for the client? By working in consultation with a physician who specializes in detoxification, the addiction counsellor can provide appropriate, efficacious treatment for the client. Science has radically improved detoxification techniques over the last two decades. The implication for addiction counselling is that by developing relationships with detox specialists, the addiction counsellor can facilitate referrals that promote continuity of care and reinforce trust and motivation by including the counsellor as a member of what becomes a multidisciplinary treatment team. This consultation is essential if assessment suggests rapid detox or outpatient detox as the treatment option.

Regardless of the detoxification model used, one common construct that an addiction counsellor must be aware of is drug withdrawal. The *DSM-IV-TR* definition of withdrawal can be summarized as significant physical, mental, or social distress or impairment caused when heavy or long-term substance use is abruptly reduced or stopped. Drug withdrawal complicates detoxification because of the number of variables at play (e.g., frequency, duration, intensity, kind of drug, and absence time without drug will impact how dramatic withdrawal symptoms can be — from mild to life-threatening). Another challenge of withdrawal is the presence of cravings, the habitual desire for the substances that created drug euphoria. In this cycle, the unconscious brain tells the client to get rid of these withdrawal symptoms quickly by just taking the drug. As a result, the client in withdrawal is challenged by both physical symptoms (e.g., alcohol withdrawal can create tremors) and the psychological (e.g., internal dialogue says: to feel good, use the drug). Narconon of Southern California, Inc. provides an excellent overview of withdrawal for the various drugs addiction counsellors face most often; this resource is online at www. addictionwithdrawal.com.

Five-step detoxification decision-making process

As with all phases of counselling along the treatment continuum, motivation is an essential component of the detoxification process (Prochaska & DiClemente, 1982). Motivational interviewing (MI) strategies (Miller & Rollnick, 1991) are helpful for assisting clients unsure of the value of detoxification to discover motivation from within themselves (for more information about MI, see page 115). The following five-step model provides the addiction counsellor with a frame of reference in aligning a client with a detoxification program:

Step 1. Assess to determine if the client is physically or psychologically dependent as per the DSM-IV-TR. An addiction counsellor can reference a **drug chart** (e-mail editor@counsellormagazine to request a copy of the drug chart) to determine the medical risks for various drugs. A quick online resource developed by the Addiction Science Network can be found at www.addictionscience.net/ASNclass.htm. Clients who meet this criterion need to be assessed by a physician for medical risk.

Step 2. Review and be clear about the physical and psychological withdrawal factors for the particular drug(s) in question. Also determine potential client resources (e.g., family, social supports, finances, living arrangements).

Step 3. Educate the client about potential withdrawal and associated health risks. Discuss how cravings can fuel an immediate relapse if not addressed in the early stages. The addiction counsellor's role is to assist the client in determining the mode of detoxification that would best meet the client's needs. If treatment suggests rapid detox or outpatient detox, it is common at this stage to bring in a physician to assist.

Step 4. After the detoxification model is selected, it is important to ensure that the client clearly understands the treatment plan and its action steps. For example, an employee assistance provider who does addiction counselling would assist the client in connecting detoxification to the client's treatment plan. However, it is vital that the client actively participates in planning his or her treatment with regard to determining space availability, insurance and financial considerations, openings, time, and who needs to be notified (e.g., family and work), so as to instill ownership into this choice of action.

Step 5. The client begins the detoxification process. Upon completion, a clear exit strategy is essential to support the client's long-term recovery. In addition, the detoxification process might include some multidimensional interventions (e.g., a psychiatrist for dual diagnosis clients who may be prescribed a medication to stabilize mental health issues).

Traditional chemical detoxification

Traditional chemical detoxification is the natural elimination of chemicals in a controlled environment until the chemical is no longer present. The goal is to manage physical withdrawal. As Seymour and Smith (2001) explain, "most withdrawal symptoms are the opposite of the drug's desired effects and as such represent symptoms that can range from things the patient would rather avoid all the way to potentially fatal effects, such as seizures" (p.67). Approximately 30 percent of opiate-dependent patients who begin detoxification as inpatients do not complete detoxification due to intense cravings and painful withdrawal symptoms during the first three days of detoxification (Addiction Recovery Institute, 2004).

There is no single "right way" to detoxify opioid-addicted patients. Traditional detoxification methods include tapering with methadone, or discontinuing opioids and administering oral clonidine to ameliorate symptoms of withdrawal. Buprenorphine is a newer agent that can be appropriate to use in a detoxification regimen. Even when pharmacological agents are utilized in the management of opioid withdrawal, there is often a significant amount of patient discomfort. Patients who are unwilling to tolerate this discomfort often terminate the detoxification process and return to opioid use (especially illicit use). Thus, relapse to active opioid addiction is a risk factor in any attempt at opioid detoxification.

Rapid detoxification

Rapid detoxification is a relatively new process in North America. It is normally a 4- to 6-hour process, conducted under the guidance and supervision of a board certified anesthesiologist, that began in Europe in the 1980's and was brought to the United States in 1996 (McCabe, 2000). This program, used primarily for clients addicted to opiates, requires the client be put under a general anesthesia, and administered a medication (two commonly used medications are naltrexone and naloxone), to counteract the physical effects of opiates and allow the body to rapidly withdraw. McCabe (2000) points out that the greatest risks of this process are the use of general anesthesia and the cost of this program, which ranges from $3,550 to $7,000, more than 2 to 3 times the cost of traditional detoxification programs.

An attractive feature of this model is that the client will experience no withdrawal symptoms, no pain, and will awaken from the process with no physical symptoms. With no symptoms comes a new start, as the client will no longer be physically dependent. While withdrawal from opiates is seldom life-threatening, it can be extremely painful and result in the client relapsing to avoid the withdrawal symptoms. Most programs will prepare the client for a recovery period in which he or she may experience mild side effects (e.g., mild nausea and diarrhea) and will recommend the client be put on an opiate antagonist for 6 to12 months. It is important to note: the exact protocols for the detoxification program as well as the exit strategy from the program will vary from program to program and client to client.

For more information on this tool and to find treatment facilities that offer this program, see www.addictionrecoveryguide.org/treatment/ patient.html.

Outpatient detoxification

Another form of detoxification that is gaining attention, because it is potentially more cost effective than inpatient programs, is outpatient detoxification. Prater, Miller, and Zylstra (1999) report, "Outpatient detoxification of patients with alcohol or other drug addiction is being increasingly undertaken. This type of management is appropriate for patients in stage I or stage II of withdrawal who have no significant comorbid conditions and have a support client willing to monitor their progress." Adequate dosages of appropriate substitute medications are important for successful detoxification; by accounting for social and environmental concerns and additional medical conditions, a physician in conjunction with a counsellor, providing supportive, nonjudgmental, yet assertive care, can facilitate the best possible chance for a client's successful recovery (Prater, Miller, and Zylstra, 1999). Outpatient programs average 3 to 14 days (Hayashida, 1998).

It is important to remember that this treatment option must be led by a physician, and the client cannot be in stage III withdrawal. There must be a designated agent who will stay with the client throughout the entire withdrawal process and the client must make daily visits to the physician who is supervising the outpatient detoxification. In order to ensure the success of this treatment program, the client will need to engage in other recovery options such as cognitive-behavioural therapy and self-help groups, counselling, or other outpatient programs. For more information about outpatient detoxification, see Morse (1999). For information about other recovery options, see Howatt (2004) and Howatt and Coombs (2003).

Pharmaceutical medical interventions

It seems that almost every day CNN is reporting a new and exciting breakthrough in brain research and biochemistry. These breakthroughs have seen drugs such as Antabuse® (disulfiram), which was first sold in 1948 and by 1986 was found to greatly improve abstinence in alcoholics. Similarly, Revia® (naltrexone), originally developed to treat opiate addiction, has been used with great effectiveness to reduce alcohol cravings almost twofold (Kurtzweil, 1996). At this point in time, medications are critical for successful traditional chemical detoxification, managing withdrawal, and harm reduction. Medications assist in reducing pain and discomfort that is associated with the addiction recovery process. Although addiction counsellors are not medical doctors who prescribe medications, it is paramount that we stay current and aware of the pharmaceutical medical interventions currently being used.

Here are a few examples of recent breakthroughs:

- Ondansetron, that was developed to prevent nausea and vomiting caused by cancer chemotherapy, radiation therapy, anesthesia, and surgery, now appears to have potential to offset withdrawal symptoms in treating early alcoholism (Food and Drug Administration, 2000).

- Drug Week introduces the potential hope of a drug called gamma-vinyl GABA (GVG) that is being used in other countries to treat epilepsy. It is showing potential for blocking the effects of cocaine because it raises levels of GABA in neural receptors (Brodie in Ritter, 2003).

- The Georgia Center for Nicotine Addiction has obtained a U.S. government patent for its one-time medical treatment it claims can eliminate urges and cravings for nicotine. Based on the research where nicotine works similarly to the chemical neurotransmitter acetylcholine, researchers have developed a nicotinergic block method using atropine and scopolamine for obtaining the neurotransmitter block. For more information, see www.nosmokeatlanta.com.

- The FDA approved two forms of buprenorphine for treating opiate addictions (Elliot, 2002). For current information on issues surrounding buprenorphine, see www.jointogether.org/sa/issues/hot_issues/bupe.

In addition to dealing with primary chemical addictions, medications are effective when managing dual diagnosis (psychiatric disorder in addictions) such as ADHD, general anxiety, posttraumatic stress disorder, depression, psychotic disorders, panic disorders, and phobia disorders. With an increase in dual diagnosis (Minkoff & Cline, 2003), it is important for addiction counsellors to refer to texts such as the Clinical Handbook of Psychotropic Drugs by Bezchlibnyk-Butler and Jeffries (2002). It will be important for addiction counsellors, as a part of a multidisciplinary team and a primary resource for clients, to keep up-to-date in terms of current medication treatments. For additional resources related to these interventions, see Barber and O'Brien (1999).

Drug testing

Today science has helped to make drug testing a more affordable option to assist clients in maintaining accountability. Drug testing can be an effective recovery tool because it provides a social contract by removing the client's ability to lie, and it promotes honesty and accountability, which can act as a guide and motivator for compliance.

There are two kinds of drug testing: performance testing (instant drug-testing kits) and toxicological drug testing (requires full-spectrum laboratory testing that is more costly and time consuming). Toxicological testing, the more accurate of the two tests, has a more detailed protocol with set standards for the chain of custody (process for taking sample, time sample is collected, process for shipping to lab, and so forth). Drug testing is commonly a four-step process: collection, screening, confirmation, and review. In drug testing, the samples are called test matrices. The most common test matrices are saliva, hair, blood, and urine. Whether or not addiction counsellors use either application of testing directly, it is helpful to be aware of them, as well as to be wary of another important factor: as sophisticated as drug tests are becoming, so are strategies and techniques to defeat them.

Addiction counsellors who are involved in drug testing must have clear testing protocols to reduce the potential of error and to increase validity of the tests. It is important with drug testing that a client's civil liberties (most notably privacy) and laws are taken into account. As drug testing by employers, the criminal justice system, and treatment centers becomes more common, the utility of drug testing will increase. With improved testing protocols and procedures, accuracy and accountability improve. Drug testing, as an accountability tool for managing recovery, is a positive instrument in facilitating recovery. It stands as a veritable recovery contract between the client and the counsellor by scientifically measuring compliance.

For additional information on drug testing, consult Baer and Booher (1994), who provide an alternative view, and visit the Drug Alcohol Industry Testing Association (DATIA) web site, www.datia.org.

The cutting edge is within reach

Managing recovery is a difficult task even with motivated clients. It is equally difficult to advocate and guide clients toward treatment options that lie on the cutting edge of science, almost beyond the traditional purview of the addiction counsellor. Awareness and education is the solution to eliminating anxiety in this process. By investigating the pros and cons of these treatment options, addiction counsellors simultaneously assert their place at the table in multidisciplinary treatment teams and position themselves to better align their clients with appropriate treatment options.

STRATEGIES FOR INCREASING CLIENT MOTIVATION

He who has a why to live can bear almost any how. — Nietzsche

"I am not sure why I am here. My wife thinks I have a problem. Sure I have a few drinks every day. What's the big deal? I bet you have a few now and then to relax, too. I do not see that I have problem. But if this will get her off my back — fine! So what are you going to do for me?"

Any addiction counsellor can relate to this scenario of rapid-fire questioning from clients lacking motivation. Regardless of where the client rests on the addictions continuum, interventions are strategies to assist in motivating a client, through non-judgmental and honest dialogue, to both accept treatment and stay in it. These strategies measure a willingness to change, while lowering the veil of resistance by building relationships and creating safe treatment environments built on trust.

The modern intervention concept is predicated on the belief that clients have the internal resources and capacities to help themselves, but will need guidance from counsellors to identify and define the life they really want when compared to a life consumed by an addictive disorder. Non-confrontational, non-adversarial interventions help clients maintain their dignity in times when they may have lost a job, money, and/or their family. Much as the initial act of an addictive disorder is the result of a conscious act, so too is the first act of treatment for that addictive behaviour.

This section will review six proven addiction recovery motivation tools that have helped counsellors successfully assess the utility of intervention and manage the process of change, as defined by Prochaska and DiClemente's Transtheoretical Model (Prochaska & DiClemente, 1982). Drawing off of a common theoretical and practical body of clinical work that advocates a non-confrontational approach to addiction recovery, each of these recovery tools — matching interventions with motivation, motivational interviewing, structured intervention, the Love First intervention, computer-assisted interventions, and Inspiring New Beginnings — embodies a unique treatment technique that mitigates defense mechanisms while harnessing client motivation.

Matching interventions with motivation

When clients come to the counsellor's doorstep with varying degrees of motivation, it is the counsellor's responsibility to match this motivation with a treatment plan. This moment of interaction, be it the first client-counsellor interview, a desperate first phone call made by the client in a moment of despair, or a dialogue in the midst of a family-sponsored intervention, is a critical juncture in the overall treatment plan. To recommend an intervention approach the client is not ready for can actually decrease the client's overall motivation to change (Coombs, 2001).

The Transtheoretical Model (also called Stages of Change) pioneered by Prochaska and DiClemente (1982) is widely accepted as a critical benchmark for determining a client's motivation for treatment (Howatt, 2000a). Prochaska and DiClemente understood that at each of the six stages of change, a client weighs the pros and cons of adopting a new behaviour. Despite the harmful side effects of an addictive substance — be it food, alcohol or tobacco, giving up the euphoria of an addictive behaviour can be a lot to ask of most clients. For most behavioural changes, the "sacrifices" are immediate, but the benefits are not. Prochaska and DiClemente call this weighing of pros and cons "decisional balance" (p. 1102). For counsellors to help clients move along the treatment continuum, a focus point is to tip the scales: to have the pros of treatment outweigh the cons of addiction.

An innovative contribution of the Stages of Change model is its emphasis on maintaining change. The model recognizes that relapse is common in the recovery process. But instead of viewing relapse as a failure (i.e., the behaviour change didn't last), the Stages of Change model uses relapse as an opportunity to teach the client how to sustain change more effectively in the future. Divided into six stages of change, each with its own set of pros and cons, the model allows the addiction counsellor to apply harm reduction and treatment strategies in the appropriate context. Once the addiction counsellor is aware of the client's present level of motivation, the appropriate intervention can be determined and implemented. As Bishop (2001) reports, this model is a powerful and effective strategy for assessing motivations and also stresses the importance of matching the client's treatment with the client's level of motivation.

Motivational interviewing

Old school, aggressive, confrontational treatment styles often can drive clients away from accepting treatment. In contrast, motivational interviewing (MI), developed in the early 1980s by William R. Miller, is a directive, client-centered counselling style. Congruent to, yet ultimately moving beyond the scope of, Roger's core conditions of empathy, congruency, and unconditioned positive regards (Rogers, 1961), MI elicits behavioural change by helping clients explore and resolve ambivalence. Compared with this style of nondirective counselling, traditional treatment approaches tend to be too action-oriented, or at least too quick to press clients into focusing primarily on making changes in their lives.

MI is based on the philosophy that "motivation for change occurs when people perceive a discrepancy between where they are and where they want to be" (Miller, Zweben, DiClemente, & Rychtarik, 1992, p. 8). MI counsellors work to develop this perception and the accompanying motivation by helping clients examine the discrepancies between their current behaviour and future goals. The counsellor facilitates this process through empathy, which involves seeing the world through the client's eyes, thinking about things as the client thinks about them, feeling things as the client feels them, and sharing in the client's experiences. Expression of empathy is critical to the MI approach. When clients feel that they are understood, they are more able to open up to their own experiences and share those experiences with others (Coombs, 2001).

Asking clients to share their experiences with you in depth allows you to assess when and where they need support, and what potential pitfalls may need to be focused on in the change-planning process. Importantly, when clients perceive empathy on a counsellor's part, they become more open to gentle challenges by the counsellor about lifestyle issues and beliefs about their addiction. Clients become more comfortable fully examining their ambivalence about change and less likely to defend ideas such as their denial of problems and reducing use versus abstaining. In short, the counsellor's accurate understanding of the client's experience facilitates change.

Used in group or in one-on-one sessions, there are several different MI strategies for increasing client motivation, such as: Drinker's Check-up (Cameron 1995), Motivational Enhancement Therapy (MET) (Miller, 1994), brief motivational interviewing (Miller 2002), and brief interventions (Webb 1999). Dunn (1996) developed the acronym GRACE to capture the application of MI concepts in a clinical environment. G stands for Gap between the client's present situations and where they would like to be; R is for Rolling with Resistance and refers to never taking the client's resistance head on (a critical element is to not confront the client, which requires flexibility); A is for Argue not, regardless of the client's responses and not to be drawn into debates; C is for Can do, all clients have the potential and skill to begin to make change; and E is Expressing Empathy.

One concern with MI is that clients often have mixed feelings about making changes. The counsellor who presses a client to make changes immediately risks evoking client resistance, promoting premature termination from counselling, and/or encouraging clients to overlook the internal and external factors that may promote relapse even following initial success in change attempts. The MI framework fits best with a view that client change is efficiently enhanced through positive reinforcement. With positive reinforcement, clients find themselves in a treatment environment that rewards trying new behaviours that fit into defined long-term goals rather than continuing addictive behaviours that provide short-term gain at the cost of long-term loss. For more information on this strategy, see Rollnick and Miller (1995) and visit the MI Web site, www.motivationalinterview.org.

Structured intervention

Developed by Dr. Vernon E. Johnson more than 25 years ago, structured intervention (SI) is a motivational strategy where family members present the client with concerns and evidence of an addictive disorder. The principle objective of the intervention is to use family member(s) as the conduit for self-realization of an addicted state/condition. Johnson's study (1973) noted that alcoholics did not seek help until a serious crisis, or collective crises, brought them to treatment. Only when their impenetrable defenses (denial system) collapsed under the weight of their alcohol-related problems did they seek treatment. Ironically, the very crises that the enabling family and friends often tried to help the alcoholic avoid were what ultimately motivated the client to seek treatment (Johnson, 1973, pp. 3-5). In this treatment approach, two things need to happen: First, family, friends, colleagues, and employers have to learn that keeping the problem a secret exacerbates the illness. Secondly, in order to get the client to treatment before he or she hits "bottom," a crisis has to be precipitated. In other words, the client's so-called "bottom" has to be raised so that he or she can see it. "Unlike hitting bottom, structured intervention provides a safe way for the denial to be broken" (Wheeler, 2001, p. 31). The idea is simple: no more secrets. What SI does, in effect, is present reality to the client in a receivable way. It forces a crisis, whereby treatment becomes the logical alternative.

SI's are led by an addiction counsellor who works with the family. The family members involved have a close relationship with the addicted family member and are willing to be a part of a loving, supportive intervention. Thoroughly planned and implemented in a safe and loving manner, SI's include the following five components:

- Decision to undertake the intervention
- Education in which an understanding of the client's defense mechanisms is reached
- Preparation for the intervention by using learning tools, such as role play
- Action/Intervention in which the actual intervention is completed
- Post-intervention follow up.

SI's generate strong emotions that are often difficult for the family member to ignore or dismiss. Provided family members adhere to the plan in a loving and patient manner, the results are often favorable, meaning that the client accepts treatment, which is the main goal of the SI. For more information, see Johnson Institute-QVS, Inc. (1996) and Global Interventions, www.intervention.net.

Love First intervention

Similar to structured interventions, the Love First intervention is a strategy for implementing a family intervention. This intervention, created by Jeff and Debra Jay (2001), is explained in detail in their book Love First. The goal of this intervention is to motivate a family member to enter treatment. This approach dispels two myths: that interventions must be adversarial and that a client must hit rock bottom. Families worrying about the harshness of forcing loved ones into treatment often overlook the option of effectively asking them to enter treatment by implementing a loving, family intervention. When the role of love takes center stage during an intervention, most families never have to resort to using tough love, in which an adversarial position is taken to place the client in treatment.

A foundation of this intervention is that love breaks through denial first. Planning meetings are used to prepare answers to all the client's objections, to line up the many details of treatment, and to unify the group. Most importantly, letters are prepared with a specific format and content, which will provide a script for the intervention. By writing everything down in advance, the intervention team can be confident that they will remain in control of the situation, delivering a powerful message to the individual with a substance abuse problem.

Each family member will write a letter to the client expressing their concerns as to how their addiction has negatively impacted them and their relationships with friends and family. Each letter will express the love and caring the family member has and "why" treatment is needed. A critical element to redirect blame and shame in the letter is how addiction is a disease. Once the letters are prepared, intervention timelines can be established. The most powerful part of the intervention happens when the letters are read aloud stating "why" the client needs to go into treatment that day. Emotions will run high and the sheer volume of unconditional love and concern often cuts through denial. The goal of this intervention is to arrive at a universal truth, that the client has an addictive disorder, and bring that construct out into the open. The authors of this treatment plan base the effectiveness of this intervention on research from Hazelden that reports that the success rate for persons going into treatment is the same regardless if they go on their own or are ordered (Jay & Jay, 2001). The bottom line is that it does not matter who is the driving force in getting a client into treatment.

This intervention has proven successful for families, older adults, and corporate executives. The authors report that families who understand the Love First process have been successful without the assistance of an addiction professional. However, in some cases, family members may request the assistance of an addiction specialist. The authors also recommend that if a family cannot find a local addiction specialist who is familiar with the Love First model, they can contact Hazelden (www.hazelden.org) and the Betty Ford Center (www.bettyfordcenter.org) for a list of interventionists who will travel the nation to do family interventions. For more information, see Jay and Jay (2001) and the Love First Web site, www.lovefirst.net.

Computer-assisted interventions

One consistent variable when exploring client motivation is that, in the end, the client is always in charge of his own motivation. For example, in the addiction field, there is a body of research that is exploring what is called spontaneous remission. In a study by Sobell, Sobell, and Toneatto (1990), the majority of excessive drinkers gave up alcohol without expert help. They were unaided and made the choice on their own to stop. Biernacki (1986) found the same results with the very challenging heroin-addicted population. Subsequently, clients, when provided with the appropriate tools, can self-monitor their recovery program.

With computers as commonplace as telephones and a level of computer literacy that now transcends generations, it is logical that the computer has been enlisted into the world of addiction treatment. Computer-assisted interventions can be used for: prevention, education, support, and self-monitoring. For clients who have access to a computer and possess basic Internet skills, this recovery tool provides clients with real-time information and interventions.

With interactive technology, even if clients lack basic technology skills, computer-assisted interventions are so effective that counsellors can teach clients to learn them at a local library or other location with computer resources. Rice (2001) explains that computer-assisted interventions have been highly effective and successful in educating clients about their addictive disorder and that they can provide the client with objective feedback. Regardless of the addictive disorder, there is the potential to design an application to assist a client, provided he or she is motivated to participate. Computers have an unlimited capacity for specialized treatment design, as well as a new kind of scheduling flexibility, because the Internet provides access from many locations at any time.

Computer-assisted interventions have many applications: they help monitor chemical use, offer learner-friendly environments, provide questions and information for self-reflection, promote the key concept that motivation is internally determined, provide clear advice on matters to do with addictions (e.g., educational facts), suggest behavioural options, provide a positive feedback support network, and offer written feedback to increase efficacy of interventions (Rice, 2001).

Similar to bibliotherapy, self-directed intervention based on reading materials, computer-assisted programs provide the client with a self-paced resource. Its success depends directly on the client's motivation and effort.

Current research suggests that clients will obtain better treatment outcomes using computer-assisted interventions than those who do not (Coombs, 2001). The key to using this recovery tool is to determine the needs of the client and then to either find or design an application. For example, *Stop That and Be Healthy: Smoke Cessation Journal* (Howatt, 2000b) is an electronic journal that the client can use for monitoring daily progress as well as obtain educational information. It is a database program that has daily templates to fill in and readings to complete. Alleman (2002) and Anthony (2003) both provide counsellors with frameworks that minimize the anxiety of working "online." The power of computer programs, databases, and the Internet provides the addiction counsellor, with minimal training, an unlimited, dynamic, adaptable resource for treating addictive disorders.

Four helpful websites for addiction counsellors to refer their clients to for computer-assisted help are: www.nasarecovery.com/interventionkit. html; www.wellnessnet.com/tests.htm; www.egetgoing.com/lowB/ index.asp; and www.habitsmart.com. See also: Coombs (2001).

Inspiring New Beginnings

The Inspiring New Beginnings model, which I have developed as an addiction counsellor and used for the past five years as a teacher of addiction studies, provides a frame of reference for the beginning, middle, and end of the process of introducing a new client to treatment planning. Grounded in theoretical underpinnings of MI, person centered therapy (Corey, 1995), and micro skills (Ivey, Pedersen, & Ivey, 2000), this dynamic approach allows for the insertion of multiple recovery and assessment tools that are appropriate for specific circumstances along the treatment continuum. This four-stage process is linear, in that each stage is to be completed before moving forward in the treatment process. This process is called Inspiring New Beginnings because addiction counsellors have the potential for inspiring change. The goal is to inspire change — not force it. In the end, clients are always in charge of motivation; the counsellor must not be a deterrent but a resource for inspiration.

Stage 1 — Discovery of Personal Resources and Needs. First, the addiction counsellor assesses: service match, client needs, scope of addictive disorder, risk-management issues, desired outcomes and goals, present medical and/or psychosocial stressors, and the point of entry to treatment (who is initiating the service). This stage is a critical part of treatment and can be done on the phone or in person. First impressions set the tone of the counselling environment. The addiction counsellor must always be non-judgmental and display a professional, caring presence.

Stage 2 — Orientation. The goal in this stage is to assess the client's present level of motivation. The motivation assessment model I recommend is the Transtheoretical/Stages of Change model (for more information, see page 174). It is important to begin treatment where the client is on the continuum. There are no magic wands in treating addictions. Treating clients with addictive disorders is complex and challenging because no two clients are exactly the same.

Stage 3 — Foundation for Inspiration. In this stage, the counsellor uses Roger's person-centered therapy core conditions (empathy, unconditioned positive regards, and congruency) and microskills questioning techniques (e.g., clarification questioning) to assist the client to start to self-evaluate her present situation. Dunn (1996) has created the acronym OARS (open-ended questioning, affirmations, reflective listening, and summaries) that captures the means to establish the foundation for inspired reinforcement of the client's treatment options in a safe and supportive environment. This foundation helps clients make internal cognitive shifts. The client can explore questions such as: will my present lifestyle lead me to where I want my life in 20 years (Bishop, 2000). Internal shifts assist the client to align present realities with internal wants. Until the client determines internally what he or she is "doing and not doing" is a problem, he or she will not be inspired to take action.

Stage 4 — Acting on Inspiration. Once the client begins expressing inspiration, this will open the door of opportunity for taking action (e.g., the client determines that he or she needs to detox). Obviously, the exact choices will depend on the client's present situation. The best action plans are ones that the client has fully bought into and is motivated to carry out. The client's ownership of the action plan is paramount.

For further information, visit the following websites — for microskills training, www.emicrotraining.com/microskills4.html; for Person Centered International, www.personcentered.com/contents.htm; and for inspiration, quotes, and insights, www.insightquotes.com/gateway.htm.

Many paths to a common goal

Each of these motivational treatment tools strives to define the responsibilities of the client in the treatment process. Determining the level of motivation a client brings to any behavioural changes is the cornerstone in developing treatment strategies. These strategies allow the client and the counsellor to manage expectations in a process that can be as difficult and arduous as it can be rewarding. While it is important for the counsellor to be cognizant of the client's state when committing to a treatment strategy, the counsellor must also be aware of his or her own strengths and weaknesses. The counsellor's ability to draw upon a litany of treatment strategies allows both the client and the counsellor to work effectively within a common treatment methodology toward a common goal — recovery.

NEW THERAPEUTIC APPROACHES:
ALTERNATIVE TREATMENTS FOR ADDICTIONS

In an average week, Americans drink 1 billion cups of coffee, 3.4 million cups of tea, 4.5 billion sugared or caffeinated soft drinks, 2.3 billion alcoholic drinks; smoke 8.25 billion cigarettes and consume 400,000 tons of sugar, and 20 million pounds of chocolate. On top of this we take 20 million antidepressants, puff our way through 25 million joints, and pop 1 million tabs of Ecstasy. Whether it's to relax, get a boost, or just plain feel good, it is clear that we are dependent on chemical stimulants.

These statistics were reported in Natural Highs, by Cass and Holford (2002), who write about the impact and effectiveness of alternative, holistic strategies for overcoming addictions and other life challenges. They promote the value of — and need for — a new set of alternative core competencies for healthier living.

Professionals in the addictions field rarely agree on the most effective treatment modalities. But when they do agree — it's on the fact that there is no silver bullet. The debate roars on as to the causes of addictions, and the most appropriate interventions.

Recovery tools help counsellors guide their clients toward important core competencies, thereby boosting their chances of a successful recovery. "Your therapeutic results will improve as you incorporate a wider variety of effective therapeutic tools in your treatment armamentarium," (Coombs, 2001).

This article explores five alternative recovery tools to help you assist your clients with their addictive disorders. We hope this review expands your awareness of alternative tools and encourages you to explore them in more detail.

Autogenetics training

Autogenetics training (AT) teaches clients how to lower their daily stress level (Linden, 1990). AT is a systematic program that helps both mind and body relax thereby enabling the person to return to a normal state. To the external observer, AT may resemble meditation, progressive muscle relaxation, or visualization. However, the internal process utilizes body sensations (e.g., person focuses on a left arm feeling heavy) as the antecedent to the healing state (mild trance).

AT teaches a person what is referred to as "self-regulation." The person is taught how to use their mind to directly influence their body's self-regulative systems: circulation, breathing, heart rate, etc. This strategy can reduce the damage of the fight or flight response.

AT has its roots in hypnosis, dating back to the last century, when a well-known German brain physiologist, Oskar Vogt, started to explore the correlation between trance and stress reduction. Another German psychiatrist, Johannes H. Schultz, developed Vogt's work into what is now known as AT. It is still being taught and has growth potential with the increasing numbers of professionals exploring alternative treatments.

AT may not presently be the first choice of recovery tools among professionals, but this may change with education. Since most addictions co-exist with stress damage, this tool lends itself to addictions treatment. Although a fairly easy strategy to teach, it may take up to six months before a client is able to realize the full potential of AT.

Research suggests AT can be as effective as hypnosis in reducing stress and anxiety (Ambulante Kurztherapie von Angstpatien-ten mit, 1994; Greenberg, 1999; Davis, Eshelman, and McKay, 1995). The latter authors advance the usefulness of autogenetics training and its potential for mainstream acceptance. Davis, Eshelman and McKay's book has sold over 400,000 copies, suggesting strategies like AT are gaining recognition in North America. Visit the following websites for more information and training opportunities:

- http://www.guidetopsychology.com/autogen.htm
- http://www.autogenics.org
- http://correspondence-courses.net/ autogenic.htm

Changing sub-modalities (Neurolinguistic programming)

Changing sub-modalities is one of the hundreds of neurolinguistic programming (NLP) techniques. Changing sub-modalities involves changing a person's perception. This process can be used to assist people with cravings that involve the five senses (sight, smell, taste, touch and hearing). For example, a person who craves chocolate can be taught to change their perception of the chocolate experience.

The client is first asked to choose two items: the food they want to stop craving, (e.g., chocolate), and a food they dislike (e.g., runny eggs.) Then the counsellor uses a checklist to survey the sub-modalities, stored by the senses, for each food. The client might be asked several questions detailing visual associations for chocolate. There are 30 questions for each food, involving each sense. Once sub-modalities are collected, the client is coached to exchange them. The client is asked to recall, for example, the visual sub-modalities of chocolate, and replace them with the visual sub-modalities of runny eggs. This technique ruins chocolate for some for a long period of time. This technique has also had good success with smokers.

NLP originated when John Grinder, then Assistant Professor of Linguistics at the University of California, Santa Cruz, collaborated with Richard Bandler, then a student of psychology. Together they developed NLP while studying Fritz Perls, Virginia Satir, and Milton Erikson (Howatt, 2000). Today NLP comprises many different strategies and techniques many of which can be used on their own as effective recovery tools.

Barlow, Esler, Vitali (1998) and Dilts (1990) extol the effectiveness of NLP in helping people change their internal belief systems. Over the last 20 years the popularity of NLP has grown and the approach appears to be assisting many people with addictive disorders who need to take charge of their lives.

Changing sub-modalities, in particular, isn't only effective in clinical settings, but has been appropriated by teachers, parents, trainers as well as corporations, wherever individuals can benefit from re-aligning their perceptions in a self-chosen direction.

Visit the following websites for training opportunities and more information:

- http://www.nlptraining.com
- http://www.nlp.com

Self-hypnosis

Self-hypnosis happens without a hypnotist, but offers the same benefits as traditional hypnosis: stress reduction, relaxation, and stimulation of the body's natural repair system (Alman and Lambrou, 1992).

A counsellor oversees the preparation steps, which entail developing a script — a story containing the suggestions the client wishes to ingrain in their sense of being. Once this is accomplished, the client may then begin work on his/her own self-hypnosis tape.

Before starting, the individual is taught guided imagery and encouraged to find a place where they feel safe practicing it. Progressive muscle relaxation also is taught to help the person calm down sufficiently to start the process.

Ultimately the person goes to their chosen quiet spot, settles down with some progressive muscle relaxation, and turns on the tape to begin their self-hypnosis. It is amazing how empowering one's own voice can be!

Hypnosis is derived from the Greek word for "to sleep," and indeed, offers many of the same benefits of dreaming sleep (REM), but without the loss of complete awareness.

One of the earliest recorded applications of hypnosis dates back to the early 1800s, when a Dr. Esdaile, a Scottish surgeon working in India, claimed to have performed several hundred painless operations using only hypnosis (mesmerism) as an anesthetic. Hypnosis has continued to have applications since that time, for both psychology and medical use, particularly in dentistry.

Addiction counsellors, therapists, hypnotists, psychologists, social workers, psychiatrists, trainers, and corporations are among those who back self-hypnosis for stress reduction.

Self-hypnosis also can help boost a person's motivation to change through self-suggestion. It can help the substance abuser connect to internal strengths he or she may have forgotten, as well as provide a framework for self-control. Self-hypnosis can help the addict discover his or her own unique path to recovery (Dubrow-Eichel, 1997).

David Spiegel, a professor of psychiatry and behavioural sciences at Stanford University argues that opinions on hypnosis can no longer be a question of belief. (For more information see "Proof of the Effectiveness of Hypnosis," The Times, February 18, 2002.)

For more information on this method, visit the following websites for training opportunities and more information:

- http://www.hypnotizeyourself.com
- http://www.selfhypnosis.com
- http://www.natboard.com

Thought field therapy

Thought field therapy (TFT) is a process that stimulates acupuncture meridians through the light tapping of meridian sites (Callahan, 1995). The area tapped is dictated by the client's concern. The cure for cravings, for example, suggests 20 taps under the eyes with both hands (Gallo, 1999). The originator, Dr. John Callahan, also developed a set of protocols for dealing with what he defines as psychological reversals, i.e., to help clients align their motivation along with their conscious desires.

The client will normally be instructed to tap with only two fingers — index and middle. In addition, the counsellor using TFT will use the technology of applied kinesiology (muscle testing) to affirm the correct tapping protocol.

According to Callahan (1995), the root cause of negative emotions is neither a traumatic event nor a person's thoughts about it. Instead, Callahan postulated that negative emotions are stored in what he called perturbations (disturbances) in the thought fields and stored throughout the body. The active storing of past negative events triggers the neurological, chemical, hormonal, and cognitive changes in the person, which result in the experience of negative emotions.

Addiction counsellors, psychologists, and social workers, are among the professionals who advocate TFT as a strategy for negative emotions and cravings.

The most prominent study on the effectiveness of TFT was conducted by Carbonell and Figley (1999), which suggested TFT is an effective intervention for emotional discomfort.

It is important to note that in recent years TFT has come under fire for its high claims of treatment success. Gaudiano and Herbert (2002) questioned the clinical effectiveness of TFT, because to date there is insufficient reliable evidence to prove its effectiveness, or confirm the success rates it claims. Many professionals have claimed great success with TFT, but no one knows why it works, and clinical evidence is inconclusive.

Visit the following websites for training opportunities and more information:

- http://www.tftrx.com
- http://www.thoughtfield.com

Timeline therapy

Timeline Therapy (TLT), a strategy with roots in NLP, focuses on influencing the client's temporal experience and changing his/her view of negative life experiences. TLT provides the client a framework with which to address past issues. Details, facts, and painful emotions are not rehashed, because in this model there is no need to know them.

TLT presents the client's entire past as a metaphor that informs their temporal experience. The goal is to release negative emotions that have remained troubling in the present.

The client is invited to change their understanding of past negative events, and separate them from the negative emotions and limiting the decisions these events precipitated. TLT can assist people with depression, anxiety, and other emotional concerns such as anger, so that they can move forward and create the future they really want.

More than any other strategy listed in this article, TLT demands effective training and awareness on the part of the addictions professional. Timeline Therapy is an outgrowth of NLP and Ericksonian Hypnosis. Tad James developed this strategy in 1985, based on co-creator Richard Bandler's studies of how people store memories, and the effects of these storage patterns on the personality of the individual (James and Woodsmall, 1988).

TLT has been used among addiction counsellors, therapists, hypnotists, psychologists, social workers, and medical doctors to help people with addictive disorders let go of harmful emotions that are holding them back — a common complication of addictions issues.

We did not find any formal clinical research on the effectiveness of Timeline Therapy, although there appears to be continued interest in Timeline Therapy among professionals who have been trained in the area of hypnosis and NLP. Dr. James claims to train hundreds of people each year in this strategy, as do trainers who teach and certify professionals. Websites proliferate hailing TLT techniques as a giant leap forward for the psychological community. As believed by Joe Kovach, PsyD, of Calumet College of St. Joseph, "By quickly getting to the heart of one's issues, Tad's work significantly cuts down long-term psychotherapy" (http://www.timelinetherapy.net).

See these websites for training opportunities and more information:

- http://www.timelinetherapy.net
- http://www.nlp.com

The search continues for effective tools to help people with addictive disorders to live happy and fulfilling lives. I have introduced you to five relatively new alternative recovery tools. To be effective, of course, each requires the appropriate application of a well-trained professional. The strategies discussed here all share the same goal of helping people take charge of their lives. We encourage you to explore the suggested websites for more information so you can make your own assessment of the potential value of these techniques.

APPENDIX A

Fight or Flight Response

By William A. Howatt, Ph.D., Ed.D., Post Doc Fellow UCLA
2003©

The quieter my mind, the less judgmental and negative I tend to be.
– Wayne W. Dyer

D ID you know that stress kills? I am sure you have heard this before. From experience, I have learned this kind of shock therapy rarely works. This brief provides an overview of how the body's natural defense system, called the *fight or flight* system, is often the body's worst enemy.

Whether the body is exposed to a single event or the reality of chronic daily stress, it can trigger the *fight or flight* response. Harvard physiologist Walter Cannon discovered this response, and taught the world how it is hard-wired into the human brain and how its sole function is to protect the body.

The intention of this response is to protect, however, science is teaching us now that *fight or flight* is either all **on or off;** you can't turn it half on or half off. The *fight or flight* cannot tell the difference or process the discrepancy between a bear and a baby! The response is designed to protect us from danger, but today some argue that it is the reason human beings are the dominant species in the world. In modern day living, do we need to still have a system that is designed to keep us from immediate danger? My belief is that we do! However, the key is for each person to learn about and understand how this system works so that they can manage it.

Today's threats that often turn on this response are, for the most part, not physical as much as they are mental. The response system will fully activate once we perceive a threat. The brain initiates the *fight or flight* defense system by triggering a series of chemical chain reactions whose purpose is to prepare the body to fight (make a stand) or flee (get to safety). Many writers also add another component called the freeze stage (person feels paralyzed), that is happening more often. This response has obvious consequences; the most damaging being the sense of having no control and feeling powerless.

Events such as occupational, family, financial, mental, and system are the root cause for many people feeling they are in danger. This leaves the person feeling unsafe and in some kind of fear, and is the root cause of why too many people's *fight or flight* systems are being activated. At the time a person is getting caught in this response, it is outside their level of awareness that it is really not in their best interest. Yes, this is an important response system when it is really needed, though many will activate it when it is not. Also, many are not aware that they have some control over this response and that they are not its prisoners. Even though it is automatic, there are choices of how not to be controlled by it.

The outcome of the *fight or flight* response that promotes aggressiveness, over-reactivity and hyper-vigilant acts or responses are really counter-productive to our survival. The real paradox here is that when the body releases chemicals that it does not need and/or use, over time they will become toxic stress hormones which will put physical survival at risk! The *fight or flight* system is an evolutional survival tool, which does not rely on the rational mind, because in all essence, it is a reflex. When a person is in a situation where they perceive a threat and then try to think, they are not able to perform to their potential.

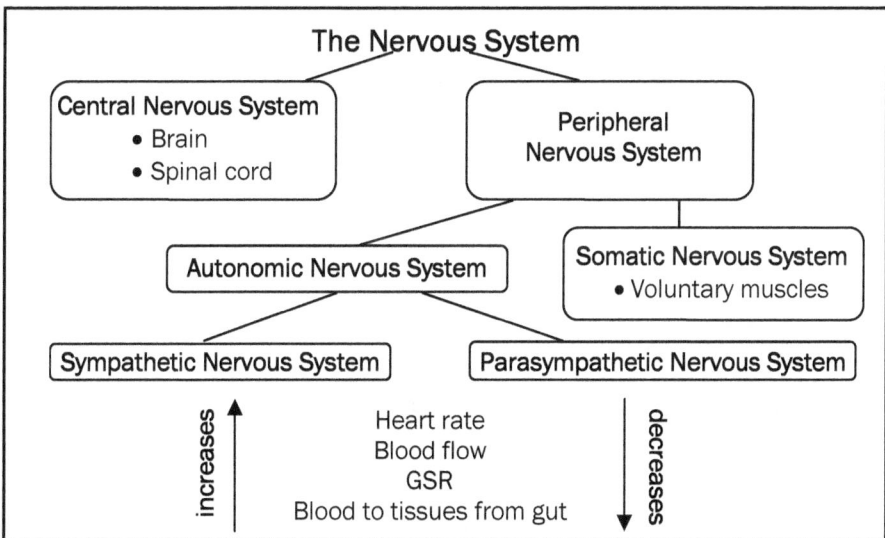

The Nervous System

Central Nervous System
- Brain
- Spinal cord

Peripheral Nervous System

Autonomic Nervous System

Somatic Nervous System
- Voluntary muscles

Sympathetic Nervous System

Parasympathetic Nervous System

increases

Heart rate
Blood flow
GSR
Blood to tissues from gut

decreases

How the *Fight or Flight* Works

Once the body perceives a threat through one of its five senses, it activates the *fight or flight* response and continues until the person's mind stops sending the danger signal. As soon as the brain detects that there is a threat, a number of its parts, such as the hypothalamus, amygdale, and pituitary gland, become activated and start communicating to each other that a threat is evident. Together, these structures start to inform the entire body through hormones and nerve impulses. The goal is to prepare the body that the *fight or flight* response is about to be fully engaged.

At this point, the body perceives there is a threat and an immediate shift occurs in the balance between two branches of the autonomic nervous system:

- *Sympathetic nervous system* – supports the *fight or flight* response system, and if turned on all the time will break down the body.
- *Parasympathetic nervous system* – the non-emergency system that allows the body to rest and heal itself. It is most active when we are in REM sleep.

During stressful conditions, the activity of the sympathetic nervous system increases to prepare the body for the *fight or flight* response. The adrenal gland's first reaction is to send epinephrine (adrenaline) into the bloodstream, which directly impacts the body (e.g., speeds up heart rate). In addition, the adrenal gland puts out more cortisol and other kinds of glucocorticoids that turn sugar in the body into energy.

Finally, the last biggest chemical released from nerve cells is norepinephrine, whose purpose is to prepare the five senses and muscles for action, making them ready for *fight or flight*. Norepinephrine is released from the adrenal medulla (the core of the adrenal glands). Neurotransmitters are powerful hormones that are secreted by the brain and nervous system and have a powerful effect on our psychological and physical health. Research reports that more than fifty different neurotransmitters have been found and more are expected.

How the body responds when the fight or flight system is turned on:

- Stored sugars and fats are released into the bloodstream to provide quick energy
- Breathing quickens to provide more oxygen to the blood
- Muscles tense in preparation for action
- Digestion ceases so that more blood is available to the brain and muscles
- Blood-clotting mechanisms are activated to protect against possible injury

- Perspiration increases to help reduce body temperature
- The pupils dilate and the sense of smell and hearing become more acute
- Increased heart rate, blood pressure, and respiration, pumping more blood to the muscles, supplying more oxygen to the muscles and heart-lung system
- Thickening of the blood – to increase oxygen supply (red cells), enabling better defense from infections (white cells) and to stop bleeding quickly (platelets)
- Prioritizing – increased blood supply to peripheral muscles and heart, to motor and basic-functions regions in the brain; decreased blood supply to digestive system and irrelevant brain regions (such as speech areas). This also causes secretion of body wastes, leaving the body lighter.
- Secretion of adrenaline and other stress hormones – to further increase the response, and to strengthen relevant systems
- Secretion of endorphins – natural painkillers, providing an instant defense against pain

The stress response hormones cause a number of biochemical and physiological changes. It is important to note that, in the short term, all of the above responses are needed to assist the human species to survive a real threat. The question that many are not aware of is what is the cost of a hyperactive *fight or flight* response system.

Cost of the *Fight or Flight* Response

One of the biggest challenges today for professionals who are under stress to the point where they keep activating their *fight or flight* response is that they lose their ability to think to their best potential. If you can imagine an employee who is faced with one or two events a day that activate this response system, you will start to draw a correlation between levels of stress and performance.

When a person goes through one of these full chemical dumps it may take the body 24-72 hours to eliminate the unneeded chemicals. People can function after a chemical dump, but when there is a recurrent pattern over a period of time, the person never returns to a 100% homeostasis state and is always behind. If they fall too far behind, something will break!

Major stresses today trigger the full activation and turn on the *fight or flight* response which can leave a person showing symptoms such as aggressiveness, hyper-vigilance (hyperactive), and over-reaction (behaving in a manner that is out of context for the situation).

When one is in this state of alert, it also negatively impacts how they perceive and process events in their world, meaning tolerances are lower and they are much more sensitive to the impact of stressors and more at risk of turning on their *fight or flight* response. This can lead a person to the point that most things in their world appear to be their enemy. Their rational and logical mind is disengaged and not working to its potential. Their conscious mind becomes focused on fear! They do not see any safety. In this mindset, the person becomes consumed by stress, and life appears to be a string of short-term crises.

When a person moves from crisis to crisis, it can lead to losing hope and/or feeling trapped in fear. Burnout or a series of health issues is inevitable and will be the person's downfall if they do not get help or learn how to take charge of this *fight or flight* response. If the chemical flooding continues and the body is not given safe time to metabolize all the chemicals over time, and the person keeps perceiving danger, epinephrine and norepinephrine will remain at levels which can negatively impact the autonomic nervous system, leading to problems such as headache, damaged arteries, irritable bowel syndrome, weakened immune and reproductive systems, and high blood pressure. The person is also at risk of disorders from hormonal and immune systems damage, such as infection, chronic fatigue, depression, and autoimmune diseases like rheumatoid arthritis, lupus, and allergies.

Once the fighting is over, and the threat—which triggered the response—has been eliminated, the body and mind return to a state of calm.

Strategies for Surviving the *Fight or Flight* Response

The first strategy is to understand that this system exists, and that by not taking action to deal with it a person is not only putting their health at risk, they are also negatively impacting their performance potential.

The *fight or flight* response does not have a warning indicator such as a light which indicates the oil in your car is low; however, the body will send messages through physical symptoms such as muscles aches, headache, upset stomach, racing heartbeat, breathing irregularities, eye twitching, and teeth grinding. It may also send messages through emotional or psychological symptoms such as anxiety, poor concentration, depression, hopelessness, frustration, anger, sadness, and fear.

When we tune in to these symptoms and pay attention, we know we need to take action or our health and performance potential will be at risk.

Seven Specific Strategies Surviving the Fight or Flight Response:

Design a Safe Environment – This includes proactive actions a person can take that are within their control for making their environment safer. Often little choices such as talking to positive peers and avoiding negative employees can help a person feel safer in their environment.

Change Internal Rules – This includes any process to change rules, attitudes, and beliefs so that life is not so hard. Often a person's biggest obstacle is overcoming their internal rules. These rules are what define fear.

Physical Exercise – Physical exercise is the best way to turn down the activity of the *fight or flight* response.

Stop Negative Thinking – When a person is caught in endless negative self-talk and judgment, they increase their level of stress and worry. There is no evidence that this kind of thinking can control anything except their health in a negative manner.

Learn About Your Personality – Type A personalities are more stressful souls; they produce forty times more cortisol (a stress hormone), four times more adrenalin (another stress hormone), and pump three times more blood to their muscles than the more laid back Type B personalities. So who is more at risk of breaking down? The point is it is important to learn how to filter and process the world, to learn strategies to cope more effectively.

Diaphragmatic Breathing – This technique consists of taking three slow breaths to slow things down. Count silently and slowly to three when you breathe in (through your nose) and push your stomach out rather than your chest. This allows you to breathe with your diaphragm and to get a deeper breath. Breathe out on a slow count of six (through your mouth). This strategy has been proven to be an effective behavioural intervention for calming a person after they have a chemical dump.

Life Balance and Stress Management Coaching – Formal adult learning is an effective process for making clear action plans for taking charge of one's health.

Closing

The rationale for becoming aware of this response is clear. It assists in overall health, quality of life, and ability to think and perform. This topic has been published in major magazines such as *Newsweek* and *Time*, as well as a great deal of research. No one is immune, and all are susceptible to the negative effects of a hyperactive *fight or flight* response. The good news is that one can learn to monitor and take charge of the effects of this response system through awareness and practice.

APPENDIX B

Screening Tools vs. Clinical Measures

By William A. Howatt, PhD, EdD, ICADC

Most addiction workers who have been properly trained understand the role, function, and difference between addiction screening tools and addiction clinical measures. They also understand that no screening tool or clinical measure alone is absolute. Similar to the prime objective of the DSM IV-TR, both have a role in assisting clinical decision-making.

This article reviews the differences between an addiction screening tool and an addiction clinical measure, and introduces a screening tool that addiction workers can incorporate into the addictive disorder screening process.

Addiction screening tools are used to assist the addiction worker and the client during the initial assessment process. The goal is to discover potential risk areas so the addiction worker selects tools that are designed to assess the risk that is being screened for. Screening tools are not designed to make clinical diagnosis; their role is to educate and identify potential risk.

A tool like the Addiction Disorder Screen (ADS) – 7[©] that has been developed for addiction screening, often lacks the statistical research needed to be proven to have internal validity and statistical reliability. This means it has not been studied to ensure it measures what it says on a consistent and regular basis. That being said, there is still a place for addiction screening tools because they are often free, in the public domain, easy to administer, fast to score, of short duration to complete, and can uncover potential risks that merit further investigation. As well, they can increase a client's internal motivation by informing and educating them about potential risks.

After a screening tool picks up a potential risk, the next step in the assessment process is to investigate it in more detail by using a diagnosing instrument that has more scientific rigor. For example, the ADS-7© for public domain use as a brief screening tool to uncover the signs and symptoms of seven addictive disorders, used alone to make an assessment would be negligent. First, it does not meet the rigor needed for a scientific clinical measure such as the Substance Abuse Subtle Screening Inventory (SASSI), nor does it have built-in sensitivities for assessing gender and diversity differences. But if an addiction worker used the ADS-7© as a screening tool and uncovered a potential risk area such as alcohol abuse or dependency, this insight would lead to further investigation. In that case this screening tool would have served an important role in the treatment continuum.

It is important to remember that clinical measures like the SASSI have been designed to assist in clinical decision-making and treatment planning. The SASSI, being a psychological instrument, has significant published clinical findings and research that can be found at the SASSI website www.sassi.com.

Perhaps one effective way to determine if an instrument should be used as a screening tool or clinical measure in the assessment process is for the addiction worker to first determine what research supports its reliability and validity. Most clinical measures, like the SASSI, that have met the scientific rigor, require clinical training so that addiction workers are certified to administer them.

There are exceptions. Some instruments, like the Beck Inventories, are extremely user friendly and do not require a lot of training or certification; and have met the scientific rigor that states they do and measure what they say. The bottom line is that addiction workers need to do their research and be clear of what tools and measures they are using in regard to clinical validity and reliability.

This brief introduction reviews the differences between a screening tool and clinical measure and their roles in the assessment process. I find it so important when I teach my addiction counselling students that they can never forgo clinical decision-making based on the results of any one instrument. I see three important elements that can influence clinical decision making and treatment planning recommendations: 1) clinical rigor – completing a detailed biopsychosocial clinical assessment, using effective screening tools, clinical measures, and clinical referring materials (e.g., DSM IV-TR); 2) experience – the more practice and coaching you have from an experienced clinician the more tacit skills you will develop; 3) intuition – trusting your gut. If you have a question or are not sure, always ask.

Introducing the ADS 7°

One of the new and exciting challenges of teaching addiction counselling in 2005 is that we no longer are just teaching our students how to assess and treat drug and alcohol concerns. The field of addiction has exploded and we are now faced with a wider continuum of addiction disorders. It seems the continuum has grown on a fairly regular basis over the last 10 years. For example, in my private practice I could not find one brief screening tool that screened potential risk behaviour across a continuum of addictive disorders such as alcohol, drug, food, gambling, work, sex, and buying that fit all the types of clients I was getting.

While working with the late Dr. Robert Coombs when I was doing my Post Doc at UCLA, I had the opportunity to be a reader for him on his book Handbook on Addictive Disorders. This expanded my scope on the topics of addictive disorders and I decided to create my own screening tool, ADS-7° that I am presenting here. Each question used in this screening tool was vetted against the literature presented by Coombs (2004) and DSM IV-TR (American Psychiatric Association, 2000) to assist in ensuring it was meaningful, accurate, and practical. Judge for yourself if you find any value in this tool.

Summary

One may ask, what about Internet addictions? Yes, I could have developed the ADS-8 by adding Internet addictions – maybe next year. And I agree the addictive disorder continuum is wider than seven categories. This tool is intended only to provide screening for seven addictions to assist in determining where further, more in-depth assessment is needed. It is imperative that addiction workers are clear about the difference between a screening tool and an addiction measure, so they do not mislead their clients or themselves.

Note: The Addictive Disorders Screen–7 (ADS-7)$^{\circ}$ 2005 is an addictive disorder screening tool to predict potential risk for seven addictive disorders: chemical dependency (drugs), chemical dependency (alcohol), compulsive buying, compulsive gambling, eating disorders, workaholism, and sex addictions. The ADS-7° has been designed to assess new clients' potential risk. This addictive disorder-screening tool is for assessing risk in the assessment process; it is not a diagnostic tool.

Addiction Disorders Screen (ADS-7) ©

Questions Over the last six months:	0 Never	1 Once	2 (Fewer than 3 times)	3 (Fewer than 6 times)	4 (More than 7 times)
1. Have family or peers expressed a concern about your drug use?					
2. Have you tried to stop gambling and been unsuccessful?					
3. Have you thought you have a problem with alcohol?					
4. Have you worried about food and calories?					
5. Have you not bought groceries or paid bills because of your buying habits?					
6. Have you lost interest in friends, hobbies, school, work, or other pursuits because of your drug use?					
7. Have partners, peers, or family members expressed a concern about your sexual behaviour?					
8. Have you noticed a connection between your financial problems and gambling?					
9. Have you purged food or used laxatives or diuretics as a strategy for maintaining body weight?					
10. Have you noticed that during weekends you cannot relax unless you are working?					
11. Have you missed work or family functions because of your sexual behaviours (e.g., people or cyber sex)?					

Addiction Disorders Screen (ADS-7) ® (Cont'd)

Questions Over the last six months:	0 Never	1 Once	2 (Fewer than 3 times)	3 (Fewer than 6 times)	4 (More than 7 times)
12. Have you driven any kind of motor powered vehicle under the influence of alcohol?					
13. Have family or friends suggested you have an eating disorder (anorexia or bulimia)?					
14. Have you started the day drinking to avoid feeling sick?					
15. Have you used sex (people or cyber sex) as a way to get away from the stress of the world?					
16. Have any relationships failed as a result of work?					
17. Have you felt depressed after a buying spree?					
18. Have you acted on an internal drive to eat large amounts of food at one sitting?					
19. Have you noticed that food seems to be a major source of pleasure for you?					
20. Have you lost time (e.g., blackouts) during a drinking episode?					
21. Have you lied about your sexual behaviours?					
22. Have you ever committed a crime to obtain drugs (e.g., stealing)?					

Addiction Disorders Screen (ADS-7) © (Cont'd)

Questions Over the last six months:	0 Never	1 Once	2 (Fewer than 3 times)	3 (Fewer than 6 times)	4 (More than 7 times)
23. Have peers or family expressed a concern over the amount of time you work?					
24. Have you used sex as a way to escape from the world?					
25. Have you noticed you gamble to escape or as a means of excitement?					
26. Have you noticed it takes more alcohol to feel good?					
27. Have you lied about your eating habits?					
28. Have you lied about your buying habits?					
29. Have you chosen drugs over people or work?					
30. Have you noticed that your sense of self-worth is directly related to your work?					
31. Have peers personally or professionally expressed concern about your drinking?					
32. Have you tried to control your sexual behaviour (people or cyber sex) and failed?					
33. Have you tried to stop drinking?					
34. Have you lied about your gambling?					
35. Have you felt regret, guilt, or remorse over your drug use?					

Addiction Disorders Screen (ADS-7) ® (Cont'd)

Questions Over the last six months:	0 Never	1 Once	2 (Fewer than 3 times)	3 (Fewer than 6 times)	4 (More than 7 times)
36. Have you noticed gambling is causing stress at home, but you continue to gamble?					
37. Have you found yourself buying things knowing you cannot afford them?					
38. Have your buying habits created money problems for you?					
39. Have you experimented with different kinds of drugs to find a better high?					
40. Have you noticed that you feel most in control when you are working?					
41. Have you felt a deep sense of depression after sex (people or cyber sex)?					
42. Have you attempted to keep your buying secretive?					
43. Have you lied to family or peers to stay at work longer?					
44. Have you used a system to increase your chances of winning when you gamble?					
45. Have you lost money gambling and felt OK?					
46. Have you spent the majority of a day obtaining drugs?					
47. Have you made projects more complex and time consuming than they need to be?					
48. Have you attempted to control your eating habits and failed?					
49. Have you noticed buying helps you feel a sense of control?					

Chemical Dependency (Drug)	Chemical Dependency (Alcohol)	Compulsive Buying	Compulsive Gambling
1	3	5	2
6	12	17	8
22	14	28	25
29	20	37	34
35	26	38	36
39	31	42	44
46	33	49	45
Total:	Total:	Total:	Total:
Risk Level:	Risk Level:	Risk Level:	Risk Level:

Food Addictions	Workaholism	Sex Addictions	
4	10	7	
9	16	11	
13	23	15	
18	30	21	
19	40	24	
27	43	32	
48	47	41	
Total:	Total:	Total:	
Risk Level:	Risk Level:	Risk Level:	

Potential Risk Levels:		
0-2	Sub clinical	May not be a concern – however, it is still important to explore this area in more detail with the client.
3-8	Medium concern	Has the potential to be a serious concern. It is recommended that the client do a more in-depth assessment in this area.
9-28	Serious concern	This score indicates the client is at risk and there is a need for a more in-depth clinical assessment.

Permission to copy the ADS-7© granted by author, William A. Howatt Ph.D., Ed.D., ICADC Post Doc Behavioural Science UCLA School of Medicine.

DRUG, ALCOHOL, AND GAMBLING SCREEN

An important component of any assessment interview is a useful measure to predict potential difficulties with addictions (drugs, alcohol, gambling). For any measure to be useful, it must be user-friendly, quick, and have validity and reliability. My students and I developed the Drug, Alcohol, and Gambling Screen (DAGS).

The DAGS is designed to be an effective screen for determining whether further assessment is required as to drugs, alcohol, and gambling. The obvious benefit of the DAGS is that it allows the assessor to confirm or develop a hypothesis of potential addiction concerns while using only one measure.

The questions on the DAGS are based upon the criteria of the *Diagnostic and Statistical Manual of Mental Disorders, Fourth Edition (DSM-IV)*. The DAGS consists of 45 questions, 15 pertaining to each of the three areas of interest. This screen is scored on a Likert Scale and the score obtained in each of the three domains indicates the severity of use. The DAGS scores indicate potential risk of addiction concerns on the following scale: mild (1-15), moderate (16-30), medium (31-40), and serious (41-60).

The DAGS is not intended to be a label maker, but to assist in discovering or ruling out potential concerns.

Drug, Alcohol, and Gambling Screen

Questions Over the last 12 months:	0 Never	1 Some-times	2 Often	3 Almost Always	4 Always
1. Do you feel the need to gamble with increasing amounts of money in order to achieve the desired excitement?					
2. Do you gamble as a way of escaping problems (work, relationships, family, school)?					
3. Have you been able to have one or two drinks and then stop drinking?					
4. Has anyone ever shown concern about your drug use?					
5. Have you missed meals because of prolonged drinking?					
6. Have you disregarded health issues in order to keep drinking?					
7. Has your use of drugs brought you in contact with the legal system?					
8. Have you driven an automobile after having used drugs?					
9. Have you ever borrowed from others (family, friends, bank, loan shark) in order to relieve a desperate financial situation caused by gambling?					
10. Have you disregarded health issues in order to keep using drugs?					
11. Do you lie to family, friends, or others to hide the extent of your involvement with gambling?					
12. Have you repeated unsuccessfully in efforts to control, cut back, or stop gambling?					
13. Do you ever go out drinking and the next day forget what happened the night before?					

Drug, Alcohol, and Gambling Screen (Cont'd)

Questions Over the last 12 months:	0 Never	1 Some-times	2 Often	3 Almost Always	4 Always
14. Do you experience feelings of remorse or guilt as a result of your drug use?					
15. Have you lost interests in activities and friends due to your drug use?					
16. Have you had problems at school or work related to your drug use?					
17. Have you attempted to hide your drinking behaviours (i.e., hiding alcohol, lying to cover up, etc.)?					
18. After losing money gambling, did you feel you must return as soon as possible?					
19. Has drinking caused problems in any of your relationships with family, friends, or significant others?					
20. Do you have difficulty in getting drinking off your mind?					
21. Have you ever sold anything to finance your gambling (family possessions, stocks)?					
22. Have you tried to cut down on your drinking and failed?					
23. Have you ever neglected family obligations because of your drug use?					
24. How often have you made efforts to cut down or quit using drugs, and failed?					
25. Have you gambled until your last dollar was gone?					
26. Have you ever been reluctant to use "gambling money" for normal expenditures?					

Drug, Alcohol, and Gambling Screen (Cont'd)

Questions	0 Never	1 Some-times	2 Often	3 Almost Always	4 Always
Over the last 12 months:					
27. Do you ever have the urge to celebrate any good fortune by a few hours of gambling?					
28. Have you drunk continuously for 12 hours or more at a time?					
29. How often do you think about cutting down, controlling, or quitting using drugs?					
30. Have you ever used drugs in large amounts over a longer period than was intended?					
31. Do you feel that you now use more of a drug to get the same effect that you got when you first were using that drug?					
32. Do you now use more alcohol to get the same effect that you got when you first stated to use alcohol?					
33. To cover up your drinking, have you ever lied about where you were going?					
34. Have you ever had difficulty sleeping because of gambling?					
35. Have you experienced "blackouts" (total loss of memory for any length of time, without passing out)?					
36. Do you experience feelings of discomfort or anxiety when you are not using drugs?					
37. Have you ever gambled longer than you planned?					
38. While drinking, do you continue to drink to excess with no regard to what your responsibilities are?					

Drug, Alcohol, and Gambling Screen (Cont'd)

Questions Over the last 12 months:	0 Never	1 Some-times	2 Often	3 Almost Always	4 Always
39. Have you ever committed illegal acts (forgery, fraud, theft) in order to finance your gambling?					
40. Has gambling jeopardized or lost a significant relationship, job, educational, or career opportunity?					
41. Has anyone ever expressed concern over your drinking behaviour?					
42. Do you consider suicide as a result of your drug use?					
43. Has the use of drugs affected how well you are able to get along with people in your life?					
44. Have you ever considered self-destruction as a result of your gambling?					
45. Do you spend large amounts of time getting or thinking about how to get drugs?					

DAGS Hand Scoring Sheet

Gambling			
1.	12.	26.	39.
2.	18.	27.	40.
9.	21.	34.	44.
11.	25.	37.	
Total:			Gambling Risk:

Alcohol			
3.	17.	28.	38.
5.	19.	32.	41.
6.	20.	33.	43.
13.	22.	35.	
Total:			Alcohol Risk:

Drugs		
14.	24.	36.
15.	29.	42.
16.	30.	45.
23.	31.	
Total:		Drug Risk:

Risk level key: Sub-clinical, 0-2; mild concern, 3-15; moderate concern, 16-30, Medium Concern, 31-40; serious concern, 41-60.

APPENDIX C

Safety First

"I listen! I heard every word you said – how else could I have told you what was wrong with it?"
– Connolly and Rianoshek, 2002

The primary goal of addiction counselling is to assist clients in finding a healthy road to recovery. This mission is important, but is secondary. The first mission is safety.

Three clear examples support this assertion: 1) client safety (e.g., safe from abuse); 2) community safety (e.g., not a danger to family or others); and, 3) counsellor's safety (both physical and psychological). All three are of equal importance.

A blind spot for new professionals is focusing on the bull's eye and being blind to the rings. Counsellors who lack experience and intuition and rely on book smarts are at risk of hyper-focusing on the obvious.

Counsellors must pay attention to their clients' safety. One behaviour that can mislead a counsellor's perception regarding a client's safety is client confabulation (e.g., leaving out information or adding false information). It is an accepted fact that in addiction assessments some clients compensate for their current circumstances by exaggerating, and they have a propensity to shade the truth and/or underscore at-risk behaviour.

Counsellors who know this keep this in mind and evaluate not only what the client is saying but also what they are not saying. For example, a 29-year-old female told me that her living situation was challenging but tolerable. She was a cocaine addict, so my gut told me to keep digging.

Upon further investigation I learned that she was living with a 58-year-old man who provided her with food and shelter, and who did not mind that she was a drug addict. As long as the client continued to engage in his sadistic sexual fantasies, such as allowing him to burn her with cigarettes, she was welcome. *Do you think this client is in a safe situation? What needs to happen before treatment can begin for this client?*

Community safety is another important factor. I recall working with a 49 year-old alcoholic who happened to live in a rural setting and was a self-employed farmer. In our first session it was clear that he was in the contemplation stage of motivation, and was struggling to make up his mind if he wanted treatment.

During this meeting it was obvious that he was drinking. He was not falling down drunk; he was still functioning. Like most 15-year-plus drinkers, this client was able somehow to present early in the day as if he were still in control. This illusion of control fools many alcoholics who happen to like to drive each day to get their daily supply of alcohol.

When I asked him how he was going to get home – since it was clear he was not ready for treatment, let alone to go through a detoxification process – he told me not to worry; he just lived down the road a few miles and he was going to drive himself home. *Do you think the community is safe in this situation? What needs to happen?*

Counsellor safety is one topic that I promote in all of my training. Counsellors do not need to take any kind of abuse or feel in danger psychologically or physically at any time. There is no level of fear that is acceptable. When a counsellor does not feel safe, they should ask for support from a supervisor, a peer, or even the police.

One day I was working with a 19 year-old male who was involved in street gang activity, whom I had seen several times before, and was a person with whom I felt I had good rapport. During the counselling session he bent over to tie his shoe, and to my shock, I noticed he had a gun in his coat. *Do you think the counsellor was safe in this situation? What needs to happen?*

A counsellor who faces situations such as these, has a safety issue that needs to be resolved so treatment can continue. In this counsellor's opinion, the top priority in these types of cases is always safety. One could argue that this is part of treatment.

I will not split hairs. The point is that counsellors need to have clear boundaries; pay attention at all times; never assume; have no tolerance for danger; and must not turn another cheek when there is a potential safety issue. We, as professional counsellors, are expected to make difficult decisions and take action to protect our clients, our community, and ourselves.

OH MY, I DID NOT KNOW THAT!

"Oh my, I did not know that."

This is a reaction I often get when teaching budding addiction counsellors who are a generation behind me and have been raised with a different set of values.

My generation has taught me there are no shortcuts and one must pay their dues, whereas the Xers (under 30) are more focused on living life and do not expect to work long hours. They expect to be evaluated not by how long they have worked but how skilled they are.

My generation is more conservative in the way we dress, express our ideas publicly, and challenge authority and the status quo. Some of these differences can generate innocent behaviours in new counsellors that if left unchecked can spark transference and/or counter transference.

These generational differences point out the need for new addiction counsellors to be trained on the ethical guidelines that protect both client and counsellor, such as managing transference and counter transference. The obvious risk is that counselling can go beyond a healthy client-counsellor relationship, called dual relationships (client and counsellor having a personal, intimate relationship outside of counselling).

Perception creates reality, so counsellors need to send a clear message that their role is to help clients facilitate opportunities for change.

Of the 20 items we discuss in detail, below are four items that could lead to misunderstandings and projections by new counsellors:

Buddy Role – A counsellor plays four roles in a counselling relationship: teacher, providing important information; counsellor, helping solve life problems; manager, helping with a crisis; and friend, a role often taken to build common ground to develop trust and rapport. If as a counsellor you are not paying attention to how much time you are spending in each of these roles, the client may become confused and think you want to be a real friend. And a friend in a client's mind may be more than just a friend. Be clear you are not a client's buddy; you are the counsellor.

Over investment in one client – I call this a favorite-client syndrome. Counsellors build relationships with clients at different degrees. You may feel you have more rapport with some clients because you have more in common. It is human nature to feel more relaxed talking to a person you feel more comfortable with. But if you have eight clients and you are spending 40 percent of your time with one who is in no more crisis or need than anyone else, what kind of message can this send to them and to other clients? Ensure you spend equal time with clients who are in equal need.

Safe dress – Before I send out young men and women on placement we have a discussion about appropriate safe dress. Most treatment agencies have a casual dress policy but I have learned that my definition of casual dress and that of the young people in my class are different. I define how important it is to dress safely so that a client does not get distracted by the counsellor's presence and can focus on what their role is, that being to counsel. I teach them to be mindful of their dress and to ask if they are unsure about what is or is not appropriate.

Giving out personal emails – There is seldom ever a good enough reason to give a client my personal email, cell phone or home number. That's why I have voice mail at my office and a business cell phone. I was surprised at how many young people were trusting and willing to give their personal contact information when I asked, "Would you give out your personal contact information so a client could call you if they needed to talk?" Do not give clients your personal contact information.

Addiction counsellors must take care of two important people: themselves and the client. Little behaviours that may not seem like a big deal can put a young counsellor in a dangerous position. Keep in mind that transference or counter transference can also occur outside the formal counselling conversation and pay attention to this reality. Freud was not kidding; this stuff can happen.

YOU ARE NOT DEAR ABBY!

One of the first things budding addiction counsellors need to learn is that that they should be careful to avoid giving advice like a Dear Abby column to friends and family.

That's one of a long checklist of guiding principles I try to get across in the first few months as I prepare to teach a new group of addiction counselling students. These are critical building blocks that will assist the new addiction counsellors' professional development.

Some of the learnings I want to teach the new professionals may be obvious but we talk about them anyway, to be sure that there are clear professional standards and boundaries that all addiction counsellors adhere to. These include such ethical considerations as avoiding dual relationships (e.g., asking a client out on a date three months after they were seen as a client).

Some expectations for professional counsellors may not always be clearly defined or talked about. We assume young professionals will get some expectations and that puts them at too much risk. So to avoid risks – whether major or minor – I make an effort to point out as many different constructs as I feel are applicable for a new addiction professional's development.

The purpose here is to start a discussion around the risk of giving advice to friends and family on addictions related topics.

Most new addiction counsellors who are healthy, motivated, and committed to a helping profession come with a tremendous amount of energy, a sense of responsibility, and compassion to help people with addiction disorders.

A hard lesson to learn is that being naïve is not a legal defense in this profession. There is an expectation that professionals will have a clear understanding of their boundaries.

Being naïve may not just expose a young professional to major ethical and legal issues; it may also lead to straining personal relationships, unwarranted blame, and criticism, as well as increased personal stress. It is important to keep in mind that good intentions can lead to serious consequences (e.g., giving advice that exposes a client to harm).

Too often, once someone hears a family member or friend is taking a course in addiction counselling they assume they have an expert resource who can give them advice when they need it. This expectation often comes from the dynamics of the relationship that of course a family member or friend would help out and give advice if needed. Thus when there is a need there is no hesitation to ask.

My message to students is, "You are not in the advice giving business and it is not a best practice to counsel a family member or friend." So each year I offer my students the following best practices for giving advice.

Best Practices for Giving Advice

- When family members come to you with addiction related issues, the best advice you can give them is a referral number.
- There is no such thing as justifying your willingness to give advice because it is only a little advice. Giving instructions or suggestions is advice.
- Avoid the temptation to give professional advice to family or friends on specific actions or taking a counselling role when you see a need. When you have a concern out of love, it is fine to say what you think and what the person could do. But as a person who is concerned. For example, saying to a loved one, "You need help with your addiction; please get help" vs. "I am an addiction counsellor and I know you meet all the requirements for the diagnosis of alcohol dependency and you need to

go to detox, then cognitive counselling and AA" is more professional advice. Be clear of your role.

- Do not pass yourself off as an expert when you are in training. Just because you are in the process of becoming an addiction professional does not mean you are qualified to give professional advice, whether it is to a friend, family member, or a client you are seeing under supervision. Know your competency levels.
- Addiction counsellors should provide advice in the counselling relationship only after they get the client's permission to offer a suggestion.
- Even with a client in counselling, never provide advice in areas such as finances in which you have no formal training or certification.

WORKING WITH CLIENTS WHO SEE ONLY NEGATIVITY

Jim is a 42-year-old alcoholic who has gambled all his money – his wife has left him; he has lost his job; and because of his alcoholic behaviour, he has lost all his friends.

Clients like Jim challenge a counsellor's ability to be positive. People need to think positive in order to act positive. Counsellors are no different when helping a person whose life is turned upside down and who appears to have no resources.

Counsellors need to stay positive and have the energy and commitment to look for potential in every client, regardless of their situation. This may be difficult and even unrealistic to do all the time, but a counsellor should not accept or buy into a client's negativity. A counsellor who takes care of their thinking has more energy, resources, and creativity to explore different strategies and solutions. If they do not constantly monitor their own thinking when working with negative people day in and day out, counsellors may be influenced to think negatively.

It can be difficult for a counsellor to maintain a positive frame of reference with challenging clients. I am referring to the ability to see a positive outcome and good opportunities for a client whenever and wherever it can be found, and to be able to express this positively when faced with one who sees only negativity, dismay, and no hope for the future. Counselling clients who are in a negative place can negatively impact a counsellor's thinking. The counsellor must strive to see more positives in challenging situations where the average lay person would say there is no hope or potential.

Carl Rogers taught the importance of believing in the potential of a client to do what needs to be done to live a quality life. As a counsellor working with high-risk clients for nearly 20 years, it is a challenge to combine theory with reality and to find potential in clients. I try not to buy into a client's negative model of the world or that of other professionals who may say the case is hopeless.

There are days when it would be much easier for me to not care, become detached to protect myself, and say there is nothing I can do because the client is in denial or is not motivated. But somehow, I have learned from brilliant mentors like William Glasser, the author of choice theory, that it is not my job to make excuses. Clients are pros at this.

My job is to assist the client to find a path to healthier choices and learn new behaviours. It is ultimately the client's responsibility, but as a counsellor, I must never give up.

What can you do as a counsellor to evaluate your current thinking? First, evaluate how you stay positive. Secondly, assess how positive your thinking is about your client's potential in general.

To do this, write down your thinking so you can analyze it without filtering it. Keep a log of your internal thinking for two weeks to define your thinking and perceptions about the client's potential. If you are not as positive as you want to be, accept this as your first win. This is important, as you have defined what you want as opposed to what you have.

Now you are ready to start to develop or implement strategies to stay positive, and to see the potential in clients regardless of their situation. These strategies include: evaluating your current life management plan to determine if it is working; assessing your professional development plan to see if you are expanding your skills as a counsellor on a yearly basis; and discussing tough cases with a mentor.

APPENDIX D

The Addiction Counsellor Tune-Up

People spend a lifetime searching for happiness; looking for peace. They chase idle dreams, addictions, religions, even other people, hoping to fill the emptiness that plagues them. The irony is the only place they ever needed to search was within.
—*Ramona L. Anderson*

As an educator, having taught college-level courses in addiction counselling since 1993, I am intrigued by acquired learning strategies and where ideas for improving educational programming originate. This interest found an unexpected conduit last month as I was buying a new Honda®. After filling out the paperwork, the sales person immediately began to discuss the importance of complying with the manufacturer's maintenance schedule. Honda® has created a comprehensive checklist that sets the standards and criteria for maintenance, with the goal of ensuring the automobile is properly maintained and road worthy.

As I was driving home, I started to reflect on the similarities between the manufacturer's maintenance schedule and the continuing education credits (CEUs) required to maintain certification as an addictions counsellor. Master mechanics have exhaustive predetermined maintenance schedule checklists that include the mundane checking of the air valves on the tires to the more complicated testing of the engine's timing. I thought to myself, why don't addiction counsellors have such a checklist for managing CEUs?

As professional counsellors, we are obligated to take a certain amount of CEU hours to maintain certification. Beyond that, continuing education is at our discretion. Much like the master mechanic who has a checklist that captures the scope of his or her professional responsibility, how can we remember to program into our development paths core skills we may overlook? A potential solution lies in the addiction counsellor tune-up checklist. Intended for addiction counsellors who work with clients daily, the purpose of this tune-up checklist is twofold: to provide you with an example of an addiction counsellor program checklist while creating an opportunity to perform a self-diagnostic overview. The checklist facilitates an interactive opportunity to self-evaluate your core skill set — the goal is to present the intrinsic and professional value of an assessment tool that leads to improved clinical efficacy. Annually identifying, in detail, a list of core competencies is helpful in determining a professional development trajectory in terms of CEUs as well as heightening an addiction counsellor's ability to keep up with the continuous changes in the growing field of addiction studies.

Addiction Counsellor Tune-up Checklist

As part of the tune-up checklist, you will be asked 18 questions that span the phases of addiction counselling. Please note that the list has no specific rationale for its order, as all listed competencies can play an important role in the treatment of persons with addictive disorders. I have developed this checklist from both my clinical and academic experiences; however, I will make no claims that this is an exhaustive list. You may invariably see the value of adding constructs and competencies that are relevant to your particular practice environment. Please take a blank piece of paper and answer the following 18 questions. It is important to write out your responses without using any kind of support or resource material so that you can accurately assess your level of competency.

1. *Addiction Definitions and Treatment Model* – What is your definition of addictive disorders, and what is your treatment model?

2. *Addictive Disorders* – Define the array of addictive disorders you will be faced with treating.

3. *Understanding Motivation for Change* – How do you conceptualize the motivation for change, and how does it impact treatment planning?

4. *Referral Resources and Case Management* – What are your referral procedures? How do you define case management and your typical role in the process?

5. *Multicultural Considerations* – How do you formally and informally screen for multicultural differences?

6. *Counselling Theory* – What are your two preferred counselling theories, and why have you chosen them?

7. *Counselling Process* – What are your counselling processes and/or therapies?

8. *Counselling Techniques* – What are your five standard counselling techniques, and why have you chosen them?

9. *Counselling Micro Skills* – What are the top five micro skills that you actively use in counselling?

10. *Addiction Clinical Measures and Screening Tools* – What are your three favored addiction measures, and what is your most useful screening tool?

11. *Addiction Recovery Tools* – What are five of your chosen addiction recovery tools?

12. *Professional and Personal Ethics* – How do you define your professional and personal ethics?

13. *Crisis Intervention* – What is your crisis intervention model? What types of crises are you prepared for?

14. *Addictions Assessment Protocol* – Describe your assessment process from beginning to end. Be specific as to how you assess physical, emotional, spiritual, and mental health.

15. *Treatment Planning* – What is your treatment planning process, and how do you develop treatment plans?

16. *Relapse Prevention* – What relapse prevention model are you currently using, and why have you chosen this one?

17. *Aftercare Program* – How do you design aftercare programs?

18. *Addictive Disorder Prevention* – What is your addictive disorder prevention model?

Please review those areas that you left blank or in which you provided a general response. They may be developmental areas that you could consider adding to next year's development plan. Even areas in which you provided detailed responses merit additional investigation as you manage your career development and clinical efficacy.

PLEASE STOP HERE AND FINISH THE ABOVE QUESTIONNAIRE
BEFORE READING ON

1. *Addiction Definitions and Treatment Models*

    - While there is no universally accepted definition for addiction, it is essential to have a clear concept of both addiction disorders and treatment models (e.g., biopsychosocial). It is critical that definitions for addictive disorders be based in clinical research (e.g., the dopamine reward system is becoming recognized as a common link for many addictive disorders).

    - An excellent resource is *Concepts of Chemical Dependency* (Brooks/Cole, 1996) by Harold E. Doweiko.

2. *Addictive Disorder*

    - There are many different addictive disorders. Those most commonly covered in the literature are: alcohol, drugs, gambling, work, sex, interactive, buying, and food. John Wiley & Sons will soon release an exciting book in press: *Addictive Disorder: A Practical Handbook* edited by Robert H Coombs.

    - It is critical that addiction counsellors understand both drug classifications and the drugs that require supervised medical detoxification (e.g., alcohol).

3. *Understanding Motivation for Change*

    - The Transtheoretical/Stages of Change model is widely accepted as a critical benchmark for determining a client's motivation and planning treatment strategies. This six-step model has utility in all aspects of treatment from intake to aftercare planning.

    - An effective resource that provides an overview of the Transtheoretical/Stages of Change model is the following journal article: Prochaska, J.O., & DiClemente, C.C. (1982). Transtheoretical therapy toward a more integrative model of change. *Psychotherapy: Theory, Research and Practice,* 19(3), 276-287.

4. *Referral Resources and Case Management*

    - Each addiction counsellor must have a current list of referral services for their region, which can be found in a number of trade periodicals, including *Counsellor*. One helpful website is: www.soberrecovery.com/links/forprofessionals.html. Addiction counsellors must be clear on the protocols for referral in their local area.

    - A text that comprehensively reviews addictive disorder case management is Becoming an Addictions Counsellor: A Comprehensive Text (Jones & Bartlett, 2000) by Peter L. Myers and Norman R. Salt.

5. *Multicultural Considerations*

- We live in a multicultural society, and it is paramount that each addiction counsellor have a built-in process to screen for multicultural needs. Addiction counsellors must challenge any potential prejudices or preconceived notions to be effective with a multicultural population.

- Addiction counsellors cannot assume that one treatment or clinical model will fit all. An excellent resource that defines the value of learning a client's frame of reference is *Multicultural Counselling Competencies: Assessment, Education and Training, and Supervision, Vol. 7* (Sage Publications, 1995) edited by Hardin L.K. Coleman and Donald B. Pope-Davis.

6. *Counselling Theory*

- Counsellors need a frame of reference that explains why people do what they do from a theoretical perspective. It is important that each addiction counsellor develop his or her own unique counselling orientation that is grounded in accepted counselling theory. The most common counselling theories used today are cognitive-behavioural (e.g., theories of Aaron Beck, Albert Ellis, and William Glasser).

- One of the most detailed books on counselling theory is Current Psychotherapies, 5th Edition (F. E. Peacock, 1995) edited by Raymond J. Corsini and Danny Wedding.

7. *Counselling Process*

- Counselling process must have a clearly defined beginning, middle, and end. Counselling processes must be proven to work with persons with addictions, like William Glasser's Choice Theory and Reality Therapy (www.wglasser.com).

- An excellent comprehensive resource is *Substance Abuse Counselling: Theory and Practice,* 2nd Edition (Prentice Hall, 2000) by Robert L. Smith and Patricia Stevens-Smith.

8. *Counselling Techniques*

- A well-developed set of proven counselling techniques is critical to the success of any addiction counsellor. Typical addiction counselling techniques include journaling, magic wand, and the triple column technique, which represent merely a sampling of contemporary techniques.

- A user-friendly resource is The Human Services Counselling Toolbox (Brooks/Cole, 2000) by William A. Howatt.

9. *Counselling Micro Skills*

- In order to keep the counselling process moving in a positive direction, addiction counsellors need to have an effective communication model that is supported by micro skills.

- There are many clinical measures and screening tools to choose from. A helpful resource is The Skilled Helper (Wadsworth, 1997) by Gerald Egan.

10. *Addiction Clinical Measures and Screening Tools*

- Addiction counsellors must be current in addiction measures, e.g., Substance Abuse Subtle Screening (SASSI) (see www.sassi.com/sassi/index.shtml) and screening tools (e.g., the portable breath alcohol tester, see www.columbialab.com) that are indigenous to their clinical environment.

- Addiction counsellors need to be familiar with the *Diagnostic and Statistical Manual of Mental Disorders, Fourth Edition Text Revision (DSM-IV-TR)* (American Psychiatric Association, 2000) as well as with psychological measures that are commonly used by their multi-disciplinary teams (e.g., dual diagnosis clients who are depressed are often monitored by the Beck Depression Inventory®).

11. *Addiction Recovery Tools*

- Addictions counsellors must have an understanding of how addiction recovery tools work. These tools will support the counselling process and treatment planning. Some common recovery tools are motivational interviewing, peer support groups, group counselling, psychoeducational programs (e.g., anger management), recovery contracts, and computer-assisted programs that are congruent with the addiction counsellor's treatment environment (inpatient or outpatient).

- One of the best resources on the market today is *Addiction Recovery Tools* (Sage Publications, 2001) by Robert H. Coombs (Ed.). See also "Psychosocial Recovery Tools for Addictive Disorders" in the August 2003 issue of *Counsellor*.

12. *Professional and Personal Ethics*

- Addiction counsellors are accountable to both a professional and personal code of ethics. Professional ethics are set by state licensing boards and national trade organizations, while personal codes of ethics are defined by the counsellor. An excellent resource is *Ethics for Addiction Professionals* (Hazelden Information Education, 1994) by Leclair Bissell and James E. Royce.

- Addiction counsellors must be aware of organizational policies and procedures, standing orders, local and national laws, and changes in legislation.

13. *Crisis Intervention*

- Addiction counsellors should have an understanding of a crisis intervention model, such as *The Six-Step Crisis Intervention Model, in Crisis Intervention Strategies*, 4th Edition (Brooks/Cole, 2001) by Burl Gilliland and Richard James.

- Addiction counsellors are advised to have basic skills in first aid, suicide intervention, and self-protection. The wrong time to prepare for a crisis situation is when a crisis occurs.

14. *Addictions Assessment Protocol*

- Structural assessments are service guides to assess clients that never replace sound clinical judgment. Formal assessments often involve multidisciplinary teams. All assessments of addictive disorders must take into consideration the potential for dual diagnosis. A useful resource is www.dualdiagnosis.org.

- A useful tool is *Assessment Handbook for Addiction Treatment Programs* (Centre for Addiction Studies and Mental Health, 1990) by Linda Palanek, Christine Bois, Darryl Upfold, Robert Murray, and Michael Gavin.

15. *Treatment Planning*

- Treatment planning can be facilitated with structured tools described in *The Addiction Treatment Planner*, 2nd Edition (John Wiley & Sons, 2001) by Robert R. Perkinson and Arthur E. Jongsma, Jr. Treatment planning must include a sound termination strategy that will ensure a smooth transition to aftercare programs.

- Treatment planning also requires effective note taking. A useful tool is *The Addiction Progress Notes Planner* (John Wiley & Sons, 2001) by David J. Berghuis and Arthur E. Jongsma, Jr.

16. *Relapse Prevention*

- Relapse prevention must be incorporated into any treatment planning. It is important that relapse prevention be discussed throughout treatment.
- Addiction counsellors need to have a proven relapse prevention model such as Gorski's Center for Applied Sciences (CENAPS®) clinical relapse prevention model (www.cenaps.com).

17. *Aftercare Program*

- When a client exits counselling, it is paramount to help the client develop a well thought out aftercare program to assist in relapse prevention. An aftercare plan, to be effective, needs to be a natural extension of the client's treatment plan.
- One effective tool for aftercare programming is *The Journey: 52 Weeks in Recovery* (Abbott-Sterling Publishing, 1995) by Jack Reid.

18. *Addictive Disorder Prevention*

- Addiction counsellors must have a clear understanding of addictive disorder prevention target areas. The three main target areas are Person (e.g., prior drug use, skills, physiological reactions, and perceptions), Situation (e.g., peer influence, family influence, opportunity, and social norms), and Environment (e.g., access, media impact, schools, and community policies and financial factors).
- Addiction counsellors need to be aware of the current thinking around primary prevention models. An excellent source is the Institute of Medicine (www.iom.edu). Another excellent resource on prevention is Substance Abuse and Mental Health Services Administration Center for Substance Abuse Prevention (SAMHSA/CSAP) (http://prevention.samhsa.gov/).

Now, plan your future

Addiction counselling is an exciting profession that is constantly changing as both a result of innovations in the discipline and the introduction of new addictions into an ever-fluid culture. It is up to each addiction counsellor to ensure that he or she stays current and is prepared to offer services of the highest quality. The tune-up checklist provides an excellent baseline against which to assess current skill sets and plan future professional development.

References

American Psychiatric Association (1994). Diagnostic and statistical manual of mental disorders (4th ed.). Washington: American Psychiatric Association.

American Psychiatric Association. (2000). Diagnostic and statistical manual of mental disorders (4th Ed., text revision). Washington, DC: Author.

Berghuis, D. J. & Jongsma, Jr., A. E. (2001). The addiction progress notes planner. New York, NY: John Wiley & Sons. Bissell, L. & Royce, J. E. (1994). Ethics for addiction professionals. Center City, MN: Hazelden.

Coleman, H. L. K. & Pope-Davis, D. B. (Eds.) (1995). Multicultural counselling competencies: Assessment, education and training, and supervision, Vol. 7. Sage Publications.

Coombs, R.H. (Ed.). (2001). Addiction recovery tools: A practical handbook. Thousand Oaks, CA: Sage.

Coombs, R. H. (Ed.). (2004). Handbook on addictive disorders, New York: John Wiley & Sons.

Coombs, R. H. (in press). Addictive disorder: A practical handbook. New York, NY: John Wiley & Sons.

Corsini, R.J. & Wedding, D. (1995). Current psychotherapies (5th edition). Itasca, IL: F. E. Peacock.

Doweiko, H. E. (1996). Concepts of chemical dependency. Pacific Grove, CA: Brooks/Cole.

Egan, G. (1997). The skilled helper. Belmont, CA: Wadsworth Publishing Co.

Gilliland, B. & James, R. (2001). Crisis intervention strategies (4th edition). Pacific grove, CA: Brooks/Cole.

Howatt, B. (2000). The human services counselling toolbox. Pacific Grove, CA: Brooks/Cole.

Meyers, P.L. & Salt, N.R. (2000). Becoming an addictions counsellor: A comprehensive text. Boston, MA: Jones & Bartlett.

Palanek, L., Bois, C., Upfold, D., Murray, R., & Gavin, M. (1990). Assessment handbook for addiction treatment programs. Toronto, Ontario: Centre for Addiction Studies and Mental Health.

Perkinson, R. R. & Jongsma, Jr., A. E. (2001). The addiction treatment planner (2nd Edition). New York, NY: John Wiley & Sons.

Prochaska, J.O., & DiClemente, C.C. (1982). Transtheoretical therapy toward a more integrative model of change. Psychotherapy: Theory, Research and Practice, 19(3), 276-287.

Reid, J. (1995). The journey: 52 weeks in recovery. Fort Lauderdale, FL: Abbott-Sterling Publishing.

Smith, R.L. & Stevens-Smith, P. (2000). Substance abuse counselling: Theory and practice (2nd edition). Englewood Cliffs, NJ: Prentice Hall.

Website References

Dual Diagnosis Recovery Network, www.dualdiagnosis.org

Glasser's Choice Theory and Reality Therapy, www.wglasser.com

Gorski-CENAPS®, www.cenaps.com

Institute of Medicine, www.iom.edu

Portable breath alcohol tester, www.columbialab.com

Sober Recovery, www.soberrecovery.com/links/forprofessionals.html

Substance Abuse and Mental Health Services Administration (SAMHSA), Center for Substance Abuse Prevention (CSAP), www.samhsa.gov/csap

Substance Abuse Subtle Screening Institute (SASSI), www.sassi.com/sassi/index.shtml